HORMONAL THEORY

THEORY IN THE NEW HUMANITIES

Series editor: Rosi Braidotti

Theory is back! The vitality of critical thinking in the world today is palpable, as is a spirit of insurgency that sustains it. Theoretical practice has exploded with renewed energy in media, society, the arts and the corporate world. New generations of critical 'studies' areas have grown alongside the classical radical epistemologies of the 1970s: gender, feminist, queer, race, postcolonial and subaltern studies, cultural studies, film, television and media studies.

This series aims to present cartographic accounts of emerging critical theories and to reflect the vitality and inspirational force of ongoing theoretical debates.

Editorial board

Stacy Alaimo (University of Texas at Arlington, USA)
Simone Bignall (Flinders University, Australia)
Judith Butler (University of Berkeley, USA)
Christine Daigle (Brock University, Canada)
Rick Dolphijn (Utrecht University, the Netherlands)
Matthew Fuller (Goldsmiths, University of London, UK)
Engin Isin (Queen Mary University of London, UK, and University of London Institute in Paris, France)
Patricia MacCormack (Anglia Ruskin University, UK)
Achille Mbembe (University Witwatersrand, South Africa)
Henrietta Moore (University College London, UK)

Other titles in the series:

Posthuman Glossary, edited by Rosi Braidotti and Maria Hlavajova
Conflicting Humanities, edited by Rosi Braidotti and Paul Gilroy
General Ecology, edited by Erich Hörl with James Burton
Philosophical Posthumanism, Francesca Ferrando
The Philosophy of Matter, Rick Dolphijn
Materialist Phenomenology, Manuel DeLanda
From Deleuze and Guattari to Posthumanism, edited by Christine Daigle and Terrance H. McDonald
Vibrant Death, Nina Lykke
Visceral Prostheses, Margrit Shildrick

HORMONAL THEORY

A Rebellious Glossary

Edited by

Andrea Ford, Roslyn Malcolm, Sonja Erikainen, Lisa Raeder and Celia Roberts

BLOOMSBURY ACADEMIC
LONDON • NEW YORK • OXFORD • NEW DELHI • SYDNEY

BLOOMSBURY ACADEMIC
Bloomsbury Publishing Plc
50 Bedford Square, London, WC1B 3DP, UK
Broadway, New York, NY 10018, USA
29 Earlsfort Terrace, Dublin 2, Ireland

BLOOMSBURY, BLOOMSBURY ACADEMIC and the Diana logo are trademarks
of Bloomsbury Publishing Plc

First published in Great Britain 2024

A catalogue record for this book is available from the British Library.

A catalog record for this book is available from the Library of Congress.

ISBN: HB: 978-1-3503-2299-8
PB: 978-1-3503-2298-1
ePDF: 978-1-3503-2300-1
eBook: 978-1-3503-2301-8

Series: Theory in the New Humanities

Typeset by Deanta Global Publishing Services, Chennai, India
Printed and bound in Great Britain

To find out more about our authors and books visit www.bloomsbury.com and
sign up for our newsletters.

CONTENTS

CONTRIBUTORS

Nayantara Sheoran Appleton is a senior lecturer at the interdisciplinary School of Science in Society, Te Herenga Waka | Victoria University of Wellington, Aotearoa New Zealand. Trained as a feminist medical anthropologist and STS scholar (with a PhD in cultural studies) she has co-edited *Methods, Moments, and Ethnographic Spaces in Asia* (2021) and *A Companion to the Anthropology of Reproductive Medicine and Technology* (2023). She is working on a monograph titled *Demographic Desires, Mediated Medicine, and Emergency Contraceptive Pills in Contemporary India*. She is the recipient of the New Zealand Royal Society's Mardsen Fast Start grant on a project titled *Social Lives of Sex Hormones*.

Tom Boylston is a senior lecturer in anthropology at the University of Edinburgh, UK. His work focuses on play, habit and ritual.

Risa Cromer is an assistant professor in the Department of Anthropology at Purdue University, United States, and affiliated faculty in the Women's, Gender, and Sexuality Studies and Critical Disability Studies programmes. Her scholarship investigates reproductive politics animating the intersections of medicine, science and technology. Her most recent book is *Conceiving Christian America: Embryo Adoption and Reproductive Politics* (2023). She co-leads 'The Reproductive Righteousness Project', an interdisciplinary feminist collaboration on right-wing extremism, and is developing a feminist data studies ethnographic project about abortion-related knowledge in the post-*Roe* context.

Cronan Cronshaw is a researcher at Lancaster University, UK, working at the intersection of feminist technoscience, sociology and creative writing.

Leah Eades is a PhD student in social anthropology at the University of Edinburgh, UK. Her research examines abortion politics and provision in the Republic of Ireland following the expansion of legal abortion in 2018. She holds an MSc in medical anthropology from University College London and a BA in English from the University of Bristol.

Sonja Erikainen is a lecturer in sociology at the University of Aberdeen, UK. Their research and publications sit at the intersection of gender and sexuality studies, science and technology studies and sport studies, focusing especially on social and ethical issues around sex and gender diversity, the medicalization of sex difference including through hormones and new and emerging biomedical technologies and approaches.

Kriss Fearon holds a FSHI Mildred Blaxter Postdoctoral Fellowship at the Centre for Reproduction Research, De Montfort University, UK, working on the theme of 'Reproductive futures: Social imaginaries and reproductive decision making in the context of chromosome disorders'. Her research with families affected by Turner Syndrome explored the social, psychological and ethical issues of reproductive decision-making, parenthood and the use of assisted conception and new reproductive technologies. She is co-author with Professor Daniela Aidley of *Doing Accessible Social Research: A Practical Guide* (2021).

The **Feminist Technoscience Governance Collaboratory** (**FTGC**) fosters engaged research through collective and collaborative feminist and queer methodologies. Recent FTGC work is part of a collective monograph, *Synthetic Becoming* (2022), and accompanying exhibit. FTGC members between 2017-2022 were: Vrisha Ahmad, April Albrecht, Sarah Hyde, Amanda Kearney, Lainie LaRonde, Jacquelyne Luce, Alek Meyer, Cassie Pawlikowski, Karisa Poedjirahardjo, Emily Pollack, Anjali Rao-Herel, and Ella Sevier.

Andrea Ford is a research fellow in medical anthropology at the Centre for Biomedicine, Self and Society at the University of Edinburgh, UK. She conducts research on childbearing, menstruation, endometriosis and 'FemTech', more broadly investigating how ideas about gender, bodies, nature and technology shape the culture surrounding medicine and reproduction. She is the author of *Near Birth: The Doula Phenomenon and American Values* (forthcoming) and numerous articles in professional and popular outlets. Currently she is working on bridging academic and non-academic spaces for research, ideas and cultural change.

Arbel Griner is an associate research scholar at Princeton University's Global Health Program, United States. With a PhD in social medicine from the State University of Rio de Janeiro, she uses her multi-disciplinary training in social medicine, social studies of science and technology and anthropology to produce a nuanced critical perspective of how ideas of pathology, normality and health are conceptualized in contemporary neuroscience and how these ideas are integrated into medicine, public health and ethical debates.

Ian Harper is a professor of anthropology of health and development at the University of Edinburgh, UK. He is the founding director of the Edinburgh

Centre for Medical Anthropology (www.edcma.ed.ac.uk) and currently acts as the coordinating editor for the fully open access journal *Medicine, Anthropology, Theory* (www.medanthrotheory.org).

Charlotte Jones is a lecturer in sociology at Swansea University, UK. Her research addresses issues of gender, sexuality, disability and health, and particularly the intersections of these areas. In this collection, she draws on her doctoral research on the medicalization of VSCs, which was completed in 2016 at the University of Sheffield. She recently led Reprofutures, a co-produced research project about reproductive justice and support communities for adults with variations in sex characteristics in the UK (https://sites.exeter.ac.uk/reprofutures).

Jacquelyne Luce is a senior lecturer at Mount Holyoke College, United States, in the Department of Gender Studies. Her teaching and research explore the interconnected worlds of health activism, scientific research and care, with a focus on rare diseases and technology governance.

Norah MacKendrick is an associate professor of sociology at Rutgers University, United States. Her research and teaching touch on the sociology of gender, food, consumer and consumption studies, medical sociology and environmental sociology. She is the author of *Better Safe Than Sorry: How Consumers Navigate Exposure to Everyday Toxics* (2018).

Roslyn Malcolm is an assistant professor in social anthropology at Durham University, UK. Her research explores practices of sociality and relatedness. She explores local understandings of the role non-humans and bodily substances play in these processes in the United Kingdom and the United States. Building on her prior research on autism, she now researches hormone models of stress, bonding and environmental toxicity.

Anne Pollock is a professor of global health and social medicine at King's College London. Her research explores feminist, anti-racist and decolonial engagements with science, technology and medicine. She is the author of three books: *Medicating Race: Heart Disease and Durable Preoccupations with Difference* (2012); *Synthesizing Hope: Matter, Knowledge, and Place in South African Drug Discovery* (2019); and *Sickening: Anti-Black Racism and Health Disparities* (2021).

Magdalena Radkowska-Walkowicz is an associate professor at the Institute of Ethnology and Cultural Anthropology of the University of Warsaw, Poland, and a member of the Childhood Studies Interdisciplinary Research Team. Her academic interest is in childhood and youth studies, medical anthropology and new reproductive technologies. She is the author of numerous articles (e.g. in

Children's Geographies, Reproductive Health Matters, European Journal of Women's Studies, Journal of Religion and Health), edited volumes and books (e.g. *In Vitro Experience: Infertility and New Reproductive Technologies from the Anthropological Perspective* (in Polish)).

Lisa Raeder is a PhD candidate in population health sciences at the University of Edinburgh, with a master's degree in gender studies from Stockholm University. Her research intersects the disciplinary fields of critical theory, gender studies and medical humanities, particularly exploring experiences and implications of hormonal contraception in the production of gender and sexuality and conceptions of health and the self.

Anjali Rao-Herel is an artist-researcher and graduate of Mount Holyoke College. Her undergraduate thesis is a graphic ethnography that articulates experiences and experiments with contested healing modalities for ankylosing spondylitis.

Celia Roberts works in the field of feminist technoscience studies and has been writing about hormones of various kinds for almost thirty years. She is based at the School of Sociology at the Australian National University, Canberra. Her forthcoming book, *Reproduction, Kin and Climate Crisis: Making Bushfire Babies*, is co-written with Mary Lou Rasmussen, Louisa Allen and Rebecca Williamson and will be published by Bristol University Press.

Fabíola Rohden is an associate professor in the Department of Anthropology at the Federal University at Rio Grande do Sul, Brazil. She is a researcher at the National Council of Scientific and Technological Development (CNPq). Her research interests focus on gender, sexuality, biomedical practices and anthropology of science. She is the author of the books *A Science of Difference: Sex and Gender in Women's Medicine* (2009) and *Decepting Nature: Contraception, Abortion and Infanticide in the Early Twentieth Century* (2003). Her most recent book is *Biotechnologies, Bodily and Subjective Transformations: Knowledge, Practices and Inequalities* (2021) in collaboration with C. Pussetti e A. Roca.

Emily Ross is a research fellow in the Department of Sociological Studies, University of Sheffield, UK. Her current project considers gestational trophoblastic disease and is supported by the Wellcome Trust. Emily's work draws on qualitative methods, medical sociology and feminist science studies to explore experiences of reproduction, cancer and novel biomedical techniques.

Mariana Rios Sandoval is an anthropologist interested in the study of chemicals as ethnographic objects, on the affective and embodied apprehension of life in times of accelerated environmental damage, on the intersections of reproductive and environmental justice and on creative transdisciplinary collaborative experiments.

Wibke Straube works as a senior lecturer and research coordinator at the Centre for Gender Studies, Karlstad University, Sweden. Their work focuses on an intersectional analysis of trans and queer embodiment, affective methodologies and possibilities to create zones of liveability. They have published in *Environmental Humanities*, *Screen Bodies*, *Lambda Nordica* and *NORA – Nordic Journal of Feminist and Gender Research*. Currently, they lead the research strand 'Environment' for the research project 'Trans*Creative: Health, Violence, and Environment in Transgender Cultural Production' (Kone Foundation, 2020–4). They also lead a research project on regional trans care seekers' access to support structures (Region Värmland, 2021–3).

Rafaela Zorzanelli is an associate professor at the Institute for Social Medicine of the State University of Rio de Janeiro, Brazil. She has been investigating the reports of people who use prescription substances regularly, especially clonazepam, in Brazil. She coordinates the website Drug trajectories (drugtrajectories.org), featuring the first batch of interviews conducted with experts in the field of drug studies, such as anthropologists, historians and sociologists.

ACKNOWLEDGEMENTS

We would like to sincerely thank all the contributors to this volume for their work, insights and editorial cooperation, as well as to Bloomsbury editors and staff and our family and friends for their support as we undertook this project. Thanks to the Centre for Biomedicine, Self and Society at the University of Edinburgh and the Edinburgh Centre for Medical Anthropology (EdCMA) for funding the initial 'What Is a Hormone?' workshop in 2020, to the Brocher Foundation for funding the 'Regulating the Hormonal Self' workshop in 2022 and to the Wellcome Trust (Grant number 209519/Z/17/Z) which supported several of the editors during the period of work on this volume. All of the editors contributed significantly to producing this volume, and all have the right to list the publication as first author in their CVs.

All images have been commissioned for this volume and are available for public use under a Creative Commons copyright license. The artist is Elsa Paulson, to whom we also owe many thanks. Support for this has generously been provided by the Wellcome Trust (Grant number 209519/Z/17/Z) and the School of Sociology at the Australian National University.

HORMONAL CASCADES

AN INTRODUCTION

ROSLYN MALCOLM, SONJA ERIKAINEN, ANDREA FORD, LISA RAEDER AND CELIA ROBERTS

What is a hormone? At first glance, this may appear to be a question with a self-evident response. Informed by natural and life sciences and biomedicine, hormones are commonly framed as chemical entities that are foundational to biological life in that they provoke, respond to and enable bodily functions and processes. Taken from the Greek term 'hormao', meaning 'to excite', these compounds set biological processes in motion, catalysing and carrying messages through systems of the body.

Yet, hormones are also cultural artefacts. They carry meaning, cascading information between people and shaping understandings and material realities of health, normalcy, sex and gender. Testosterone, for example, is heralded as 'the male hormone' and oestrogen as 'the female hormone'. These hormones act as messengers of sex and gender, carrying gendered meanings throughout the body (Roberts 2007). However, as has been powerfully detailed by science and technology studies scholars, among others, these meanings are deeply rooted in prevailing biomedical and social constructs of what male and female bodies are and ought to do (Oudshoorn 1994; Roberts 2007).

While hormones are often primarily associated, both scientifically and culturally, with reproduction and sex or gender, they cascade across the vast majority of bodily processes. Hormones mediate our response to stress, processes of digestion, metabolism, growth and immunity, and even our psychological functioning. Like knowledge about sex hormones, knowledge about these myriad hormonal interactions is enmeshed in cultural meanings, mediating our understandings of bodies and their relations within and to the world. Despite being involved in complex and varied processes that span different functions and areas of the body, knowledge about hormones often reflects pre-existing social categories, through which hormones become associated with or are made to represent singular kinds of cultural and social phenomena. Cortisol becomes a messenger of stress (Roberts and McWade 2021); dopamine of pleasure; oxytocin of social bonding, care and love – just as testosterone becomes the messenger of masculinity and oestrogen of femininity (Roberts 2007).

Hormone talk in science, medicine, media and popular culture has become particularly salient in recent years as part of a growing 'molecularization of life' (Rose 2007). Hormones are central to medical and other body-shaping practices, emerging sciences such as epigenetics and environmentalist discourses about pollution and human and more-than-human health. Increased access to synthesized hormones and hormone blockers – used in contraception, fertility treatments, cancer treatments, psychiatric interventions and gender affirmation – combines with wider acknowledgement of their ability to modulate human (and animal) biologies. For example, endocrine-disrupting chemicals that are widespread in our manufactured and post-industrial environments are emerging as a potent site for situating and reflecting upon environmental degradation (Murphy 2008; Pollock 2016). As Jean-Paul Gaudilliére notes, with the discovery of sex hormones came an 'endocrine style of thought' (2004: 542). Roslyn Malcolm (2021) relatedly argues that we are living through the broader emergence of hormone thinking as a mode of understanding the lived body, beyond sex hormones.

Although hormones constitute forms of material substance, they also extend beyond their position within biological spheres, shaping biological, social, cultural and political forces, while simultaneously being shaped by them. In so doing, they challenge the very separation between the biological and the social or cultural as differentiable phenomena. Due to their capacity to flow across and enact biological and social processes, and to blur conceived boundaries between meaning and matter, hormones are a signature material-semiotic entity, to use Donna Haraway's (1991) term. As such, hormones not only reinforce but also trouble commonly taken-for-granted understandings of biomedical, technoscientific and cultural categorizations.

Why hormonal theory?

The editors of this volume share a strong interest in exploring how to engage with hormones and their biocultural meanings and effects. In May 2020, during the first wave of the Covid-19 pandemic, we organized an interdisciplinary academic workshop titled 'What is a Hormone?' The event was motivated by our curiosity about the plural knowledges and roles of hormones in biomedical, social scientific, humanities and public discourses, and the disruptions they enact as they blur boundaries between the biological and social, natural and cultural and inside and outside. In asking 'what is a hormone', we sought to explore how hormones are configured in current framings of the biology-society nexus and what is at stake in these configurations. We hoped to understand the kinds of material-semiotic flows that hormones set in motion as well as to catalyse interdisciplinary conceptual and methodological approaches to make sense of the complex biosocial ontology of hormones in the contemporary world. This event sparked a cluster of interdisciplinary conversations and collaborations as well as public engagement activities, culminating in this book.

Hormonal Theory explores various approaches to engaging with hormones, taking their complex and multiple biosocial currents and material-semiotic ontologies as a starting point. Entries attend to hormones' proliferating, shape-shifting expressions by following the ways in which hormones cascade across multiple dimensions and what they do as they move. Foregrounding spaces where multiple kinds of hormone knowledges, medical and social practices and cultural imaginaries converge, the authors explore why and how hormones create plural, intersecting realities. In centring these complex cascades, the book illuminates how hormones permeate every sphere of our lives.

Mapping hormonal theories

In forging theoretical approaches to engaging with hormones, this book builds on and expands existing conceptualizations of the biosocial meanings and roles of hormones and their fluid or cascading actions. Some of this work focuses on pharmaceuticals. Anita Hardon and Emilia Sanabria (2017), for example, have shown how synthesized pharmaceuticals (including hormones) are not 'discovered' but rather made and remade through social relations and commodity chains, contributing to our understanding of chemical and molecular fluidity and movement through their analysis of the social production of pharmaceutical objects. As they state, 'there is no pure (pharmaceutical) object that precedes its socialization' (2017, 117). Sandra Bärnreuther (2018) has offered a concrete example of this process in her analysis of the relational infrastructures through which the hormone human chorionic gonadotropin (hCG) moves globally. She details how low-caste pregnant women in India are encouraged – through narratives of a transnational shared motherhood – to donate their urine to expectant mothers in IVF clinics in the United States and Europe. Through a process akin to alchemy, the waste product gifted by women in the Global South is processed, repackaged and turned into figurative gold, with consumers in the Global North having no knowledge of the origins of the treatment. Nayantara

Sheoran Appleton (2022) has similarly detailed the commodity chains through which hormones move, highlighting the stratification of women in Delhi, India, through differential access to the emergency contraceptive pill (ECP). She shows how wealthy elite women are given access to these pills and relatedly access to an emerging contraceptive modernity, a cosmopolitan imaginary of emancipated womanhood. Yet such treatments remain inaccessible for the majority. These analyses highlight the ways in which hormones gain multiple meanings as they flow across complex global and local networks of social relations, often as a commodity. In so doing, they function as a nexus that links biomedical processes and entities with unequal social power relations.

A substantial body of work focuses on the fluidities of the so-called sex hormones. Due to their central role in the sexing/gendering of bodies and social relations, sex hormones have been an important object of feminist and queer studies of the science-society relationship and of hormones as material-semiotic actors. This work brings to the fore how hormones both break down and reinforce social categories and binaries between the biological and social, natural and cultural and sex and gender. Paul B. Preciado's *Testo Junkie: Sex, Drugs and Biopolitics in the Pharmacopornographic Era* (2013), for example, examines the role and effects of hormones in the 'pharmacopornographic era', an era characterized by a storm of modes of late capitalist production, hormone synthesis and hyper-binarization of male and female, which are deployed to reproduce the somatic fiction of a 'natural' heteronormative gender binary. Reporting on an ethnographic study, Sanabria's *Plastic Bodies: Sex Hormones and Menstrual Suppression in Brazil* (2016) details manifold practices and bodily manifestations enacted via hormone flows. Focusing on menstrual suppression, Sanabria shows how sex hormones are enrolled to both discipline and mould subjectivities and social processes in relation to existing categories that are often figured as natural, including sex difference and gender, yet hormones also enact and embody fluidity in the very notions of nature and the natural that are being produced. Rebecca Jordan-Young and Katrina Kazarkis's *Testosterone: An Unauthorized Biography* (2019) similarly unpacks and dismantles the accepted or 'authorized' biomedical and social representations of testosterone as a substance that naturally represents and carries masculinity, providing an 'unauthorized' critical biography of testosterone as a complex biosocial entity, in ways that mirror and motivate the experimental approach of this glossary.

These accounts of sex hormones build on earlier works, including Nelly Oudshoorn's *Beyond the Natural Body: An Archaeology of Sex Hormones* (1994), which unearths the 'discovery' of sex hormones to show how they came to simultaneously disrupt, reinforce and reconfigure notions of sex difference and gender relations. Celia Roberts's (2007) *Messengers of Sex: Hormones, Biomedicine and Feminism* further highlighted and defined the role of hormones as material-semiotic messengers – carriers of social and cultural meaning as well as biological action. In *Puberty in Crisis: The Sociology of Early Sexual Development*, Roberts

(2015) continues this thread, showing how the sex panic around hormonally mediated early-onset puberty emerges from synergies of biological, psychological and social processes, including the increased surveillance of childhood development.

The existing scholarship offers critical analyses of hormones as material-semiotic entities that are both shaped by sociocultural processes and relations and have the capacity to disrupt and unsettle these processes and relations especially as they pertain to gendered systems of materiality and meaning making. Bringing together a set of entries about a wide range of hormones, *Hormonal Theory* uses the metaphor of cascades to theorize hormonal actions across the biological and social and the material and semiotic in highly diverse contexts – from equine therapy to gaming, from medical treatments of sexual dysfunction to plant gynaecology and racialization of heart disease. Read as a whole, the book makes an empirically as well as theoretically rich contribution to recent scholarship on the fluidity of human and other-than-human biology (see e.g. Pitts-Taylor 2016; Myers 2015).

Outline of the glossary

Hormonal Theory is a playful take on a biomedical glossary, bringing together a range of humanities and social scientific scholars to think with hormones as the focus and vehicle of scientific, ethical and political concerns. It is not an edited collection in the conventional sense but rather a resource to excite new ways of hormonal thinking. The glossary format is inspired by Rosi Braidotti and Maria Hlavajova's (2018) *Posthuman Glossary* for Bloomsbury Academic Press. Each entry takes a biomedically recognized hormonal compound as its starting point yet works to complicate, elaborate and confound biomedical understandings of hormones. Over the course of the book, the entries collectively highlight how hormones cascade into one another and across human and non-human bodies and their socio-ecological surroundings. This glossary, then, is not simply a qualitatively rich companion to medical knowledge about hormones but a challenge to the conceptual underpinnings of currently dominant understandings of hormones and the various social and material spheres in which they operate, including disease, wellness and normalcy.

In taking on the appearance of a conventional alphabetical medical glossary, the book appropriates scientific modes of producing knowledge about hormones while simultaneously rebelling against and destabilizing them. Each entry moves across biomedical, social, political and/or experiential ways of understanding hormones. In so doing, they challenge the separation between biomedical and social forms of knowledge and illustrate how hormones elude this separation by existing at the boundaries and intersections where multiple knowledges collide. The entries also 'rebel' against strictly discussing one chemical entity, illustrating how different hormones and hormonal processes collide with and affect each other.

The entries in this glossary are informed by posthumanism, new materialism, feminism, queer theory and eco-criticism but also venture beyond their theoretical boundaries, contributing towards thinking a 'nature' that is fluid, open and unfolding. This approach follows from and resonates with Indigenous epistemologies and ontologies (e.g. Million 2017), a relationship which Nayan Sheoran Appleton explores in this volume. This book is thus both an exploration into and an experiment with interdisciplinary ways of making sense of the incessant slippage that hormones provoke across different spheres of matter, meaning and life. The book can be read sequentially to engage with an overall argument about the biosociality of hormones or instead read by entry according to readers' interests.

Contributors are scholars from a variety of disciplines, including many with an interdisciplinary orientation, and indeed the editorial collective is similarly composed; as such the book both challenges conventional disciplinary boundaries and provides multiple lenses through which to understand what hormone theory and hormonal cascading might look like. Entries are written by scholars at a wide variety of career stages, and the editorial collective's five members range from senior and junior faculty to pre- and postdoctoral researchers based at a range of international institutions.

From angiotensin to cortisol, testosterone to progestogens and dopamine to endocrine disruptors, the book is a compendium of hormones, offering nineteen entries that explore the inextricability of societal, political, ecological and physiological tensions. They show the entanglement of personal experiences of the embodied self with medical models of the hormonal body, and of cultural, biochemical and environmental disruptions. Entries are organized alphabetically to appropriate the format of conventional glossaries. However, in the following text we group them thematically, to guide the reader to the argument offered by the book: hormones flow biosocially, acting as carriers of biological change that are simultaneously able to mediate and modulate social meanings and as manifestations of socio-environmental experience that carry physiological consequences.

The glossary entries have diverse formats. Some actively play with academic writing conventions – such as Cronon Cronshaw's entry on gonadotropin-releasing hormone agonist (GnRHa), which takes the form of a subversive patient information leaflet (PIL), and Ian Harper's reflections on hydrocortisone and life after pituitary embolism, which offer a powerful autobiographical narrative. Others adhere to more standard academic writing formats. The diversity of styles and theoretical approaches represented across entries in this volume mirrors the book's overarching articulation of hormonal multiplicities and the way that their movement and agencies are unruly, deflecting attempts towards cohesion and order.

Outline of entries

The glossary opens with Celia Roberts's entry, which explores how adrenaline and the 'stress response' are understood to span highly divergent contexts, from a snakebite scare to extreme sports and enduring interpersonal violence. Describing the neurological and endocrinological pathways through which stress is said to 'get under the skin', the entry problematizes conventional understandings of adrenaline as an evolutionarily ancient biological entity. Engaging with contemporary exhortations encouraging us to learn how to 'control' our adrenaline, Roberts points to the paradoxical figurations of adrenaline as a basic survival mechanism and a potential object for self-improvement projects. Starting with a story about an encounter between herself, her dog and a highly poisonous snake, the entry also explores multispecies flows of stress and threat.

Following on the theme of stress, Anne Pollock's entry on angiotensin illuminates the inextricability of societal and physiological tensions in bodies. Pollock explores layered biomedical engagements with angiotensin, showing that chronic stress participates in the dysregulation of the renin-angiotensin system, providing a physiological pathway for the stress of racism to become embodied. Through this lens, she interrogates the simultaneously social and physiological phenomena of risk and receptivity as instantiated in bodies navigating structurally racist societies. Angiotensin is considered an 'endogenous' hormone – that is, one having an internal cause or origin. As such this contribution offers a useful launching point for exploring hormone cascades, by linking 'endogenous' bodily and 'exogenous' social forces.

In her entry on cortisol cascades, Roslyn Malcolm follows a connected thread, exploring how the stress of ableism becomes embodied in the context of autism. This entry unearths a model of autistic experience that evokes a cascade of hormones and related bodily systems in relation to social environs. Here, heightened sensory experience and the 'fight-or-flight' (or stress) response mediated by the brain are understood as irreducible from the human and non-human environments in which autistic people live. Cortisol – like adrenaline, popularly known as a 'stress hormone' – features centrally within this biosocial model of the autistic body, acting as a chemical connection that makes visible the intertwinement of social environments with hormonal flows. Malcolm draws from her ethnographic research on the perceived efficacy of horse-based therapies for autism, situating this phenomenon within a 'therapeutic ecology' of multispecies resonances and transcorporealities across material, affective, atmospheric and architectural scales.

Ian Harper's entry on hydrocortisone – a 'replacement' drug for cortisol – offers personal reflections on suffering a bleed into the pituitary and the consequences of living with hypopituitarism and cortisol deficiency. Reflecting on his own experience of dependency on hydrocortisone, Harper points to how biomedical understandings of the pituitary are broken into the functions of individual hormones and poses the critical question – do we expect too much of medicine when we hope it would pay greater attention to the person as a whole, rather than their atomized fragments?

Oxytocin, popularly labelled the 'love hormone', is often posed in opposition to stress hormones (see Malcolm's and Ford's entries). Arbel Griner and Rafaella Zorzanelli, however, take things in a different direction, elaborating oxytocin's role in the neurobiological 'love complex', a composite of neurohormones and neuropeptides that, according to neuroscientific literature, interacts to guarantee human reproduction and survival. The authors reflect on the construction and implications of the love complex as scientific fact and an epistemic entity that involves chemically based treatment protocols and enhancement practices. Their entry illuminates such therapies' generative power in reiterating scientific and culturally hegemonic affective arrangements and relations – those that are heterosexual, long-lasting, child-centred and economically productive.

Andrea Ford's entry offers another example of how oxytocin – which is not usually associated with so-called 'reproductive hormones' because these are generally glossed with the 'sex hormones' of testosterone, oestrogen and progesterone – is increasingly central to reproductive narratives. It examines Pitocin, a synthetic oxytocin used in medical procedures during birth that is vilified by many for interrupting the cascade of oxytocin and related hormones that 'naturally' occurs during birthing. Unlike externally applied Pitocin, endogenous oxytocin not only causes uterine contractions but also further works to provide pain relief and help initiate breastfeeding and bonding between the birthing person and their infant. Based on ethnographic research, Ford investigates birth narratives where medical spaces, personnel and procedures are all implicated in triggering (un)desirable hormonal cascades. She shows how competing narratives of hormone cascades during birthing respond to ideologies about 'natural bodies' while simultaneously articulating bodies as deeply enmeshed with their surroundings and as sites for self-cultivation.

Many of the entries critically examine so-called sex hormones. Fabíola Rohden's contribution explores testosterone, commonly defined as the 'male' hormone, discussing the ways this hormone is used to construct and treat a broad and varied swathe of problems related to 'female sexual dysfunction' in Brazil. In her ethnographic research, Rohden investigates the phenomenon of intense medicalization and pharmaceuticalization of female sexuality particularly present in middle- and upper-class women with access to private medical services. Here, she explores the ways in which sexual desire is defined empathically as the presence of a greater or lesser amount of testosterone, a standard associated primarily with biological definitions of gender difference.

In her entry on progesterone, Nayantara Sheoran Appleton rethinks the ways in which Euro-American scientific, biomedical and public discourses have historically framed progesterone and progesterone receptors as 'female'. Exploring the nuances of the Te Reo (Maori) term for this hormone, 'Takai Tūmua', Appleton exhorts us to pay close attention to the cultural freight carried in scientific languages. What happens, she asks, if we use a term that does not prioritize the reproduction-related actions of this hormone but instead takes account of its actions across multiple biosocial domains?

Building on existing scholarship on 'sex-hormones'' ability to carry messages regarding gendered norms, Kristine Fearon and Charlotte Jones critically examine oestrogen. Through exploring the significance and signification of oestrogen 'deficit' for women with sex variations, the authors investigate how this hormone and its effects are constructed by, and constructors of, the somatic, biomedical and social stages of life women are expected to travel through: menarche, reproduction and menopause. Drawing from the experiences of women and parents of children with clinically diagnosed 'disorders/differences of sex development' (DSDs), the authors explore the role of oestrogen in the imagination of these gendered biosocial communities.

Magdalena Radkowska-Walkowics's entry on recombinant growth hormone (rGH) takes up a synthesized molecular intervention into growth as its focus. This entry explores the role of rGH as a medical technology and biosocial actor in experiences of Turner syndrome, a condition that causes a complete or partial absence of an X chromosome in women and girls and affects height. Drawing from anthropological research, Radkowska-Walkowics interrogates the ways in which rGH therapies to promote growth in girls with Turner syndrome reflect social entanglements and expectations related to the meaning and embodiment of a 'normal' life, including aesthetic patterns around height and mitigation against short stature. At the same time, striving towards a 'normal' life through rGH obscures how different actors, including doctors and parents of girls with Turner syndrome, may actually not want to reverse the symptoms because 'normal' life is a relative concept that depends only to a small extent on centimetres.

In his entry on gonadotropin-releasing hormone agonist (GnRHa) Cronan Cronshaw details the pharmaceutical chemical used to 'block' the production of hormones such as oestrogen and testosterone to postpone the onset of puberty. This entry mimics and subverts a PIL on GnRHa, otherwise known as 'hormone blockers', illuminating essentialist notions of sex and gender in both such leaflets and GnRHa therapies themselves. GnRHa therapies, used to pause pubertal development in young people diagnosed with gender dysphoria, work by intervening in hormonal messaging between the brain and the gonads. Cronshaw explores GnRHa therapies as envoys of neoliberal values and ideals, such as choice, individualism and control, and exposes the many contradictions and nuances of the social realities that accompany taking these drugs, which are biosocial agents in producing sexed and gendered subjectivities.

Risa Cromer's entry on follicle-stimulating hormone (FSH) and luteinizing hormone (LH) traces a history of stimulating excitement about and interest in (hormonally assisting) reproduction within scientific, clinical, religious, national, ethical and market forces. It does so by investigating the generation of landmark gonadotropic therapeutics, Pergonal and Gonal-F, by the Italian pharmaceutical company Serono. Cromer explores how stimulating reproduction decentres hormones and considers the conditions, minds and agents that activate their production and excite broad social engagement in assisting reproduction.

Leah Eades's entry on Mifepristone and Misoprostol similarly offers a critical analysis of abortion drugs, agency and reproductive governance. Here, Eades speaks specifically to the social and political situatedness of Mifepristone and Misoprostol as hormonal drugs with agency in disrupting relations of power as well as terminating pregnancies. Eades explores the ways they rebel against and complicate dominant modes of categorizing and regulating bodies, with implications for maternal-foetal politics, clinical hierarchies and power relations. Through an investigation of how abortion medication contests biopolitical forces of reproductive governance, Eades argues for a nuanced reading of abortion medication that attends to how their development, uptake and use disrupts systems of knowledge production and political economies of medical expertise.

In another entry that exposes complexities around the pregnant body, Emily Ross highlights the instability of biological facts through the slippage at play in biomedical knowledges regarding Human Chorionic Gonadotropin (hCG). Ross interrogates how the hormone hCG is constituted as both a marker of pregnancy and a marker of cancer. Drawing on document analysis and patient and practitioner experiences relating to gestational trophoblastic diseases, in which cancerous growths incite signs of pregnancy, she offers a critical investigation of the seemingly 'natural' distinctions, boundaries and relationships between women and foetuses, bodies and cancers and corporeality and technology.

Mariana Rios Sandoval's entry on progestogens brings critical accounts of gender, sex and pregnancy into conversation with concerns about hormones in the environment. It presents an ethnographic account of the progestogenic entanglements taking place among French feminist self-gynaecology groups that have (re)emerged in contestation to a highly medicalized and coercive contraceptive apparatus centred around hormonal interventions in female bodies. Exploring the variety of progestogens present in these conversations – those in bodies, in contraceptive pills, in plants and in industrial pollutants – Sandoval makes visible how young feminists rekindle relationships with their bodies and environments and points to an expansive space of hormonal action that is not contained within the limits of the skin.

Also speaking to expansive hormonal action across the assumed boundary of the skin, several entries interrogate leakages and flows from the environment 'in' to bodies via chemical pollution. In their entry, Jacquelyne Luce and Anjali Rao-Herel, working with the Feminist Technoscience Governance Collaboratory, explore how diethylstilbestrol (DES), a synthetic oestrogen and the prototypical endocrine-disrupting chemical (EDC), functions as a chemical potentiality for sex, gender and sexuality. Drawing on interviews with people with documented or suspected exposure to DES, they analyse how temporally unbound and (re) spatialized understandings of DES, and the potential effects it may have, engender particular narrations of sexual difference, gender identity and sexuality that have a complex relationship with the notion of 'toxicity'.

Norah Mackendrick's entry on dichloro-diphenyl-trichloroethane, the pesticide commonly known as DDT, continues this thread, examining cultural and social anxieties about this pollutant which can simultaneously mitigate against some risks (the spread of malaria) and heighten others (global chemical pollution that gives rise to health concerns). Interrogating the 'threat of feminization' that DDT is seen to pose for both humans and the wildlife as a chemical pollutant, Mackendrick considers how different kinds of risks and the tensions between them are navigated in gendered ways in relation to each other and in relation to concerns over the future of the human species as a whole.

In their entry on endocrine disrupting chemicals, more generally, Wibke Straube highlights the potential implications for gender non-conforming people in drawing attention to the hormonal effects of environmental toxicity. Considering both scientific research that links environmental pollution with gender/sex and the social media uptake of such research, Straube explores how scientific research into EDCs brings about discussions of naturalness in new forms that can be threatening to the well-being of gender non-conforming people, particularly youth, even when it purports to help them. Yet Straube emphasizes the importance of critical science investigating environmental pollution and suggests a disclosure mechanism to help keep such research from inadvertently causing harm.

Lastly, and bringing this introductory walk-through full circle, Tom Boylston's entry on dopamine discusses hormonal environments, agency and self-crafting. In interrogating discourses on dopamine in online publics that congregate around video games, technology use and productivity, Boylston asks how ideas about dopamine shape understandings and practices of selfhood and desire. Based on an exploration of how people in these virtual public spheres understand desire and compulsion in critical, intersubjective and environmental terms, Boylston argues that dopamine thinking should be understood within a wider field of 'hormone heuristics'. This challenges popular notions of the brain as a relatively fixed and monistic organ, instead highlighting hormonal cascades not only within bodies but also between bodies and in conversation with social and physical environments.

All entries in this glossary play on and challenge the biomedical notion that hormones can be conceived as discrete entities. *Hormonal Theory* draws from this wealth of humanities and qualitative social science research to illustrate, and provoke further exploration into, how hormones mediate bodies, relations and affects in complex ways that exceed the biophysical. Together, the entries show how the various chemicals classified as hormones or that interact with hormonal processes not only constitute bodies and their experiential realities (as is commonly reflected in medical explanations) but also how experiential realities in turn constitute the chemical processes of bodies. Collectively, the entries explore how hormones are increasingly a site for managing social and ecological relations and how this can result in both the biomedicalization of relations and affects and resistance to such medicalization.

References

Appleton, N. S. (2022), 'Critical Ethnographic Respect: Women's' Narratives, Material Conditions, and Emergency Contraception in India', *Anthropology of Medicine* 29 (2): 141–59.

Bärnreuther, S. (2018), 'Suitable Substances: How Biobanks (Re)store Biologicals', *New Genetics and Society* 37 (4): 319–37.

Braidotti, R. and M. Hlavajova (2018), *Posthuman Glossary*, London: Bloomsbury.

Gaudilliére, J.-P. (2004), 'Genesis and Development of a Biomedical Object: Styles of Thought, Styles of Work and the History of the Sex Steroids', *Studies in History and Philosophy of Science Part C* 35 (3): 525–43.

Haraway, D. (1991), *Simians, Cyborgs and Women: The Reinvention of Nature*, New York: Routledge.

Hardon, A. and E. Sanabria (2017), 'Fluid Drugs: Revisiting the Anthropology of Pharmaceuticals', *Annual Review of Anthropology* 46: 117–32.

Jordan-Young, R. and K. Karkazis (2019), *Testosterone: An Unauthorized Biography*, Cambridge, MA: Harvard University Press.

Malcolm, R. (2021), '"There's No Constant": Oxytocin, Cortisol, and Balanced Proportionality in Hormonal Models of Autism', *Medical Anthropology* 40 (4): 375–88.

Million, D. (2017), '7. Indigenous Matters', in S. Alaimo (ed.), *Gender: Matter*, 95–110, Farmington Hills, MI: MacMillan.

Murphy, M. (2008), 'Chemical Regimes of Living', *Environmental History* 13 (4): 695–703.

Myers, N. (2015), *Rendering Life Molecular: Models, Modelers, and Excitable Matter*, Durham: Duke University Press.

Oudshoorn, N. (1994), *Beyond the Natural Body: An Archaeology of Sex Hormones*, New York and London: Routledge.

Pitts-Taylor, V. (2016), *The Brain's Body: Neuroscience and Corporeal Politics*, Durham and London: Duke University Press.

Pollock, A. (2016), '7: Queering Endocrine Disruption', in K. Behar (ed.), *Object-Oriented Feminism*, 183–99, Minneapolis: University of Minnesota Press.

Preciado, P. B. (2013), *Testo Junkie: Sex, Drugs and Biopolitics in the Pharmacopornographic Era*, London: The Feminist Press.

Roberts, C. (2007), *Messengers of Sex: Hormones, Biomedicine and Feminism*, Cambridge: Cambridge University Press.

Roberts, C. (2015), *Puberty in Crisis: The Sociology of Early Sexual Development*, Cambridge: Cambridge University Press.

Roberts C. and B. McWade (2021), 'Messengers of Stress: Towards a Cortisol Sociology', *Sociology of Health and Illness* 43 (4): 895–909.

Rose, N. (2007), *The Politics of Life Itself: Biomedicine, Power, and Subjectivity in the Twenty-First Century*, Princeton University Press. https://doi.org/10.1515/9781400827503/pdf

Sanabria, E. (2016), *Plastic Bodies: Sex Hormones and Menstrual Suppression in Brazil*, Durham and London: Duke University Press.

1 ADRENALINE

CELIA ROBERTS

Beni and I were walking on Mt Majura, enjoying our local bush track. Beni is a young energetic dog, who walks with great enthusiasm, thrusting his nose into scent trails and rising up on his hind legs to catch a glimpse of the kangaroos or foxes he detects. We constantly negotiate how we are going to walk together, to manage my desire to keep going forward, his to stop and read the land; mine to walk quickly, his to at least trot. On this hot, sunny day, the long grass, weighed down by seed, was rippling in the breeze, capturing my attention. Suddenly, Beni sprung vertically in the air. Looking down I saw a gleaming Eastern Brown snake escaping across the narrow path. Beni turned back to sniff this strange creature. I heard a short, high scream and ran, hauling the dog away. The scream was mine. My heart banged and my limbs felt trembly. Such a near miss! Both Beni and I on top of Australia's most deadly snakes! And I had done the wrong thing: you are supposed to stand still. Beni, sensing my concern, jumped up like a puppy, as if I could take him into my arms for protection. We walked home along the wider path; all three creatures shaken by our undesired encounter within our daily shared space.

Adrenaline is a hormone secreted from the adrenal glands as humans (and other non-human vertebrates) experience something fear-inducing. The experience of adrenaline coursing through our bodies is, in some ways of looking at it, fear itself. Importantly adrenaline moves far faster than cognition, so it can generate muscular actions, including running and screaming, before we have any chance of thinking. It can make humans – and other non-human animals – incredibly strong and nimble: we can leap out of the way of a charging beast, arching snake or runaway machine, and we can lift extremely heavy objects off someone else's body. Lives can be saved because of adrenaline. Great harm can also occur: snakes strike at lightning speed when threatened; dogs can bite; and humans can shoot or use their bodies to attack others without conscious thought.

Adrenaline is often described as a 'rush' because of its speed of action. This term also indicates the potential pleasures of this hormone – its flows can create intense feelings of aliveness. Some people go to enormous lengths to experience this – climbing mountains or leaping off cliffs (see e.g. Jacobson 2020); while others seem to search for it in less socially approved ways – driving fast, fighting in gangs, taking drugs (see e.g. Duffy 2020).[1] For others, as discussed later, frequent surges of adrenaline become part of an embodied experience of undesired danger, over time leaving a trail of negative health implications, including insomnia, jitteriness, metabolic issues and high blood pressure.

In scientific terms, adrenaline is part of the 'flight-or-fight' response to threat. This response has two key pathways: the hypothalamic-pituitary-adrenal (HPA) axis, a set of hormonal 'cascades' connecting the brain, the brain stem and the adrenal glands in times of physiological or psychological stress or danger; and the sympathetic-adrenal-medullary (SAM) axis, a neuroendocrine system connecting the brain to various parts of the body including the adrenal glands. When the brain experiences a threat, often parsed in the scientific literature as 'stress', the hypothalamus sends hormones to the pituitary gland, which in turns hormonally messages the adrenal glands above the kidneys. The adrenals secrete cortisol into the bloodstream, thereby entering a negative feedback loop with the brain, facilitating some physiological responses (increasing heart rate and blood pressure, for example) and inhibiting others (like digestion). At the same time, but with much greater speed, the hypothalamus sends noradrenaline (a neurotransmitter) through the spinal cord to various organs, including the heart, eyes and lungs, *and* to the adrenal medulla and adrenal glands. These glands then secrete adrenaline and more noradrenaline (which is also a hormone) to get the body ready for action, increasing heart rate, dilating pupils, increasing blood sugar levels and pumping more blood to muscles. Alongside the HPA axis, then, the hormonal patterns constituting the SAM axis helps the body to act in self-defence by running away or fighting. In times of extreme fear, human and other animal bodies can also freeze, faint or dissociate. Neurologist Stephen Porges describes this as 'an evolutionarily ancient shutdown system' which is activated when the 'flight-or-fight' processes do not lead to safety (Porges 2018: xxi). In my snake encounter, I ran, but my snake-handling sociologist colleague Gavin Smith tells me that some people faced with an Eastern Brown try to kill it (which is illegal – these snakes are a protected species), while others freeze. As Porges (2018: xxi) explains, in evolutionary terms 'this immobilization response was the body's attempt to become inanimate in the presence of a predator'.

Despite its importance to survival and the significance of fear in human societies, there is very little critical social scientific work about adrenaline compared to other hormones in this volume. This is despite the fact that adrenaline is relatively well known. The term 'adrenaline junkie' appears frequently in cultural texts to describe people who deliberately engage in activities that provoke adrenaline flows. The term 'adrenaline rush' is also commonly used. Taken together, both phrases carry highly problematic moral freight, signalling a connection between the 'loss of control' associated with adrenaline flows and the experiences of people using illicit substances, specifically heroin.[2] Both this commonly made analogy to drug-taking *and* the biological details of adrenaline flows remain largely unexamined, even in social scientific texts that refer to adrenaline in exploring people's engagements with fear-inducing activities such as war (see e.g. Braender 2016a).

In some ways, the absence of critical analysis of adrenaline makes sense: its actions within the sympathetic nervous system are about as far away from social science or cultural theory as one can think. Understood as part of a survival mechanism, adrenaline is associated with humans' most animal-like qualities, described in scientific texts (and those citing them) as a 'primitive' or 'reptilian' element of human neuro and endocrine physiology. In such texts, human reactions to threat are understood as important evolutionary connections between all vertebrates: even reptiles 'flight, fight or freeze' when threatened. (The snake I encountered, for example, moved quickly to escape my dog and me and probably saved its own and my dog's life in so doing.) Adrenaline is understood, in other words, to work beyond conscious thought and thus outside social life.

In this entry, I want to challenge this figuration of adrenaline and argue instead for its significance in understanding the biosocial world. As I have argued previously in relation to oestrogen, testosterone (Roberts 2007) and cortisol (Roberts and McWade 2021), adrenaline plays a hugely important role in messaging between social and biological worlds and, in so doing, troubles conventional social scientific understandings of the distinction between them. I take the idea that adrenaline is, like cortisol, a 'messenger of stress' from scientific texts but want to reshape this notion to encompass a more critical understanding of the significance of the social – of meaning making and culturally shaped forms of embodiment – to human and non-human animal lives.

'Getting under the skin': The biology of stress

In biological research, threat, or more broadly 'stress', is often described as a social or 'environmental' phenomenon that 'gets under the skin' via hormonal cascades (McEwan 2012). In these literatures, the hormones adrenaline, noradrenaline and cortisol form bidirectional bridges between social worlds and (human and non-human) bodies, carrying messages of stress both from the world and to it, sometimes causing individuals to respond to real danger and at other times to overreact to relatively safe situations, often causing suffering to themselves and others (Roberts and McWade 2021).

As many social scientists have argued, the term 'stress' has a complex history and a somewhat diffuse and broad meaning in scientific texts (see e.g. Young 1980; Jackson 2013). Building on the work of pioneering stress physiologists Walter Cannon and Hans Selye (Jackson 2013: 222), contemporary neuroscientists such as Bruce McEwan, Robert Sapolsky and Michael Meany, for example, argue that it is important to distinguish between 'good' stress – that which motivates humans and other animals to move, explore and live – and 'bad' stress, which can create long-term toxic effects on the brain and body via hormonal pathways. This distinction, as we will see later, is often repeated in popular accounts. Scientists also draw distinctions between acute and chronic stress: encountering a snake in a one-off event is biologically a very different experience to experiencing relentless interpersonal violence, even though adrenaline and cortisol are involved in both cases.

With its rapid flows and strong and sudden physiological impacts, adrenaline teaches us how to survive. For several weeks after my encounter with the Eastern Brown, I avoid that part of my regular walking trail, sticking to wider and clearer paths. These changes to my patterns are not conscious decisions; I just find myself doing them. My body remembers the snake and the unpleasant – and pedagogic – adrenaline of our encounter. Social life, or 'experience', clearly intersects with adrenaline here: what happened to Beni and me makes me cautious and changes our patterns of living. (I'm also hoping that the snake now avoids that path!)

In other sorts of adrenaline-related circumstances, however, hormonal life lessons can become confused and potentially harmful. For humans (and other animals such as dogs), repeated or chronic exposure to stress and/or high levels of adrenaline can lead our brains and bodies to believe we are threatened when we are not. Hormonal and neurohormonal cascades involving cortisol, adrenaline and noradrenaline can, in these cases, be activated by apparently benign material or emotional experiences: a particular smell, raised voices or the sensation of being touched, for example. Sometimes people with repeated exposure to serious threat (e.g. those working in the military or emergency services or people exposed to familial or community violence) can also develop post-traumatic stress disorder (PTSD), a psycho-physiological condition involving flashbacks or recurrent memories of stressful events. During these flashbacks, hormonal flows can be triggered as if the person is materially back in the dangerous situation, resulting in high levels of cortisol and adrenaline (Levine 2018; National Health Service 2022).

These situations highlight the complex nature of adrenaline as both a necessary survival mechanism and a potentially harmful entity. In popular discourses, the troubling connection to addiction is sometimes deployed to articulate this 'polyvalence'. On the website 'Exploringyourmind.com', for example, psychologist Valeria Sabatar describes the 'dark' and 'addictive' qualities of adrenaline, somewhat paradoxically giving it credit for *producing* 'the anxiety and chronic stress that many people suffer from':

> Adrenaline is what makes us feel good when we exercise. It gives us butterflies in our stomach when we're attached to someone and enables us to react to everyday dangers. In addition to helping with performance and activation, however, adrenaline has a dark side. In excess, it has serious side effects. **Adrenaline is a polyvalent substance, just like dopamine and oxytocin.** It also acts as a neurotransmitter and affects our behaviour more than almost any other hormone. For example, adrenaline activates our survival instincts but also give us a tendency towards addictive behaviors. It can provoke the kind of anxiety and chronic stress that many people suffer from. (Sabatar 2021; bold in original)

Scientific research highlights the long-term health impacts of repeated exposure to stress (see also Pollock, this volume). Many scholars in this field use the term 'allostatic load' (McEwan and Stellar 1993) to describe the biological burdens (hormonal and otherwise) of accumulated stress, documenting their epigenetic (and potentially intergenerationally transmissible) impact on inflammation levels and individuals' risk of illnesses such as heart disease, cancer and stroke (Guidi et al. 2021). As Pollock discusses in her entry on angiotensin, this research also articulates the interconnections between wider sociocultural stresses, such as racism and socio-economic status, on individual and population health (see e.g. Massey 2004; Paradies et al. 2015; Slopen et al. 2016).

Importantly, and somewhat paradoxically, repeated exposure to stress can also produce atypically low levels of cortisol (Sherin and Nemeroff 2011; Roberts and McWade 2021). Porges (2018: xxii) argues that such cases demonstrate the significance of the 'freeze' response to extreme stress: trauma survivors, for example, sometimes experience a 'down regulation of the sympathetic nervous system and HPA axis convergent with personal experiences of shutdown, immobilization, and dissociation'. Military experience may also lead to habituation to adrenaline-triggering events. Here, the idea of 'addiction' again comes into explanatory play. Sociologist Morten Braender, for example, describes the Danish soldiers in his survey-based study as people who 'just like real drug addicts build up a physiological tolerance to narcotics . . . can become "adrenaline junkies" because their tolerance towards excitement is "pushed upward" by being exposed to danger' (Braender 2016a: 3). He argues that we must understand these patterns of attraction as both physiological and social. In his podcast about this article, Braender (2016b) also reports that soldiers call those who have been deployed many times 'adrenaline junkies': this way of thinking about adrenaline clearly has both social and scientific resonance (see also Caddick, Smith and Phoenix 2015; Carter 2019).

Taking control

People who may be experiencing 'too much' adrenaline in the absence of materially dangerous threat are advised by health authorities to do yoga, laugh or be massaged, among other things, in order to regulate their bodies' reactivity to stressful situations via hormones (Healthdirect 2021). As with cortisol (Roberts, Mackenzie and Mort 2019: 74), learning to breathe deeply and slowly is said to reduce 'excessive' amounts of adrenaline (Bancos 2022). Various modes of somatic therapy also teach clients to notice when they might be experiencing 'fight-or-flight' responses and to make connections between these experiences and their personal histories of trauma or abuse (Porges and Dana 2018).

In popular health discourses, the consequences of not addressing your adrenaline levels are said to be serious, even ruinous. In the following example, addiction again appears as a warning figure ('if we need to have this feeling every day . . .'):

When we go through difficult, comfortable situations that threaten our physical and emotional balance, **our brain interprets them as a danger**. That's when adrenaline comes onto the scene, and when we must act efficiently. However we don't always do that, and that's when adrenaline builds up and causes changes in our bodies (high blood pressure, rapid pulse, digestive problems). Our health is compromised and we put our lives at risk. It's not something we can just brush aside, nor should we put it off until tomorrow or next week . . . In conclusion, we can say that **adrenalin fulfills its 'magic' purpose as long as it is released at the right time**. In those situations, it acts as a vital impetus to help us react, keep us safe, make us adapt better to certain situations. But if we need this feeling every day or allow tension and fears to take over, adrenaline can have the worst effect possible: it can ruin our health. (Sabatar 2021, bold in original)

As modern subjects, all of us (but especially those suffering from 'excessive' adrenaline) are exhorted to learn to control our 'reptilian' brains; to use our evolutionarily higher mammalian capacities to understand and, when necessary, resist our biological responses to perceived threat (even as such responses are described as natural, even magical). In tune with the scientific concept of endocrinological homeostasis, such control is often described as promoting 'balance' and therefore good physical and mental health. Engaged citizens are taught to think of themselves in hormonal terms and to act accordingly. In the following advice from Healthline.com, for example, readers are advised to 'learn technique' to 'activate your parasympathetic nervous system', the physiological counterbalance to the SAM axis. Such activation, we are told, will 'allow the body to rest and repair itself':

How to control adrenaline

It's important to learn technique to counter your body's stress response. Experiencing some stress is normal, and sometimes even beneficial for your health. But over time, persistent surges of adrenaline can damage your blood vessels, increase your blood pressure, and elevate your risk of heart attacks or stroke. It can also result in anxiety, weight gain, headaches and insomnia. To help control adrenaline, you'll need to activate your parasympathetic nervous system, also known as the 'rest-and-digest system'. The rest-and-digest response is the opposite of the flight-or-fight response. It helps promote equilibrium in the body, and allows your body to rest and repair itself. (Carfasso 2023, bold in original)

Part of being able to 'control' adrenaline is coming to understand and recognize its effects. Future biosensing technologies and wearables may help in this regard – adrenaline is measurable in sweat – although the technical and practical complexities of possible biochemical biosensing devices are many (Perez and Orozco 2022). Like cortisol biosensing (Roberts, Mackenzie and Mort 2019), adrenaline biosensing would also be confounded by hormones' inherently fluctuating nature and, in this case, adrenaline's characteristic rapidity. Coming to know adrenaline's physiological traces – increased heart rate, shakiness, dry mouth and so on – is a more likely route towards 'control' than any direct measuring of hormone levels.[3]

Intervening in fear cascades need not be conscious or even done by the individual concerned. Parents, for example, often use calming strategies – tone of voice, physical touch, explanation – to modulate the adrenaline and cortisol flows of their children (Mackenzie and Roberts 2017). Sports coaches and military officers use spoken and physical strategies (bodily patterns such as marching or team movement patterns) to manage their charges' physiological states (Cuncic 2023; Williamson and Barker 2021). Like dog trainers, snake handlers similarly use calming strategies of voice, movement and self-awareness to increase the safety of capturing and relocating snakes (Smith 2021). Adrenaline-reducing actions can also be undertaken by non-human others. Dogs can be trained to respond to the signs of elevated stress hormones in humans with PTSD, joining in negative feedback loops through actions such as pressing against their companion to bring these levels back to homeostasis (https://ptsddogs.org.au; see also Malcolm, this volume).

Biosocial flows

The term 'cascade' is used in biology to refer to a chain of events in which each is dependent on the previous one. Borrowing from cascade's other meaning – a steep, usually small waterfall – the term implies a form of unstoppability of flow or connection. In relation to stress hormones, 'cascade' carries a sense of inevitability, contributing to a cultural narrative that leaves adrenaline in the realm of biology, far away from social science. Diving deeper into popular and scientific accounts of adrenaline's actions, however, shows that flows of this hormone – like all the others in this volume – are profoundly connected to social life in multidirectional ways.

I noted at the start that some experiences of adrenaline are enjoyable: others are unbearable and are avoided at all costs. In a parallel apparent contradiction, adrenaline flows are described as both instinctive and addictive and as something we should and could learn to control. Adrenaline messages across social and biological and human and more-than-human worlds, connecting worlds of conscious and unconscious meaning and barely signified felt experiences. As an actor in biosocial cascades, adrenaline is far from 'simply biological' or 'primitive'. Like all the other hormones in this volume, then, it could and should be an object of critical social scientific study. Beni's and my encounter with the Eastern Brown snake certainly involved physiological responses that went faster than conscious thought – but this does not mean that our encounter was not biosocial in its nature and its effects. All three of us hopefully learnt something important about the dangers of sunny paths that can accompany their many pleasures. Smith is currently developing a 'snake sociology', arguing that it is important that we humans and our companion animals learn to share space with these beautiful creatures and understand their actions in more complex ways. His focus on snake-human relations is instructive here. Similarly, I want to suggest a critical analysis of adrenaline that engages with both its material actions in human and non-human animal bodies and its representations in scientific and other texts. Such analysis would help us to think in more depth about how adrenaline's actions shape human and more-than-human lives and to move (as we must with regard to snakes) beyond discourses of 'control', and its 'loss', towards practices of recognition and careful attention.

Acknowledgements

With special thanks to Andrea Ford, Sone Erikainen, Gavin Smith and Adrian Mackenzie for discussing this piece with me.

Notes

1   Despite using the phrase 'adrenaline junkie' in his book title, psychologist Kenneth Carter (2019) argues that seeking the feeling of adrenaline is not a strong motivating element in those who engage in sensory-seeking activities.

2   The idea that taking illicit drugs involves 'loss of control' is hotly debated within critical drug studies, as is the suggestion that people can become 'addicted' to internal hormonal and other biochemical flows (Fraser and Valentine 2008; Weinberg 2013; Fraser, Moore and Keane 2014; Boylston this volume).

3   Although see Pykett et al. (2020) for an interesting suggestion for citizen science projects involving stress biosensing.

References

Bancos, I. (2022), 'Adrenal Hormones', Available at www.endocrine.org/patient -engagement/endocrine-library/hormones-and-endocrine-function/adrenal -hormones, (accessed 1 February 2023).

Braender, M. (2016a), 'Adrenalin Junkies: Why Soldiers Return from War Wanting More', *Armed Forces and Society* 42 (1): 3–25.

Braender, M. (2016b), 'Why Soldiers Return from War Wanting More', *Podcast*, Available at https://journals.sagepub.com/doi/10.1177/0095327X15569296 (accessed 8 February 2023).

Caddick, N., B. Smith, and C. Phoenix (2015), 'Male Combat Veterans' Narratives of PTSD, Masculinity, and Health', *Sociology of Health and Illness* 37 (1): 97–111.

Carfasso, J. (2023), 'Adrenaline Rush: Everything You Should Know', Available at www
.healthline.com/health/adrenaline-rush (accessed 1 February 2023).

Carter, K. (2019), *Buzz! Inside the Minds of Thrill-Seekers, Daredevils and Adrenaline
Junkies*, Cambridge: Cambridge University Press.

Cuncic, A. (2023), 'How to Handle Performance Anxiety', Available at www.verywellmind
.com/how-do-i-handle-performance-anxiety-as-an-athlete-3024337 (accessed
13 February 2023).

Duffy, E. (2020), *The Speed Handbook*, Durham: Duke University Press.

Fraser, S., D. Moore, and H. Keane (2014), *Habits: Remaking Addiction*, New York:
Palgrave Macmillan.

Fraser, S. and K. Valentine (2008), *Substance and Substitution: Methadone Subjects in
Liberal Societies*, New York: Palgrave Macmillan.

Guidi, J., M. Lucente, N. Sonino, and G. A. Fava (2021), 'Allostatic Load and its Impact on
Health: A Systematic Review', *Psychotherapy and Psychosomatics* 90 (1): 11–27.

Healthdirect (2021), 'Adrenaline'. Available at www.healthdirect.gov.au/adrenaline
(accessed 1 February 2023).

Jackson, M. (2013), *The Age of Stress: Science and the Search for Stability*, Oxford: Oxford
University Press.

Jacobson, K. J. (2020), *The American Adrenalin Narratives*, Athens: University of Georgia
Press.

Levine, P. (2018), 'Polyvagal Theory and Trauma', in S. W. Porges and D. Dana (eds),
Clinical Applications of The Polyvagal Theory, 3–26, New York and London: WW
Norton and Company.

Mackenzie, A. and C. Roberts. (2017), 'Adopting Neuroscience: Parenting and Affective
Indeterminacy', *Body & Society* 23 (3): 130–55.

Massey, D. (2004), 'Segregation and Stratification: A Biosocial Perspective', *DuBois Review:
Social Science Research on Race* 1 (1): 7–25.

McEwan, B. S. (2012), 'Brain on Stress: How the Social Environment Gets Under the Skin',
Proceedings of the National Academies of Science 109 (Supplement 2): 17180–5.

McEwen B. S. and E. Stellar (1993), 'Stress and the Individual. Mechanisms Leading to
Disease', *Archives of Internal Medicine* 153 (18): 2093–101.

National Health Service (2022), 'Causes – Post-traumatic Stress Disorder', Available at
www.nhs.uk/mental-health/conditions/post-traumatic-stress-disorder-ptsd/causes/
(accessed 1 February 2023).

Paradies, Y., J. Ben, N. Denson, A. Elias., N. Priest, et al. (2015), 'Racism as a
Determinant of Health: A Systematic Review and Meta-Analysis', *PLOS ONE* 10 (9):
e0138511.

Pérez, D. and J. Orozco. (2022), 'Wearable Electrochemical Biosensors to Measure
Biomarkers with Complex Blood-to-Sweat Partition Such as Proteins and Hormones',
Microchimica Acta 189: 127.

Porges, S. W. (2018), 'Preface: Why Polyvagal Theory was Welcomed by Therapists', in S.
W. Porges and D. Dana (eds), *Clinical Applications of The Polyvagal Theory*, xix–xxv,
New York and London: WW Norton and Company.

Pykett, J., B. Chrisinger, K. Kyriakou, T. Osbourne, B. Resch, A. Stathi, E. Toth,
and A. C. Whittaker (2020), 'Developing a Citizen Social Science Approach to
Understand Urban Stress and Promote Wellbeing in Urban Communities', *Palgrave
Communications* 6: 85.

Roberts, C. (2007), *Messengers of Sex: Hormones, Biomedicine and Feminism*, Cambridge:
Cambridge University Press.

Roberts, C., A. Mackenzie, and M. Mort (2019), *Living Data: Making Sense of Health Biosensing*, Bristol: Bristol University Press.

Roberts, C. and B. McWade (2021), 'Messengers of Stress: Towards a Cortisol Sociology', *Sociology of Health and Illness* 43 (4): 895–909.

Sabatar, V. (2021), 'Adrenaline, the Performance and Activation Hormone', Available at https://exploringyourmind.com/adrenaline-the-performance-and-activation-hormone/ (accessed 1 February 2023).

Sherin, J. E. and C. B. Nemeroff (2011), 'Post-traumatic Stress Disorder: The Neurobiological Impact of Psychological Trauma', *Dialogues in Clinical Neuroscience* 13 (3): 263–78.

Slopen, N., Y. Chen, N. Priest, M. A. Albert, and D. Williams (2016), 'Emotional and Instrumental Support during Childhood and Biological Dysregulation in Midlife', *Preventive Medicine* 84 (March): 90–6.

Smith, G. (2021), 'Good Luck Fella, Stay Safe: A Snake Catcher Explains Why Our Fear of Brown Snakes is Misplaced', *The Conversation*, January 4. https://theconversation.com/good-luck-fella-stay-safe-a-snake-catcher-explains-why-our-fear-of-brown-snakes-is-misplaced-150783 (accessed 1 February 2023).

Weinberg, D. (2013), 'Post-humanism, Addiction and the Loss of Self-control: Reflections on the Missing Core in Addiction Science', *International Journal of Drug Policy* 24 (3): 173–81.

Wilkinson, A. and J. Barker (2021), 'What Stress Does to the Body – And How Practice Can Help Athletes React Better Under Pressure', *The Conversation*, 15 July. Available at https://theconversation.com/what-stress-does-to-the-body-and-how-practice-can-help-athletes-react-better-under-pressure-164281 (accessed 8 February 2023).

Young, A. (1980), 'The Discourse on Stress and the Reproduction of Conventional Knowledge', *Social Science and Medicine*, 14B: 133–46.

2 ANGIOTENSIN

ANNE POLLOCK

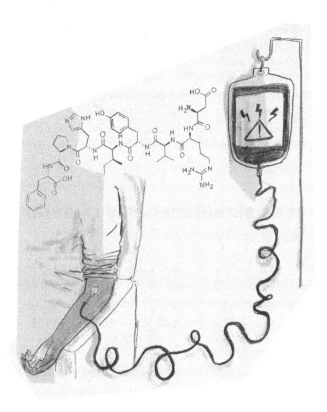

Angiotensin is a hormone that causes vasoconstriction, which is to say, narrowing of the blood vessels. Angiotensin also has impacts on the nervous system that can be sensed – inducing thirst and desire for salt – and wide-ranging systemic effects. Operating in close relationship with the kidney enzyme renin in what is often referred to as the renin-angiotensin system or the renin-angiotensin-aldosterone system that regulates salt and fluid retention, angiotensin plays a key role in regulating blood pressure and the fluid balance of the body.

In principle angiotensin levels might be too high or too low, but it is heightened levels of angiotensin that attract the bulk of medical interest, because of its role in high blood pressure, which is one of the most well-established risk factors for multiple forms of heart disease as well as stroke. Angiotensin has been a subject of increased biomedical interest with the emergence of Covid-19, because the SARS-Cov-2 virus that causes the disease enters the cells of the body via angiotensin-converting enzyme 2 (ACE2) receptors. As we will see, the role of angiotensin is sometimes invoked in discussions of racial disparities in morbidity and mortality from these diseases, and although this is sometimes done in a retrograde biologically essentialist way, it can also be fodder for a more dynamic analysis of mechanisms by which social inequality gets under the skin.

After introducing angiotensin as an object, and tension more broadly as a rich site of material and semiotic consideration, this entry examines layered engagements with angiotensin across wide-ranging bio/medical disciplines. Doing so illuminates the fundamental inextricability of societal tensions from physiological tensions and, by articulating an avenue by which social inequality becomes embodied, a route into engaging with race and biology that eschews biological reductionism.

Tension as simultaneously material and semiotic

The substance now known as angiotensin was identified in 1939 by two different research groups: one based at the University of Buenos Aires that named it 'hypertensin' and one based at Eli Lilly in Indianapolis that named it 'angiotonin' (Milei 2010: 260). The two groups' leaders 'arrived at the compromise nomenclature' amicably 'while enjoying martinis' at a meeting at the University of Michigan in 1957 (Milei 2010: 263), and the compromise name was taken up among hypertension researchers across regional contexts in the early 1960s (Basso and Terragno 2001: 1248). If the new moniker made up of two halves with root words from each group was a politically savvy way to resolve the discrepancy between groups of researchers, angiotensin's etymology is also effectively descriptive because it combines two Greek roots: angi, vessel of the body, and tónos, stretching, strain, tension.

The presence of the word stem for tense in the name angiotensin is much more broadly evocative. Tension names an embodied quality that is simultaneously material and semiotic, and this makes it an apt topic for feminist technoscience analysis. The positing of bodies as material-semiotic has been foundationally argued by Donna Haraway: 'bodies as objects of knowledge are material-semiotic generative nodes' (Haraway 1988: 595), and this whole volume illuminates how this is true, as it were, all the way down. This entry specifically explores angiotensin as an object of knowledge that can be drawn upon to expand understandings of both matter and meaning.

Tension is an inevitable element of contemporary life, in ways that are not merely figurative. In their recent book *The Urban Brain: Mental Health in the Vital City*, sociologists Nikolas Rose and Des Fitzgerald move from an informant's invocation of the potential deadliness of 'tension' to a consideration of the simultaneously social and biological condition of 'stress':

> Stress is not just a part of the language with which they [urban dwellers] describe the feelings of pressure, anxiety, tension, strain, and hassle that pervade urban existence, nor is it only a state of mind, but it is also a state of the body – of blood pressure, hormones, nerves, and neurons. (Rose and Fitzgerald 2022: 117)

While Rose and Fitzgerald focus primarily on the inextricability of neurological and mental life, the more capacious list here is suggestive: stress as a 'state of mind' is simultaneous with stress at the level of elevated blood pressure, and angiotensin is a biological material that plays an important role in embodied stress.

The embodiment of stress with and through hypertension is both constantly reinforcing and cumulative. If we consider the body itself as built environment, angiotensin plays a role in its continual construction. Angiotensin causes hypertension, and, over long periods, the artery walls respond by laying down more collagen – the protein with the greatest tensile strength – thickening and stiffening to push back on the pressure of the blood pushing on the artery walls. This arterial thickening becomes an additional layer of embodiment: the arteries themselves go through structural change such that even if angiotensin levels are lowered, there are physical structures remaining that cause the health issues to continue.

Rose and Fitzgerald situate their argument about the urban brain as building on the imperative posited by feminist social scientists that we 'take seriously' what it means for 'humans to be "embodied"' (Rose and Fitzgerald 2022: 2), and I take the same starting point. In a way that is resonant with feminist theorist Elizabeth Wilson's (2004) contention that neurological research can offer resources for feminist theory, and biomedical research into angiotensin can offer resources for thinking through the inextricability of psyche and soma. Notably, angiotensin offers an analytical entrée that is not centrally situated in the neuro. As I have argued elsewhere (Pollock 2015), the heart and the cardiovascular system more broadly offer an as-yet underexplored domain for feminist theorizing. The renin-angiotensin system provides an additional example of the simultaneity of matter and meaning that STS scholars of neuroscience have illuminated, and it opens new analytical avenues as well.

The renin-angiotensin system as a site of (racialized) risk

The role of angiotensin in vasoconstriction and fluid levels makes it central to understanding blood pressure and the risks that follow from its elevation.

Hypertension as a risk factor was canonically recognized in the landmark Framingham Heart Study that has been running since the post-Second World War years of heightened concern about heart disease morbidity and mortality (Kannel et al. 1961). That is why preventive cardiologists have long been interested in angiotensin and especially in its inhibition.

The inhibition of angiotensin is typically accomplished by intervening on the renin-angiotensin system. In a nutshell, the renin-angiotensin system operates through an emergent interaction between four key biological materials: the renin enzyme produced in the kidneys; the angiotensin hormone produced in the liver; the aldosterone steroid hormone produced in the adrenal gland; and the angiotensin-converting enzyme produced in the capillaries of the lungs that makes angiotensin biologically active. A key pharmaceutical route to intervening on this system in order to lower blood pressure is to inhibit angiotensin's biological activity.

There are two classes of drugs that operate on angiotensin to decrease blood pressure: ACEs and ARBs. 'ACE' here is shorthand for 'ACE inhibitor' – 'angiotensin-converting enzyme inhibitor', which is to say that this class of drugs inhibits the angiotensin-converting enzymes that are essential to making angiotensin biologically active. The first ACE inhibitor was developed from a peptide found in the venom of a Brazilian pit viper, and analogous substances with fewer side effects would become the basis of this highly profitable class of drugs (Bryan 2009). 'ARBs' are angiotensin receptor blockers that reduce angiotensin's action. Developed as a way to generate a novel route to achieving the physiological and commercial success of ACE inhibitors, many ARBs have become blockbuster drugs as well (Bhardwaj 2006). Since the renin-angiotensin system has been characterized as 'a crossroad from arterial hypertension to heart failure' (Pugliese, Masi, and Taddei 2020), among other dangerous outcomes, it is a primary site of preventive intervention.

These drugs that aim to lower blood pressure by intervening on angiotensin emerged at a historical moment of the increasing prominence of race in pharmaceutical research. As sociologist Steven Epstein (2007) has persuasively argued, in the 1990s when the US Food and Drug Administration began requiring the inclusion of members of racialized minorities in drug research and the reporting of any differences between racial groups, this laid the groundwork for an 'inclusion-and-difference paradigm' in which pharmaceutical research would be increasingly attuned to potential racial differences in pharmaceutical efficacy. Contested claims of lower efficacy of ACE inhibitors in African American patients have been a prominent site of debates about whether and what role race should play in pharmaceutical prescribing (Pollock 2012: see especially pp. 135–6; the debate is still unresolved, see Helmer et al. 2018).

Indeed, if angiotensin has been of widespread interest in understanding and preventing cardiovascular diseases broadly across the whole population, it has also been enrolled in understanding particular risks and the unequal distributions thereof. Hypertension has been a principal site of durable preoccupations with racial differences in cardiovascular disease research (Pollock 2012), and so angiotensin is often invoked in discussions of the increased risk of hypertension – and its sequalae ranging from heart failure to stroke – in Black populations, especially African Americans.

Angiotensin dysregulation as biological reductionism?

The stakes of exploring the role of dysregulation of the renin-angiotensin system have become even more heightened since 2020, a time in which interest in angiotensin and its receptors and inhibitors has extended well beyond the domain of cardiovascular disease. Since 2020, researchers from many more biomedical fields have taken greater interest in it, because the ACE2 receptor in the capillaries of the lungs is the physiological route by which many coronaviruses, including the one that causes Covid-19, enter host cells and enrol the cells' materials in viral reproduction. ACE2 is also involved in the disease course: the ACE2 receptor on the lung epithelial cells plays a role in Covid-19's lung damage, and the ACE2 receptor on the endothelial cells plays a role in Covid-19's cardiovascular complications. This, in turn, has been fodder for explanations for why African Americans have suffered such a heavy burden of morbidity and mortality from the pandemic. One characteristic example from the medical literature puts it this way: 'dysregulation of the renin-angiotensin system may place African Americans at disproportionate risk for severe COVID-19 outcomes' (Ajilore and Thames 2020: 66).

This may seem like standard-issue dubious racial science, suggesting that differences that are imagined to be innate somehow cause health inequalities. Indeed, that kind of thinking is sometimes at play in the medical literature and is contested by both biomedical researchers and by ethicists and social scientists (Cardeña 2021). It is infuriatingly common to see angiotensin-related aspects presented as an alternative to racism as an explanatory mechanism for disparities in the medical literature. For example, this paper from the *Journal of Human Hypertension* on Covid-19 disparities is quite typical:

> The higher mortality rate in African–Americans raises questions about the underlying mechanisms behind these racial disparities. Several known mechanisms might be implicated, including increased comorbidities, inequalities in healthcare access, and socioeconomic factors. However, we propose that another mechanism might be also implicated: the renin-angiotensin system. (Doumas et al. 2020: 764)

This and other medical studies that conceptualize risk in these binaries in which nature and nurture are alternative explanations misconstrue our simultaneously material and social world.

When these papers on Covid-19 health disparities present angiotensin as an alternative to structural inequality rather than a mechanism by which inequality becomes embodied, they build on a long-standing literature that invokes angiotensin in retrograde racializing ways. This is starkest when speculated static racial differences in genetic polymorphisms are invoked, rather than recognizing the renin-angiotensin system as a dynamic system. That is, when 'racial analysis of the distribution of genetic polymorphisms associated with elevated angiotensin I-converting enzyme' is pursued instead of social analysis (Obasogie et al. 2015: 3110).

Of course we should be immediately sceptical about any leap from claims about the distribution of genetic polymorphisms to claims about race. The distribution of genetic factors related to renin-angiotensin regulation does not follow racial lines but varies considerably within racial groups; indeed, this is further evidence that racial categories are not biological in any essentialist sense, and that environmental factors explain the differences in rates between Black groups and other groups (Rotimi et al. 1996). But what if the renin-angiotensin system is not an alternative to explanations rooted in social inequality but precisely a mechanism by which social inequalities contribute to unequal health?

Thinking with angiotensin to understand how social inequality becomes embodied

It is not necessarily the case that claims of differences between racial groups in the renin-angiotensin system exemplify racial essentialism, because some scientists can and do understand dysregulation itself to be a consequence of living in an unequal social world. Thus, the dysregulation of the renin-angiotensin system can also be a rich analytical site for avowedly anti-racist and anti-essentialist scientists such as biological anthropologist Lance Gravlee, who has described it together with inflammation as emblematic of the ways in which systemic racism becomes embodied – through diabetes, hypertension and (thus) Covid-19 (Gravlee 2020). Gravlee is among the many natural scientists interested in the impact of racism on health who have been drawn to the study of angiotensin, because the role of chronic stress in the dysregulation of the renin-angiotensin system provides a physiological pathway by which the stress of racism can become embodied.

One high-profile domain of bioscience research that engages with such processes of biological becoming is gene-environment interaction research. Gene-environment interaction research straddles the uneasy territory between the damnable essentialism and the laudable indictment of the biological effects of social inequality. For example, consider the perspective of one researcher involved in gene-environment interaction research on air pollution and heart disease, quoted by social scientists and ethicists Sarah Ackerman, Kate Weatherford Darling, Sandra Soo-Jin Lee and colleagues (2017). The scientist was proud of his decades-long work building up 'the groundbreaking data that's showing that the long-term exposure to air pollution is related to cardiovascular mortality' that has strengthened the case that regulators and industry need to spend significant sums to decrease harm (Ackerman et al. 2017: 367). However, the same scientist also reveals awareness of an important risk of this 'high stakes business' of gene-environment interaction research, which is that it can inadvertently put the responsibility on individuals rather than industry: 'We're not going to say that people who have a variant in the angiotensin receptor gene should all move away from big cities . . . I don't think we should go there' (ibid.). For Ackerman and colleagues, that normative argument does a lot of work: 'he argued that knowledge about GEIs [gene-environment interactions] should contribute to collective efforts to clean up unhealthy environments, rather than create new forms of individual responsibility' (ibid.). This is a vital imperative that can be challenging to realize. Indeed, if we want to avoid both genetic determinism and the imposition of individual responsibility for risk reduction, gene-environment interaction studies are likely not the best place to start.

There are alternative ways to understand the developmental biology of hypertension. Feminist biologist and STS scholar Anne Fausto-Sterling provides an insightful alternative approach, and it is one that centres hormones. She does not name angiotensin in particular, but we can be confident it is part of what underlies the system that she describes as setting blood pressure via 'multiple, mutually reinforcing mechanisms' including 'hormones affecting blood vessel diameter' as well as 'hormonal control of blood volume' (Fausto-Sterling 2004: 29). Fausto-Sterling persuasively argues against a 'homeostasis' model of understanding blood pressure levels as if they were operated by a thermostat and instead posits that we should understand blood pressure regulation through an alternative model called 'allostasis', in which 'blood pressure does not seem to return to a single set point, but instead is regulated to match anticipated demand' (Fausto-Sterling 2004: 27). Rather than hunt for genes to explain hypertension's disproportionate prevalence in Black populations, she argues:

> The allostasis model does not ratchet up the hunt for a 'broken' gene to explain essential hypertension. Instead, it proposes that hypertension is an orchestrated response to a predicted need to remain vigilant to a variety of insults and danger – be they racial hostility, enraging acts of discrimination, or living in the shadow of violence. Over time, all of the components that regulate blood pressure adapt to life under stress. (Fausto-Sterling 2004: 28)

For Fausto-Sterling, this provides a basis for critique of both gene-environment interaction research and of the development of race-based pharmaceuticals. She notes that drugs can sometimes be effective to control dangerously elevated blood pressure – albeit often not effective for long, for many people – but argues that a more effective solution still would be a more fundamental one, which would be to achieve social transformation such that the stress of living in a racist society would be radically diminished. I would resist Fausto-Sterling's call to take sides between either intervening pharmacologically or intervening socially: access to pharmaceuticals is not intrinsically an alternative to demanding social justice but can be a high-stakes component of it (see Pollock 2012). Yet Fausto-Sterling is absolutely right that the biological harms of the stress of racism cannot ultimately be eradicated without dismantling racism entirely.

Engaging bios beyond determinism

With its layers of social and biological meaning, angiotensin offers a rich site for feminist technoscience consideration. Tension is a vital aspect of our material and semiotic bodies, our vasculature and our sense of how we negotiate the world. The inequalities in that world, in turn – notably including racialized inequalities – become embodied as they become lived.

For feminist and anti-racist STS, the primary value of this material-semiotic contemplation is to offer resources for meaning making, in a way that complements and extends the robust literature of race and genetics beyond determinism. Tension is fundamental to life, both in its biographical sense and in its biological one. Considering angiotensin in this way resonates with sociologist Alondra Nelson's (2008) evocative framing of genetic root-seeking as 'bio science' – in which, for Black people pursuing genetic research into their African ancestry, biological markers do not determine social identities, but rather biological and social identities are co-produced. In Nelson's account:

> a genetic 'match' is just the beginning of a process of identification, rather than its conclusion. After test results are rendered, root-seekers endeavor to translate them from the biological to the biographical, from a pedigree of origins to a satisfying life story. They attempt to meaningfully align bios with bios. (Nelson 2008: 775)

Applying 'bio science' to the present context, tension exists both within our biological bodies and within our individual and collective life narratives in a way that is co-produced and emergent rather than deterministic.

As with health disparities research broadly, documenting the harms of racism is not enough (Paine et al. 2021): material-semiotic contemplation does not by itself work to develop anti-racist praxis, and the pursuit of more biomedical research is distinctly secondary in importance to the pursuit of social justice.

And yet employing a material-semiotic approach – for example, by attending to the dynamism of the renin-angiotensin system – illuminates how building a more just world would transform our social lives and our biological lives for the better.

Acknowledgements

Thanks to those who provided helpful feedback on drafts of this chapter: Maital Dar, Emma Kowal and Manu Platt, as well as collection editors Sone Erikäinen and Roslyn Malcolm.

References

Ackerman, S. L., K. W. Darling, S. S.-J. Lee, R. A. Hiatt, and J. K. Shim (2017), 'The Ethics of Translational Science: Imagining Public Benefit in Gene-Environment Interaction Research', *Engaging Science, Technology, and Society* 3: 351–74.

Ajilore, O. and A. D. Thames (2020), 'The Fire this Time: The Stress of Racism, Inflammation and COVID-19', *Brain, Behavior, and Immunity* 88: 66–7.

Basso, N. and N. A. Terragno (2001), 'History about the Discovery of the Renin-angiotensin System', *Hypertension* 38 (6): 1246–9.

Bhardwaj, G. (2006), 'How the Antihypertensive Losartan was Discovered', *Expert Opinion on Drug Discovery* 1 (6): 609–18.

Bryan, J. (2009), 'From Snake Venom to ACE Inhibitor — The Discovery and Rise of Captopril', *The Pharmaceutical Journal* 282: 455–6.

Cerdeña, J. P. (2021), 'Race-Conscious Bioethics: The Call to Reject Contemporary Scientific Racism', *The American Journal of Bioethics* 21 (2): 48–53.

Doumas, M., D. Patoulias, A. Katsimardou, K. Stavropoulos, K. Imprialos, and A. Karagiannis (2020), 'COVID19 and Increased Mortality in African Americans: Socioeconomic Differences or does the Renin Angiotensin System also Contribute?', *Journal of Human Hypertension* 34 (11): 764–7.

Epstein, S. (2007), *Inclusion: The Politics of Difference in Medical Research*, Chicago: University of Chicago Press.

Fausto-Sterling, A. (2004), 'Refashioning Race: DNA and the Politics of Health Care', *Differences: A Journal of Feminist Cultural Studies* 15 (3): 1–37.

Gravlee, C. C. (2020), 'Systemic Racism, Chronic Health Inequities, and COVID-19: A Syndemic in the Making?', *American Journal of Human Biology: The Official Journal of the Human Biology Council* 32 (5): e23482.

Haraway, D. (1988), 'Situated Knowledges: The Science Question in Feminism and the Privilege of Partial Perspective', *Feminist Studies* 14 (3): 575–99.

Helmer, A., N. Slater, and S. Smithgall (2018), 'A Review of ACE Inhibitors and ARBs in Black Patients with Hypertension', *Annals of Pharmacotherapy* 52 (11): 1143–51.

Kannel, W. B., T. R. Dawber, A. Kagan, N. Revotskie, and J. Stokes III (1961), 'Factors of Risk in the Development of Coronary Heart Disease—Six-year Follow-up Experience: The Framingham Study', *Annals of Internal Medicine* 55 (1): 33–50.

Milei, J. (2010), 'A Cornerstone in the History of Hypertension: The Seventieth Anniversary of the Discovery of Angiotensin', *Journal of Cardiovascular Medicine* 11 (4): 260–4.

Nelson, A. (2008), 'Bio Science: Genetic Genealogy Testing and the Pursuit of African Ancestry', *Social Studies of Science* 38 (5): 759–83.

Obasogie, O. K., J. N. Harris-Wai, K. Darling, C. Keagy, and M. Levesque (2015), 'Race in the Life Sciences: An Empirical Assessment, 1950–2000', *Fordham Law Review* 83 (6): 3089–154.

Paine, L., P. de la Rocha, A. P. Eyssallenne, C. A. Andrews, L. Loo, C. P. Jones, A. M. Collins, and M. Morse (2021), 'Declaring Racism a Public Health Crisis in the United States: Cure, Poison, or Both?', *Frontiers in Public Health* 9: 676784.

Pollock, A. (2012), *Medicating Race: Heart Disease and Durable Preoccupations with Difference*, Durham: Duke University Press.

Pollock, A. (2015), 'Heart Feminism', *Catalyst: Feminism, Theory, Technoscience* 1 (1): 30.

Pugliese, N. R., S. Masi, and S. Taddei (2020), 'The Renin-Angiotensin-Aldosterone System: A Crossroad from Arterial Hypertension to Heart Failure', *Heart Failure Reviews* 25 (1): 31–42.

Rose, N. and D. Fitzgerald (2022), *The Urban Brain: Mental Health in the Vital City*, Princeton: Princeton University Press.

Rotimi, C., A. Puras, R. Cooper, N. McFarlane-Anderson, T. Forrester, O. Ogunbiyi, and L. Morrison Ryk Ward (1996), 'Polymorphisms of Renin-Angiotensin Genes among Nigerians, Jamaicans, and African Americans', *Hypertension* 27 (3): 558–63.

Wilson, E. A. (2004), *Psychosomatic: Feminism and the Neurological Body*, Durham: Duke University Press.

3 CORTISOL

ROSLYN MALCOLM

'Cortisol, cortisol, cortisol'

A central feature of being autistic for many autistic people is heightened sensory experience. This emerged during the ethnographic research I carried out over the last ten years with autistic people and those they share their lives within the United Kingdom and the United States. In our interactions, a model of autism was formed around this notion of heightened sensory experience. Ways of being autistic were defined in terms of sensory alterity and, relatedly, a 'fight-or-flight' (or stress) response particularly sensitive to neurotypical atmospheres and architectures. As therapists understood it, Living in worlds lacking affordances for neurodiverse ways of being led to 'overload' and 'meltdown', severe stress and, if left unchecked, chronically high cortisol levels. Such states were understood to be ameliorated by regulatory movement practices known by my interlocuters as 'stimming' and 'autism-friendly' environments.

In 2015/16 I spent sixteen months in England, UK, and a southern state of the United States researching a horse-based, autism-specific kind of therapy. This therapeutic milieu was a context where the model detailed above was particularly salient. I carried out participant observation and interviews with therapy practitioners, their autistic clients, parents, carers and teachers, alongside working with young autistic adults learning horse training and care. Amy, an autism therapy practitioner, described the effects of such embodiments of 'overload' and 'meltdown' by dramatically referring to the rapid release of flows of 'cortisol, cortisol, cortisol' into the bloodstream. Processes of 'overload', 'meltdown' and the workings of 'fight or flight' were commonly described in hormonal terms. However, as I show here, this was not a simple biological reduction of 'autism' to flows in the blood. Hormones were used to articulate cascades of biosocial flows across environments (human and built) and embodied living, and a therapeutic ecology of equine therapy. I seek to articulate these uses here.

Cortisol was used by practitioners to acknowledge a negative spiral of stress (Milton 2013) caused by inhabiting worlds where one's needs are deemed secondary to the dominant majority and therefore unimportant. I explore wider narratives of cortisol and chronic stress in the UK alongside their perceived alleviation through animal-assisted therapies in the context of autistic children and adults. By exploring an autism-specific type of horse-riding therapy I show that increased contemporary fluency with hormone knowledges facilitates a linking of health to particular environments of stress for autistic people. This reflects the ability of cortisol and 'fight or flight' to articulate broader concerns around the ecological situatedness of human health.

In her work on hormonal contraceptive use in New Delhi, India, Nayantara Sheoran Appleton (2015) explores differential access to emergency contraceptive pills (ECPs). Wealthy, elite women easily access ECPs within private clinics. Women in the adjacent slums cannot. Sheoran very usefully traces a process of what she terms 'stratified contraception'. Here I travel in a similar vein yet expand this notion to non-reproductive and non-synthesized hormones (cortisol, oxytocin). I propose the notion of *hormonal stratification* to encompass processes like stratified contraception so well articulated by Appleton. Yet I depart from a focus on the ingestion of synthesized hormones to which one has stratified access and instead engage with the stratification of endocrine systems more broadly.

The notion of hormonal stratification encompasses the endogenous hormonal effects of living in environments of inequality. In this entry, this offers a way to appreciate the biosocial effects of living in neurotypical worlds that create significant amounts of stress for autistic people. Tracing examples of hormonal stratification allows us to see the ways that autistic people and their therapists (and arguably people more broadly) in the United Kingdom and the United States are currently operationalizing endocrinological knowledge – and the stress response system in particular – as a legitimate way of articulating these concerns.

Situating autistic experience

As part of this project, I attended an annual general meeting of a local branch of the National Autistic Society (NAS), a UK-wide autism support organization. One of my autistic interlocutors, Thomas, was there to present to the group, which consisted predominantly of parents of autistic children or non-autistic providers of care. He eloquently spoke about his experiences of being autistic. His tics and 'stimming'[1] emerged every so often. He brought his hands quickly to his face and made his fingers flicker rapidly in front of his eyes. Sometimes he shook his head and giggled. This happened mostly when he was pleased or excited about something. He told the crowd, 'I was diagnosed late. I constantly asked "why am I different from the other kids at school? Why do I feel different? Why am I so anxious?"', before explaining the significance of sensory experience in his life:

> There's a lot of change just now and people are interested in autism. It's an interesting time to be autistic. But what people need to understand is that nothing changes about your autism from when you are little to when you grow up. The sensory problems and social problems and stimming are all there. You just learn better coping strategies.

Here Thomas signals to the importance of relations with other people in the production of his difficulties at school and with performing as a good student.

For him, being taught by teachers with no understanding of his needs would send him into overload and meltdown.

> I struggled at school . . . too much information at once. My brain was like 'arggggghhhh', . . . I tried hard, but I couldn't cope. That's why I say, 'I don't have a learning disability, I have an educational problem'.

School was particularly hard for him, yet being outside, in the countryside, caring for his horse furnished Thomas with an environment full of positive embodiments. Commonly described negative 'triggers' for sensory overload are supermarkets with their bright lighting, array of smells including synthesized cleaning solutions, echoing atmospheres and large volume of people. Thomas therefore didn't feel that 'autism' was something situated in his brain alone but in his relations with the human and built environment. For Thomas being autistic was a condition emerging from his situation within worlds that did not understand him or make affordances for different ways of being. He clearly felt that embodiments of anxiety were exacerbated by sensory and social worlds designed for neurotypical people and by spaces that took no account of the particular needs of neurodiverse people, especially those with enhanced sensory sensitivities (Malcolm 2021).

As part of the fieldwork I travelled to a ranch in a southern state of the United States. I took training in a method of autism-specific horse therapy and was taught that 'natural' environments were stress and anxiety relieving and could modulate hormonal flows in the blood. As such, it was thought that the open fields and countryside of the farm-like spaces, where horses and other animals were kept, were by design effective in helping to calm sensory overload and meltdown. Part of the method training included guidance on how to enhance these effects, by accessing (or planting) a woodland trail, riding to a river or stream or by simply adding spaces where engagement with the elements and a range of 'natural' textures could be encouraged (water troughs, sand pits, muddy areas).

By default, the more natural spatial design of the horse farm was a significant part of what made horse therapy in particular so useful for helping ease the chronic stress of autistic people. The trainer reflected significant current focus on the health benefits of 'nature' in the United Kingdom and the United States. They also invoked salient ideas circulating in the UK about the somatic effects of stress. These models of autistic ways of being speak to very contemporary, widely mobilized concerns with chronic stress and the human condition, and more specifically, a perceived bodily incompatibility with the urban, industrial milieu.

Cortisol cascades

Hormones act as messengers (Roberts 2007) cascading information around the body and between biological processes. Yet they also effect a cascade of information in the shape of meanings passed between persons. They are a particularly striking example of a material-semiotic actor (ibid.). Hormone knowledges have emerged in a range of arenas to articulate the human condition beyond reproduction and now circulate in public narratives as a powerful heuristic for understanding physiological manifestations of social and sensory worlds and states of mind. Oxytocin for bonding, care and love; dopamine for pleasure; cortisol for stress and anxiety. In focus here, and in response to my interlocutors' uptake of the terms and knowledges that surround them, are the flows of cortisol. Despite significant difficulty with studying the role of cortisol in biological processes in the body, these chemicals broadly act as a 'messenger of stress' (Roberts and McWade 2021). Cortisol was central to how horse therapy practitioners understood the embodied effects of being autistic and inhabiting worlds that do not take differences – in this case autistic sensory and communicative needs – into account.

Like other hormones, cortisol cascades. It does not flow in isolation but rather always in relation to other 'internal' bodily processes and endocrinological flows and 'external' features of one's environs. Surging cortisol flows in particular were deemed to be the result of living in sensorially stressful worlds and both the cause and effect of a cyclical, spiralling chronic stress. In this context cortisol sets in train a cascade of information communicating the embodied experience of autism to wider publics, due to the wider salience of cortisol as a carrier of meanings about stress. This action importantly situates the condition (1) beyond the flows of isolated hormones and into the stress response of the body and (2) in environments extending beyond the molecular flows of the individual, human body. This action of cortisol as a carrier of meaning intimately echoes its perceived bioecological cascades, making the 'interior' of the body permeable to 'external' forces. I expand on this later in the entry.

A therapeutic ecology: Environments, limbic systems and endocrine flows

Paul was the father of an autistic son and the chairperson of the local branch of a national autism society in the UK. He told me that when living and working with autistic kids and adults it is key to 'generate a calm, trusted environment'. Thinking about the lived environment and not only the hormonal flows or neurological processes in the individual body was central to engaging sensitively and respectfully with autistic people. Paul spoke to the cascading action of hormones when he told me that by effecting a safe environment 'cortisol levels come down. Adrenaline levels come down; noradrenaline levels come down . . . It takes some kids a while to trust the environment.' Paul also noted that 'good horse people' (horse trainers) had long-term experience in working sensitively with horses, herd animals that are particularly sensitive to bodily communications. As such they were cast as well placed to engage sensitively, in non-verbal and embodied ways, with autistic clients. Human and built environments were therefore intimately linked to the flow of cortisol which was in turn intimately linked to the flows of other hormones.

This cascading was central to the model of autism being promoted in this autism-horse therapy nexus. This kind of embodied hormonal model of autism as something inseparable from one's environs emerged strongly throughout my fieldwork with autistic children and practitioners providing autism-specific horse riding. The method used was 'back riding' where an instructor sits in the saddle with the child. From this proximity, the instructor can control the horse, keeping the child safe. This means that faster paces can be used than when a child rides alone in the saddle. During my first induction into the activities at the largest riding centre offering back riding, I was told that the faster pacing of trot and canter (rather than walking) 'gets the hips moving which releases the feel-good hormones, oxytocin, serotonin, and reduces cortisol'. As I've explored elsewhere (Malcolm 2019, 2021) back riding was deemed able to modulate the hormonal flows of the body and in a more concentrated way, compounding the benefits of moving through 'natural', calm environment of the riding centres and engaging with people with sensitive bodily ways of communicating, as described by Paul. Horses therefore became part of what I call the perceived 'therapeutic ecology' of horse-assisted therapy (2019, 2021).

Practitioners particularly focused on cortisol's relationship to the flow or blockage of oxytocin, the 'love' or 'bonding' hormone. The two were perceived to exist in proportional balance with one another with horse therapy described by some practitioners as a way of redressing an 'imbalance' of (too little) oxytocin and (too much) cortisol in the blood (Malcolm 2021). We can see that stress and cortisol were central to understanding lived bodies in embodiments of stress, yet never in isolation from related bodily systems, other hormones or environments.

Therapy practitioners' focus on the 'fight-or-flight' response worked to entwine the limbic system, the endocrine system and the digestive system. Paul's words and allusions to cortisol flows speak to a hormonal model of autism, yet also importantly to a focus on lived experience as something enacted through complex interactions of the entire, situated body. Both of these notions were utilized by the people I got to know to understand autistic ways of being. Sympathetic and parasympathetic nervous systems (rather than only the central nervous system) were invoked – shifting autism from being perceived as a psychiatric condition of the brain to one enacted via lived, material embodiments.

The articulation of living breathing bodies through the language of hormonal and other systemic bodily flows is of course not limited to these very specific models of the autistic body. Autistic people's ways of articulating their experience are just as deeply situated within contemporary models of the body as those of non-autistic people, despite long-standing and incredibly problematic declarations of autistic people's irreducible isolation from social worlds and environments (see Bettelheim 1969) and ontological positioning as somehow alien to human experience (Hacking 2009). On the contrary, these models speak to very contemporary concerns with the human condition and chronic stress and a perceived bodily incompatibility with the urban, industrialized milieu. As Fitzgerald and Rose (2022) detail, these concerns have very long histories.

Stress, fight or flight and the limbic system

Hormones are increasingly used by a range of publics to articulate bodily inhabitations and are bound up in burgeoning notions of the porosity of the body to its environs. Cortisol, the 'stress hormone', is central to daily bodily functions of waking, yet it is deemed to spiral out of control in response to intensely stressful worlds too fast to be kept up with without overload and burnout. In my experiences from fieldwork and from the popular science media it is evident that cortisol talk almost always involves a mention of or implies the activation of what is known as 'the stress response'. Also referred to as 'fight or flight', this process is a function of the limbic system and endocrine systems of the brain and body, respectively. Walter Bradford Cannon (1932) coined the term in his fluid matrix model of the body referring to 'fight or flight' as an integral part of 'the wisdom of the body' for its action of returning internal homeostasis, or balance, after the experience of an external threat.

Acting as messengers of stress (Roberts and McWade 2021) cortisol (and the stress response) offers a relevant language to sensitively articulate the lived experience of autistic ways of being in ways that can be understood by non-autistic publics. By actively highlighting, in a culturally salient way, that particular social and built environments affect sensory issues and anxiety for autistic people, these biological articulations can be used to encourage non-autistic people to learn about the experience of being autistic. In so doing, they can make living, breathing somatic affordances for such ontologies, altering what we might call the infrastructures of feeling produced by the social and built environment.

The normative force of ideas about hormones that are either balanced (and normal) or imbalanced (and pathological) requires critical attention. This is certainly true in the case of autism where dubious hormonal therapies in the shape of oxytocin nasal sprays and luteinizing hormone-releasing agonists for reducing testosterone are sold as 'treatments'. Yet there exist tensions and ambiguities between the reductive biologization, on one hand, and the disruptive power, on the other, of hormone thinking. These ambiguities within the realms of the biosocial require careful unpacking (Mackenzie and Roberts 2017, 137). It is imperative that we remain open to the potential new models of the body that hormone thinking facilitates and what this can tell us about contemporary understandings of situated embodiments in the context of autism and beyond.

In short, the earlier discussed models of hormones, the limbic system and their inherent relation to the environment speak to the real-world impacts of living in spaces designed for neurotypical people, as these models become important for autistic people's understandings of their condition as situated in and produced by relations with the world. These considerations acknowledge the role of poverty and social inequalities in the activation of 'fight or flight' otherwise known as 'the stress response' in the context of autism and beyond. They act widely as potential aetiologies for ill health which problematically molecularize life (Rose 2007) by situating autism in the molecular flows of the biological body. Yet, they also speak to the de-individualization of conditions like autism (and other groups of people whose quality of life is deemed less important than dominant majorities). That is, they simultaneously alter the site of autism, moving 'it' from pathologized individual bodies to something enacted in the interactions of lived bodies within stressful environments that lack affordances for different ways of being. In new ways then, this quantifies the deleterious effects of, for example, inhabiting poor housing, insecure work or continual threats of and experiences of incarceration, discrimination and violence that ultimately emerge from a significant lack of understanding of autistic sensitivities and ways of being.

Hormonal stratification and transcorporeality

Stacy Alaimo (2010) proposes the term 'transcorporealities' to speak to 'the imbrication of human bodies, not only to each other, but with non-human creatures and physical landscapes' (15). In her final work, *The Transmission of Affect* (2004), feminist scholar Theresa Brennan (2004, 1) relatedly speaks to the bodily transmissions of feeling. She tells us that the

> transmission of affect, whether it is grief, anxiety or anger is social and psychological in origin. But the transmission is also responsible for bodily change; some are brief changes, as in a whiff of a room's atmosphere, some more longer lasting. In other words, the transmission of affect, if only for an instant, alters the biochemistry and neurology of the subject.

The 'atmosphere' or environment literally gets into the individual. Building on Alaimo's notion of transcorporeality (2010) and Brennan's transmission of affect (2004) we can see that the bodily affects expressed by practitioners speak to a system of biofeedback loops with the bio-referring to a deeply subjective material body and the feedback emerging from the atmosphere of the environment. The notion of, and lived experience of, 'stress' is a central feature of current models of the body, affecting people in variegated and stratified ways – across gender, disability, socio-economic status and those who are the subject of racialization.

Building on earlier work on discourses of race, hypertension and heart disease in the United States Anne Pollock (2012) has more recently explored how racism and discrimination are understood to become embodied through the lens of the hormone angiotensin (2023, *this volume*). In her ethnographic work Nayantara Sheoran Appleton (2015) engages directly with the ways that hormones can enact stratification. She details the differential use of and access to the ECP by women from different castes and socio-economic backgrounds in Delhi, India. Sheoran builds on Shellee Colen's (1989) invaluable notion of stratified reproduction and delineates women's stratified access to emergency contraception with a focus on 'stratified contraception'.

Here I speak to a broader process of hormonal stratification, beyond reproduction or synthesized hormones, that my interlocutors suggested seeped into bodies, linking normative architectures, 'natural' green spaces and their accessibility (or lack thereof), the living, breathing effects of discrimination and ultimately (embodied) mental health and illness. In the context of autism and horse therapy in the United Kingdom and the United States, and arguably more broadly, cortisol and 'fight or flight' have become salient mediators of meaning about the lived embodiments of inequalities in the United Kingdom and the United States and beyond. They facilitate the therapeutic ecology crafted by my therapist interlocutors to understand the real-world effects of equine therapy for autistic people.

Conclusions

Cortisol cascades as a material-semiotic messenger of stress, in the context of autism and horse therapy and arguably more broadly. In this entry, I have established my interlocutors' understanding of a negative spiral of stress (Milton 2013) caused by inhabiting worlds where one's needs are deemed secondary to the dominant majority and therefore unimportant. I have described particular environments designed to alleviate sensory discomforts through enhancing 'good' sensory triggers, reducing 'bad' sensory triggers and teaching non-autistic people about autistic modes of communication and sociality as a way to improve the human environment. These can be seen as living affordances for autistic ways of being. This alleviation is perceived to be enacted via engaging in ways attuned to the 'fight or flight' response and transcorporeality (Alaimo 2010) affording the transmission of affect (Brennan 2004) between people (and mammals in general). This model of stress was situated in one's embodied experience of the environment and articulated via a very contemporary fluency with hormone knowledges.

This approach allows us to delve 'in' to the body, illustrating what was understood by my interlocutors to be a deeply enmeshed person-in-action, taking autism beyond the individual body. By engaging with the notion of hormonal stratification produced by particular built and human environments we can see the emergence of hormonal ways of thinking that acknowledge the slow structural violence of living in worlds designed for an assumed neurotypical majority. This reflects broader contemporary concerns around stress in the United Kingdom and the United States, signalling cortisol's ability to communicate significant disparities in the embodied effects of living as a minority.

Note

1 Stimming is a term used by autistic people to refer to self-stimulatory movement practices, described as practices used for either pleasurable engagement with one's environs or for soothing anxiety and sensory overload.

References

Alaimo, S. (2010), 'The Naked Word: The Trans-corporeal Ethics of the Protesting Body', *Women and Performance* 20 (1): 15–36.

Bettelheim, B. (1969), *The Empty Fortress: Infantile Autism and the Birth of the Self*, New York: the Free Press.

Brennan, T. (2004), *The Transmission of Affect*, New York: Cornell University Press.

Cannon, W. B. (1932), *The Wisdom of the Body*, London: Kegan Paul, Trench and Trubner & Co., Ltd.

Colen, S. (1989), '"Like a Mother to them": Stratified Reproduction and West Indian Childcare Workers in New York', in F. Ginsburg and R. Rapp (eds), *Conceiving the New World Order: The Global Politics of Reproduction*, 78–102, Berkeley: University of California Press.

Fitzgerald, D. and N. Rose (2022), *The Urban Brain: Health in the Vital City*, Princeton: Princeton University Press.

Hacking, I. (2009), 'Humans, Aliens and Autism', *Daedalus* 138 (3): 44–59.

Mackenzie, A. and C. Roberts (2017), 'Adopting Neuroscience: Parenting and Affective Indeterminacy', *Body and Society* 23 (3): 130–55.

Malcolm, R. (2019), 'Rhythms That Matter: The Kinetic Melodies and Matterings of Autism and Equine Therapy in the UK and USA', Doctoral Thesis. University of Edinburgh, Edinburgh.

Malcolm, R. (2021), '"There's No Constant": Oxytocin, Cortisol and Balanced Proportionality in Hormonal Articulations of Autism', *Medical Anthropology* 40 (4): 375–88.

Milton, D. E. M. (2013), 'Reversing the Negative Spiral of Stress – A Personal and Philosophical Reflection', *Stress and Autism: Combating Stress, Lightening the Load, Research Autism Conference*, London, 14 May. (Unpublished).

Pollock, A. (2012), *Medicating Race: Heart Disease and Durable Preoccupations with Difference*, Durham: Duke University Press.

Pollock, A. (2023), 'Angiotensin', in S. Erikainen, A. Ford, R. Malcolm, L. Raeder, and C. Roberts (eds). *Hormonal Theory*, London: Bloomsbury Academic.

Roberts, C. (2007), *Messengers of Sex: Hormones, Biomedicine and Feminism*, Cambridge: Cambridge University Press.

Roberts, C. and B. McWade (2021), 'Messengers of Stress: Towards a Cortisol Sociology', *Sociology of Health and Illness* 43: 895–909.

Rose, N. (2007), *The Politics of Life Itself: Biomedicine, Power, and Subjectivity in the Twenty-First Century*, Princeton: Princeton University Press.

Sheoran, N. (2015), '"Stratified Contraception": Emergency Contraceptive Pills and Women's Differential Experiences in Contemporary India', *Medical Anthropology* 34 (3): 243–58.

4 DIETHYLSTILBESTROL (DES)

JACQUELYNE LUCE, ANJALI RAO-HEREL, AND THE FEMINIST TECHNOSCIENCE GOVERNANCE COLLABORATORY

Diethylstilbestrol (DES) is a synthetic oestrogen synthesized in England in 1938 by Charles Dodds et al.. They discovered that DES behaved similarly to 'natural oestrogen', holding the possibility to bring about similar results in therapeutic application. During the 1920s, hormonal response stimulation was viewed as a source of sexual rejuvenation and longevity (Pettit 2013; Logan 2013), followed in the 1930s by the use of oral and intravenous injections of synthetic hormones. Concurrently, oestrogen therapy by injection was emerging within the field of gynaecological health as researchers gained more understanding of the role of oestrogen within the menstrual cycle (Bell 1995). The approval of DES by the newly formed Food and Drug Administration (FDA) in 1941 introduced synthetic hormones as a regular component of clinical care, first in relation to treating 'symptoms' of menopause and, beginning in 1947, as a means of alleviating the risk of miscarriage.[1] Never patented, and easy to self-administer, in the United States DES promised to greatly increase access to oestrogen therapy. In assigned female at birth individuals, oestrogen levels decrease with menopause and it was thought that replacing lost oestrogen with DES 'would control a woman's body and ensure that it functioned smoothly' (Bell 1995: 480). Oestrogen levels increase in an individual during pregnancy. Oestrogen deficiency was thought to contribute to miscarriage, rendering DES a possible preventative therapy (Troisi, Hatch and Titus 2016).

Initially understood to be the first 'transplacental carcinogen' (Bell 2009: 17), DES is now also recognized as the prototypical endocrine-disrupting chemical (EDC), a term coined in the early 1990s to describe chemicals with properties that can disrupt endocrine system functioning (Colborn et al. 1996; see also Abboud 2018). DES exposure is associated with anatomical differences in the genital and reproductive tracts as well as menstrual irregularities, potential increases in testicular and breast cancer and autoimmune conditions.[2] Claims have also circulated about DES's possible role in shaping gender identity and sexual orientation of those exposed (Kerlin 2004; Hines 2003). Feminist scholarship focusing specifically on DES examines its role in transforming patient advocacy and health activism (Bell 2009; Cody 2008) and shaping the history of pharmaceutical regulation and environmental justice initiatives (Bell 1995; Langston 2010). This literature most often portrays DES as a hormone of the past, albeit one that holds significant lessons for the present and future. There is very little known about the current lived experiences of DES-exposed individuals and how they navigate emerging knowledge about DES. As part of a larger project,[3] we spoke with twenty-five individuals in their late fifties through early seventies about their experiences of learning about DES and how this knowledge has shaped their lives. Drawing on interviews with individuals who believe themselves to have been exposed to DES, in this entry we examine the contemporary significance of knowledge about DES in shaping interactions with other exogenous hormones. We illustrate the ways in which interviewees articulate their perspectives within frameworks of chemical toxicity or chemical potentiality, contributing a plurality of perspectives on the temporalities of (DES) toxicity. Scientific and public knowledge about DES is replete with uncertainty. By attending to the ways in which such uncertainties are taken up, we hope to encourage critical engagement with the long-term and enduring entangled impacts of toxic social and chemical exposure.

Emerging understandings of DES toxicity

DES was thought of (and marketed) as a 'wonder drug' with the potential to prevent pregnancy loss and promote foetal growth and healthy weight babies (Troisi, Hatch and Titus 2016).[4] Between 1947 and 1971, DES was prescribed in various regions of the United States as an increasingly routine component of prenatal care (not only for those at risk of pregnancy loss) (Troisi, Hatch, and Titus 2016), resulting in the in utero exposure of an estimated 5 to 10 million individuals.[5] In 1971, clinicians reported an association between in utero exposure to DES and rare clear cell adenocarcinoma of the vagina in young women (Herbst, Ulfeder and Poskanzer 1971). While cases of rare vaginal and cervical cancers remained relatively low in relation to the number of individuals exposed to DES, during the 1980s in utero DES exposure was associated with widespread infertility and pregnancy complications (Troisi, Hatch, and Titus 2016; Bell 2009). In 1992, dedicated government funding was approved to support a long-term DES Follow-Up Study to track the health effects of in utero DES exposure.[6]

When DES was first assessed for approval by the FDA, toxicological risk assessment was based on knowledge about natural (not synthetic) toxins, whereby acute poisoning was associated with high doses (Langston 2010: 5). Although a carcinogen (and despite studies showing the carcinogenic effect of DES exposure in animals), DES was not expected to have negative health impacts on humans as the amount of exposure would be relatively low. Foetuses were understood to be protected by the same mechanisms which prevent endogenous oestrogen that circulates in the pregnant individual's body from impacting foetal development (Langston 2010). A genetic 'preformationist' model of foetal development (whereby foetal genes would not be influenced by environment) and a continued belief that the placenta was an impermeable protectant against contaminants challenged any idea that low doses of DES could have a negative impact (Langston 2010). Furthermore, Langston (2010) explains that, at the time, toxicity was understood to be immediately apparent; it was difficult to imagine a delayed manifestation of toxicological effects. Emerging knowledge of EDCs offered new understandings of the effects experienced by exposed individuals decades later. Not only were toxic effects of DES possible at low doses, it became clear over time that negative effects could manifest over the life course and across generations (Langston 2010; Titus et al. 2019).

Chemical toxicity or chemical potentiality?

During the 1970s and 1980s, concurrent with growing awareness about the effects of in utero DES exposure, the use of hormones within medical care was increasingly common in the form of birth control, menopause-related hormone replacement therapy (HRT), emergency contraception, fertility treatment and, to a lesser extent, sexgender (Cavar 2020) medical transition. Those exposed to DES in utero (whether or not they knew of their exposure) during the late 1940s and 1950s were among the early potential users of these hormone therapies. In 1979, the newsletter of a prominent DES advocacy and education group cited national and global experts and organizations that articulated concerns about the cumulative effects of oestrogen exposure and advised DES-exposed women to avoid exposure to additional oestrogen (Editorial: DES Daughters and the Pill 1979: 1, 8).

Several cisgender individuals we interviewed had received such warnings and approached hormones and other chemicals, whether in the environment or in the form of medication, with great caution. Quinn-Anne recalled her doctor advising: 'Besides your thyroid medicine, don't take any other form of hormones, because you're a walking timebomb for this because of DES.' Lena expressed strong trepidation surrounding the use of hormonal supplements to help with the chronic pain she experienced with menstruation and menopause:

> Because of my DES exposure . . . I was very nervous about 'better living through chemistry'[7] after my early life experience. I don't like to put anything in there that I don't have to put in. I just felt like I'd been so drastically influenced by chemicals in my early onset that any chemicals I didn't need, I wasn't about to take.

Carolyn noted:

> I would have never gone on estrogen replacement therapy because, just psychologically, to go on a synthetic hormone, would have been, uh, I don't know, it would have felt like I was taking poison.

These brief remarks highlight these interviewees' awareness of DES as something that is a part of them, not just a synthetic hormone to which they were exposed as a foetus. Several interviewees attributed experiences of intense menstrual cramps, fertility difficulties and menopausal concerns to their DES exposure. Paradoxically, these concerns are typically 'treated' with some form of hormonal intervention (birth control, fertility drugs, HRT). Thus, despite the warnings mentioned earlier, most interviewees used some form of exogenous oestrogen over their life course. Interviewees in this group who used forms of hormonal therapy described navigating the risk related to hormone use in relation to the possible benefits and health goals (preventing a pregnancy, having a child, alleviating chronic pain). Very often interviewees distinguished between the non-consensual exposure to an unsafe synthetic hormone (DES) and consensual exposure to more modern (safer and studied and/or temporarily necessary) hormonal therapy.

Other interviewees, cisgender and transgender, engaged with hormones within what we call a framework of chemical potentiality, using hormones in projects of self-making. For these interviewees, the chemical toxicity of DES could be countered by the chemical potentiality of contemporary hormones. Hormones could be used for balancing purposes and restorative practices of self-care. For example, Ingrid noted that she had become quite skilled at self-assessment and recognizing the ways in which she could restore balance:

I think that my experience personally in my body has taught me that I have to really work at balancing my hormones and I have to supplement them in order to get out of bed, you know? So, I do take supplemental hormones, some estrogen, some DHEA [Dehydroepiandrosterone], progesterone, and testosterone, and we are doing a constant balancing act to try and balance the needs of one specific system in my body with the needs of every other system in my body.

Hormones also offered means to achieve a particularly gendered sense of self. Rachel visited a hormone wellness clinic, reporting having seen 'women on TV [who] said how wonderful they feel ten thousand dollars later'. She attended the clinic to address 'energy, libido, just all of those things'. She stated, 'I was great, you know, for the two months that I [took hormone supplements].' Rachel's descriptions are reminiscent of the aspirations behind hormone rejuvenation practices of the 1920s and 1930s (Pettit 2013; Logan 2013). However, instead of being presented as experimental science, or the more medicalized representations of HRT to address ageing-related bodily changes, hormone wellness is embedded within an ethos of self-care. It was Rachel's primary care physician who advised her to stop taking the supplements, reintroducing a notion of risk associated with chemical toxicity.

The concept of hormone restoration also emerged in interviews with transgender interviewees who speculated that their transness was a result of their exposure to DES. During the 1990s and early 2000s, numerous studies and media reports emerged about the so-called 'feminizing' impact of chemicals with estrogenic properties on the reproductive and sexual behaviour of wildlife. Scientists, journalists and activists drew attention to the 'gender-bending' effects of EDCs – referring to sex changes and/or intersex traits observed in fish and wildlife – as a means of calling for public and regulatory attention to the impact of EDC pollution. *Our Stolen Future: Are We Threatening Our Fertility, Intelligence, and Survival? – A Scientific Detective Story* (Colborn et al. 1996) was one of the first trade books to bring many of these examples together (see also Rudacille 2006). Di Chiro (2010), Pollock (2016) and Ah-King and Hayward (2013) examine such stories of 'gender bending' that continue to populate the media, critiquing the queer and transphobic depictions of the heteronormative natures and societal futures that are being disrupted. As Di Chiro states, 'What are presented by many environmentalists as critical scientific facts (and quite rightly worthy of alarm) can, however, work to create a "sex panic," resuscitating familiar heterosexist, queerphobic, and eugenics arguments classifying some bodies as being not normal: mistakes, perversions, or burdens' (2010: 201–2; see also Veselá et al. 2022). This same period generated theories about prenatal hormone influences on the formation of non-heteronormative gender and sexuality, with some studies in psychology and neuroscience specifically focusing on DES (Meyer-Bahlburg et al. 1995; Hines 2003). As we write elsewhere (Feminist Technoscience Governance Collaboratory 2022), queer and trans individuals we interviewed embraced these theories as possible explanations of their sex/gender/sexuality non-normativity. Extending theories about the 'gender-bending' properties of EDCs to humans, interviewees suggested that DES (a very potent EDC) could have disrupted an intended sex/gender pathway, resulting in transness and/or queer desires. Hormonal intervention, for the purpose of transitioning, is then narrated as a means of restoration. This differs from a more common, but certainly not uniform, narrative in which a trans individual seeks alignment with who one truly is or a growing practice of transitioning to transness rather than to a binary sexgender. Hormones offer a means of restoring a process of gendering that was chemically disrupted. Terry noted:

I'm on hormones and I have surgery – facial lift and breast augmentation – scheduled so that I can transition completely. I'm sixty-one years old and I'm kind of like, it's never too late. So, I'm really looking forward to that. I was denied those surgeries already twice, so I was in an appeal process for [quite some time]. I'm in the process of breaking out like a butterfly and being me . . . I've never been happier in my life actually. There are so many things going on and it feels right.

Sam, who also wondered if their transness was caused by exposure to DES, noted:

I started doing a little research into it and I discovered plant estrogens. I started taking those because I didn't have a prescription. I started taking them and I noticed a little bit of a change, a little bit of budding up here. I said, 'Wow, I must be really susceptible to this stuff.' I really am just affected very easily by it.

For Sam, their body's responsiveness to hormonal intervention reaffirms their understanding that exposure to DES could have influenced their gender development in utero. For some, articulating the individual nature of responsiveness to hormones explained why not everyone who was exposed to DES is trans. Dose, timing of exposure and susceptibility to the hormone all played a role, defining the specific effect that DES might have on any particular individual.

Temporalities of (DES) toxicity

The impact of DES exposure continues to be experienced, and knowledge about DES continues to shape the lives of millions who identify as DES exposed. As we've shared, the most significant finding was a distinction between viewing hormones within a framework of chemical toxicity or chemical potentiality. Looking more closely at which interviewees aligned with which framework, our observations led us to think more closely about the temporalities of toxicity. Our interviewees shared a view that DES exposure was harmful, that DES was toxic. How might timing – of exposure, encounters with knowledge about DES or identification as DES exposed – shape the ways in which individuals engage with other hormones?

During the 1970s and 1980s much of the public discourse about DES exposure centred on its carcinogenic effects and reproductive health impacts (Cody 2008). Beginning in the mid-1990s, case studies of DES as an EDC (Colborn et al. 1996; Hines 2003) expanded public perceptions of who might have been exposed, how one might know whether they had been exposed and what the effects could have been. Shawn and Casey, interviewees who were both closely involved with a large DES health advocacy organization, referred to an observation by a former director that people were often active members of the organization (or active consumers of the information it circulated) during the time periods in their lives when they felt most affected. For some, that was when first learning of their DES exposure, for others it was while experiencing fertility difficulties or when confronted with a cancer diagnosis. In the past couple of decades, it seemed to also be upon reading that DES might be a possible cause of transness and then seeking out further information.

In the first set of examples shared earlier, in which interviewees echoed the idea that additional oestrogen use might compound the effects of DES, interviewees had known about their DES exposure from quite early on in life, usually in their teens or twenties. Their familiarity with the toxic effects of DES stemmed from the impact it had on their lives in the form of vaginal cancer, infertility, severe menstrual cramps and cycle irregularity and/or regular extensive vaginal and cervical cancer screening as recommended for those exposed. Interviewees in this set of interviews identified with the 'slow toxicity' of DES; they understood this toxicity as long term, replete with uncertainty about possible new effects.

The examples these interviewees shared drew on experiences that were in fairly close temporal proximity to the warnings that circulated about the potential harm of cumulative exposure. At the time of the initial reports about EDCs, and the identification of DES as an EDC, most of these individuals were aware of their exposure. Most of these interviewees, who are all assigned female at birth individuals, were also aware of the widespread marketing of HRT to treat menopausal symptoms and the abrupt discontinuation of a Women's Health Initiative study in 2002 due to evidence of increased health risks in women taking combination oestrogen and progestin HRT.[8] Their use of other oestrogens was framed as necessary and often due to the harm caused by DES. These interviewees did not imbue hormones with 'potentiality' – an open-ended sense of possibility for reshaping and rebalancing the self. Instead, their engagement with hormones was inflected with a sense of order, control and purpose. As with the original prescription of DES that resulted in their exposure, if these interviewees engaged with hormones, it was as necessary and within the conventional medical sphere.

Interviewees who identified as DES exposed and embraced the chemical potentiality of hormonal engagement seldom had direct experience with the more commonly known physical effects of DES exposure and/or came to identify as DES exposed later in life. Rachel, for example, seemed primarily concerned about the effects of her in utero DES exposure on her son and engaged minimally with any sense of risk to herself. The visibility of emerging knowledge about third-generation impacts informed her concerns for her son's health but did not resurface concerns for her own. Other interviewees spoke about the impact of DES on the foetus but did not express a sense that the effects of exposure might continue to unfold over a lifetime. DES was perceived to have changed their life, their brain-body experiences, to have done harm. But the toxicity of DES had already manifested. For some, this led to a perspective that the in utero toxicity generated a unique chemical make-up, which necessitated a more constant bodily awareness of endocrine system flows to be addressed through hormonal engagement. For others, including transgender assigned male at birth individuals, information about DES and their own potential exposure was sought as an explanation for something that had already happened. The toxicity of DES was viewed as significantly different from the potentiality ascribed to knowledge about DES's possible effects, and to other hormones, including various forms of oestrogen.

Although active prescription of DES is a practice of the past, DES remains a hormone that is shaping our present. Exploring the narratives of those who believe themselves to have been exposed offers insight into the contemporary life of DES, highlighting discursive and embodied engagements with frameworks of chemical toxicity and chemical potentiality. By thinking through narratives of chemical toxicity and chemical potentiality, and the 'temporalities of toxicity', we hope to further feminist conversations about how emerging knowledge about not only hormones and their effects but also normative expectations of gender/sex/sexuality embodiment converge to shape understandings of the self that people often carry with them for decades.

Notes

1 DES was also used to 'treat' non-normative and pathologized bodies and behaviour, including homosexuality (via 'chemical castration'), intersex variations

(Gill-Peterson 2018: 105, 108) and above-average height in assigned female at birth individuals (Lee and Howell 2006), topics beyond the scope of this entry.

2 To access key scientific publications see the DES Follow-Up Study webpage (https://dceg.cancer.gov/research/what-we-study/des-study#publications) and the DES Action USA website (desaction.org).

3 'Embodying Transgenerational Exposure: Gender/Sex/Sexuality and Experiences of being DES-Exposed' (The DES Project) was approved in September 2017 by the Institutional Review Board at Mount Holyoke College and supported with funding from DES Action USA and Mount Holyoke College. The project included research in the DES Action USA archive at Smith College; twenty-four in-depth interviews with US-based trans, cis, straight and queer individuals ranging in age from fifty-nine to seventy-one who identify as DES exposed and one with an individual who had taken DES; and analyses of blogs, reports and public narratives about DES. All names of interviewees in this entry are pseudonyms.

4 DES's 'prescriptive peak' was during the 1950s (Bell 2009: 17). Based on available demographic data, DES was mostly prescribed to white assigned female at birth individuals. See descriptions of the research participants in DES-focused publications: https://dceg.cancer.gov/research/what-we-study/des-study#publications.

5 DES was marketed under approximately 200 different names, and accurate accounts of prescriptions between 1947 and 1971 are unavailable. See: https://www.cancer.gov /about-cancer/causes-prevention/risk/hormones/des-fact-sheet (last accessed 12 February 2023). For full analyses of the regulatory processes related to the approval of DES see Bell (1995), Langston (2010) and Langston (2014).

6 See dceg.cancer.gov/research/what-we-study/des-study and https://www.cancer.gov/ about-cancer/causes-prevention/risk/hormones/des-fact-sheet (both last accessed 8 January 2023).

7 This was an advertising slogan adopted by the pharmaceutical company Du Pont.

8 https://www.womenshealth.gov/30-achievements/25.

References

Abboud, A. (2018), *A Biography of Endocrine Disruptors: The Narrative Surrounding the Appearance and Regulation of a New Category of Toxic Substances*, PhD thesis, Arizona State University ProQuest Dissertations Publishing, 10788210.

Ah-King, M. and E. Hayward (2013), 'Toxic Sexes—Perverting Pollution and Queering Hormone Disruption', *O-Zone: A Journal of Object Oriented Studies* 1: 1–11.

Bell, S. (1995), 'Gendered Medical Science: Producing a Drug for Women', *Feminist Studies* 21 (3): 469–500.

Bell, S. (2009), *DES Daughters: Embodied Knowledge and the Transformation of Women's Health Politics*, Philadelphia: Temple University Press.

Cavar [s] (2020), 'Enacting Transbutch: Queer Narratives beyond Essentialism', [Undergraduate thesis, Mount Holyoke College], Mount Holyoke College Institutional Digital Archive, Available at: https://search-ebscohost-com.proxy.mtholyoke.edu:2443 /login.aspx?direct=true&AuthType=ip,sso&db=cat09205a&AN=mhf.oai.edge.fiveco

lleges.folio.ebsco.com.fs00001006.01df1204.16c2.5466.b07c.53532a13863f&site=eds-live&scope=site&custid=s8884507.

Cody, P. (2008), *DES Voices: From Anger to Action*, Columbus: DES Action.

Colburn, T., D. Dumanoski, and J. Peterson Myers (1996), *Our Stolen Future: Are We Threatening Our Fertility, Intelligence, and Survival? – A Scientific Detective Story*, New York: Dutton.

Di Chiro, G. (2010), 'Polluted Politics? Confronting Toxic Discourse, Sex Panic, and Eco-normativity', in C. Mortimer-Sandilands and B. Erickson (eds), *Queer Ecologies: Sex, Nature, Politics, Desire*, 199–230, Bloomington: Indiana University Press.

Editorial: DES Daughters and the Pill' (1979), 'Editorial: DES Daughters and the Pill', *DES Action Voice* 1 (3): 1, 8.

Feminist Technoscience Governance Collaboratory (2022), 'Retrospective Exposure: Tracing Narratives of Chemically Induced Transgressions', in L. Veselá (ed.), *Synthetic Becoming*, 138–56, Berlin: K. Verlag.

Gill-Peterson, J. (2018), *Histories of the Transgender Child*, Minneapolis: University of Minnesota Press.

Herbst, A., H. Ulfeder, and D. Poskanzer (1971), 'Adenocarcinoma of the Vagina — Association of Maternal Stilbestrol Therapy with Tumor Appearance in Young Women', *New England Journal of Medicine* 284 (15): 878–81.

Hines, M. (2003), *Brain Gender*, Oxford: Oxford University Press.

Kerlin, S. (2004), 'The Presence of Gender Dysphoria, Transsexualism, and Disorders of Sexual Differentiation in Males Prenatally Exposed to Diethylstilbestrol: Initial Evidence from a 5-Year Study', Paper Presented at 6th Annual E-Hormone Conference New Orleans, October 27–30. Available at https://diethylstilbestrol.co.uk/the-presence-of-gender-dysphoria-transsexualism-and-disorders-of-sex-differentiation-in-males-prenatally-exposed-to-des/ (accessed 8 January 2023).

Langston, N. (2010), *Toxic Bodies: Hormone Disruptors and the Legacy of DES*, New Haven: Yale University Press.

Langston, N. (2014), 'Precaution and the History of Endocrine Disruptors', in S. Boudia and N. Jas (eds), *Powerless Science? Science and Politics in a Toxic World*, 29–45, Berghahn Books.

Lee, J. M. and J. D. Howell (2006), 'Tall Girls: The Social Shaping of a Medical Therapy', *Archives of Pediatrics & Adolescent Medicine* 1 (October): 1035.

Logan, C. (2013), *Hormones, Heredity, and Race: Spectacular Failure in Interwar Vienna*, New Brunswick: Rutgers University Press.

Meyer-Bahlburg, H. F. L. et al. (1995), 'Prenatal Estrogens and the Development of Homosexual Orientation', *Developmental Psychology* 31 (1): 12–21.

Pettit, M. (2013), 'Becoming Glandular: Endocrinology, Mass Culture, and Experimental Lives in the Interwar Age', *American Historical Review* 118 (4): 1052–76.

Pollock, A. (2016), 'Queering Endocrine Disruption', in K. Behar (ed.), *Object-oriented Feminism*, 83–199, Minneapolis: University of Minnesota Press.

Rudacille, R. (2006), *The Riddle of Gender: Science, Activism, and Transgender Rights*, New York: Anchor Books.

Titus L, E. E. Hatch, K. M. Drake et al. (2019), 'Reproductive and Hormone-Related Outcomes in Women whose Mothers were Exposed in utero to Diethylstilbestrol (DES): A Report from the US National Cancer Institute DES Third Generation Study', *Reproductive Toxicology* 84 (March): 32–8.

Troisi, R., E. E. Hatch, and L. Titus (2016), 'The Diethylstilbestrol Legacy: A Powerful Case Against Intervention in Uncomplicated Pregnancy', *Pediatrics* 138 (1): 42–4.

Veselá, L. (ed.) (2022), *Synthetic Becoming*, Berlin: K. Verlag.

5 DICHLORO-DIPHENYL-TRICHLOROETHANE (DDT)

NORAH MACKENDRICK

Dichloro-diphenyl-trichloroethane (DDT) is an organochlorine pesticide that is banned in some parts of the world and permitted for limited use to control the spread of malaria in others. First synthesized in 1874, it was not until 1939 that DDT was discovered to be an effective insecticide, spurring its widespread production and adoption to control flies and mosquitoes and to (misguidedly) slow the spread of polio (Carson [1962] 2002; Conis 2022).[1] DDT was banned in the United States in 1972, more than twelve years after the emergence of strong evidence that it caused serious harm to living organisms. Most famously, DDT was the subject of Rachel Carson's groundbreaking environmentalist book, *Silent Spring* (Carson [1962] 2002). DDT belongs to a class of chemicals called organochlorines, and it is not a hormone.

It belongs in this glossary, however, insofar as it unleashes an endocrine response in birds, fish, amphibians and humans that can be characterized as estrogenic (Wolff 1995). Exposure to DDT early in life is thought to raise one's risk for breast cancer in adulthood. The presence of DDT in the environment, its 'feminizing' effects on wildlife and its presence in human breastmilk have prompted cultural and social anxieties around the future of the human species. As this glossary entry outlines, the safety calculus arising from the question of 'what to do about DDT?' places undue responsibility on female and maternal bodies and reflects a risk society where one catastrophic risk (malaria) is evaluated next to another (global pollution), with no single entity clearly responsible for creating these risks in the first place.

Hormones are powerful biological substances that are delicately calibrated in the biological body through various feedback loops. Exogenous hormones and hormone mimics are compounds that behave like hormones once metabolized by the body and can elicit an endocrine response even at very low doses of exposure. Exogenous hormones have long been used as therapeutics in transgender medicine or as tools in the treatment of various conditions (e.g. menopause) and illnesses (e.g. prostate cancer), with too much or too little hormone dosing potentially deleterious to health. Hormone mimics or endocrine disruptors are synthetic compounds found in pollution and other by-products of industrial expansion and global capitalism. Exposure to them is unintentional. Endocrine disruptors have generated considerable social and ecological anxiety owing to their carcinogenicity and ability to interfere with reproduction and foetal development (McLachlan 2001).

Just as we carry the building blocks of our own biological hormones, our bodies carry traces of DDT. Recent biomonitoring surveys in the United States show that most American adults have detectable levels of DDT and its metabolites (though much lower levels than in earlier decades) in their bodies, despite the fact that the compound was banned fifty years ago in that country (CDC 2021). Globally, all body burdens of DDT and its metabolites have decreased over time, most significantly in the United States, Canada and Western Europe, yet levels are comparatively higher in Africa and Asia, as DDT is still used to control mosquito populations in regions with high rates of malaria (WHO 2011, 2015). Populations living in the Arctic also have high body burdens of DDT, owing to how this compound biomagnifies in the food web, accumulating in fish and aquatic mammals that migrate north and are important traditional and subsistence foods for northerners (Laird, Goncharov and Chan 2013). The Arctic also acts as a sink for persistent environmental chemicals, as global flows of air and water deposit DDT and other toxins at the poles (AMAP 2002). Thus, while the harms of DDT appear to be of less urgent concern to countries that have banned its use, this pesticide remains a real health risk for those living in the far North and the Global South. In short, as a hormone mimic, DDT circulates through the global ecosystem just as it circulates within individual bodies, yet the burden of exposure is highly unequal.

When DDT was first promoted for use in agriculture and as a preventative measure for the spread of polio, there was significant public pushback (Conis 2022). Rachel Carson's *Silent Spring* most famously raised the alarm. In that book, Carson made a connection between DDT and bioaccumulation (Carson [1962] 2002). Bioaccumulation refers to the gradual accumulation of a contaminant as it moves up a food chain – for example, DDT moves from the soil into fish and from fish into fish-eating birds and mammals. Thus, the concentration of DDT in organisms at the top of the food chain is much higher than those at the bottom. Carson's book made a compelling case for taking seriously the ecological impacts of DDT. She expressed alarm over declining bird populations and the effects of high levels of DDT in fish, which subsequent research has confirmed. Even moderate use of DDT is associated with eggshell thinning in birds, thereby impairing their reproduction, and is toxic to fish and aquatic life (WHO 1989). Carson also warned about the widespread use of DDT and rising cancer rates in people, especially in children. While these concerns were voiced in scientific publications and among ecologists, Carson made a convincing case to a public audience and brought together disparate bodies of evidence in ways that galvanized the scientific community (see e.g. Griswold 2012). One of her concerns was how DDT and other pesticides interfered with the liver, a vital organ that regulates sex hormones and other hormones in the body. Reflecting on animal studies demonstrating that organochlorines like DDT damage liver cells, Carson wrote that 'the road to cancer may be an indirect one [. . .] important examples are cancers, especially of the reproductive system, that appear to be linked with disturbances of the balance of sex hormones' (Carson 2002 [1962]: 235). The excess of oestrogen associated with liver damage, she reported, is also associated with higher incidence of uterine cancer and kidney cancer (Carson 2002 [1962]: 236).

For years after the publication of *Silent Spring*, the main concern related to human exposure to DDT was the carcinogenicity of this compound, yet evidence was mixed – sometimes DDT exposure was associated with a higher rate of cancer (especially breast cancer) but not always (Soto and Sonnenschein 2015). Endocrine disruption theory helped specify how DDT threatened human and ecological health and it emerged as a result of scientific and policy work in the 1980s investigating ecological decline (Krimsky 2000). More specifically, in the mid-1980s, zoologist and World Wildlife Fund researcher Theo Colborn examined threats to living organisms in the Great Lake regions of Canada and the United States by systematically reviewing a large body of published scientific literature and government papers from many scientific disciplines, such as biochemistry, toxicology and developmental pharmacology, as well as the biological sciences, including wildlife biology and reproductive biology (Krimsky 2000). Drawing from the theory of 'environmental estrogens' Colborn and others formulated a hypothesis that industrial pollution posed a significant threat to human reproduction, in addition to wildlife populations (Colborn and Clement 1992).

Key to her discovery was that even low-dose chemical exposures could have long-term, subtle effects on the reproduction and behaviour of living organisms (Vandenberg et al. 2012). That is, levels of exposure that do not generate a toxic response (severe illness or death) can still be deleterious to organisms. By acting upon the endocrine system, endocrine-disrupting compounds like DDT interfere with metabolic, reproductive and neurological processes (Kabir, Rahman and Rahman 2015). Colborn's discoveries challenged traditional toxicology and received widespread attention. Together with Pete Myers and Diane Dumanoski, Colborn published *Our Stolen Future*, which cast pollution as a threat to male and female reproductive health and the future of the human species (Colborn, Myers and Dumanoski 1996). Indeed, scientific research conducted since the publication of *Our Stolen Future* has found that high levels of exposure to DDT increase the risk of neurological impairments – particularly among children exposed in early childhood or in utero – as well as breast cancer, diabetes, miscarriage and lower semen quality (Eskenazi et al. 2009).

From a feminist and science and technology studies perspective, what is especially problematic in the social and biomedical 'discovery' of DDT as an endocrine disruptor is how the female body has become the dominant vector transmitting the risk of this pesticide to unborn children and infants and therefore the vector that is worthy of social control and biomedical (and cultural) concern. For instance, biomedical research identifies 'early windows of exposure' to endocrine disruptors as setting the stage for future disease, such as fertility problems, neurological problems and cancer, meaning that the social and ecological anxiety surrounding DDT has continued to centre on female reproductive bodies as vectors of transmission for the harm of this pesticide, along with other endocrine disruptors (MacKendrick 2018; Roberts 2007). Early life exposure to DDT, particularly during foetal development, is considered a risk factor for developing breast cancer later in life (Cohn 2015; Soto and Sonnenschein 2015). Managing this risk therefore implicates female bodies because DDT builds up in fatty tissues over the life course, and during periods of rapid growth, gestation and breastfeeding it is released back into bloodstream as the body mobilizes fat tissues to fuel growth and breastmilk production. DDT also crosses the placenta during pregnancy and is delivered when infants are breast or chest fed.[2]

DDT acts upon hormone receptors in the cells of living organisms and can therefore be considered a kind of hormonal technology. Unlike therapeutic hormones (like thyroxine, oestrogen, testosterone and progesterone) that require a prescription from a medical professional and are regulated by government bodies charged with ensuring the safety of pharmaceuticals, DDT enters the body unknowingly and acts upon it through a form of toxic trespass (Cranor 2011). In a modern risk society, large-scale, potentially catastrophic hazards – like global pesticide pollution – are forced upon individuals who have no direct say in the production of these hazards but are encouraged to develop the 'right' safety calculus to decide how much to worry about risk at a given moment and whom or what to hold accountable in the production of risk (Beck 1995). While the state and the companies that make and distribute pesticides are ultimately responsible for global pesticide pollution, it is the bodies and behaviours of pregnant people and women of reproductive age that have become sites of intense scrutiny and intervention for managing this risk in the short term (MacKendrick 2018).[3] Indeed, public health programmes frequently target the health behaviours of these groups in the name of protecting foetuses, infants and young children from harm. In the United States, environmental groups warn pregnant people and parents of young children about the deleterious impact of toxic chemicals on their child's growth and development (MacKendrick and Cairns 2019). Exposure to toxic chemicals early in life is thought to be linked to learning disorders, cancer and reproductive problems (Birnbaum 2013). Attention to the dangers of DDT and other endocrine disruptors to developing foetuses and breastfeeding infants reflects not only the 'state of the science' but also cultural anxieties around the riskiness of mothers' bodies and actions in relation to children's health and future potential (Lappé, Jeffries Hein and Landecker 2019; Mansfield 2017). In casting DDT as an environmental threat, female bodies become sites of concern because biomedical experts typically conceptualize the 'environment' as the pregnant body and sphere of control a pregnant or breastfeeding person has over their surroundings and everyday activities and choices (see e.g. Lappé 2016; Malcolm 2021; Valdez 2021; Lappé and Hein 2022). Such an understanding is internalized by mothers who feel personally responsible for their child's exposure to toxic substances (Cairns, Johnston and MacKendrick 2013; MacKendrick 2014, 2018; Valdez 2018, 2021).

The scientific research on DDT and endocrine disruptors more generally has generated substantial socio-ecological anxiety surrounding environmental destruction and human reproductive futures. Exposure to DDT has been associated with 'feminization' of males in birds and other animals, as males fail to fully develop male reproductive organs, develop female reproductive characteristics or display altered mating behaviour (Milnes et al. 2006). As a feminizing influence, DDT threatens the gender binary and the normative model of successful and normal reproduction, creating what Celia Roberts calls a 'sex panic' (Roberts 2003, 204). When the feminization and endocrine disruptor research captured public attention in the 1990s, some activists and scientists predicted a gradual 'feminization of the planet' (Duncan 1995, LI25) with, as the title of a popular 1994 British documentary proclaimed, the 'assault on the male' from environmental oestrogens well underway (Cadbury 1994; see also Roberts 2003). Such fears surrounding the impact of endocrine disruptors on sex and sexuality coincided with broader cultural anxieties about the decline of men and masculinity (Kimmel 1996; Messner 1997; Daniels 2006). In the 1990s, multiple books and editorials raised alarms about the threat of feminism to traditional masculinity and men's falling social and economic position as a consequence of single motherhood (and, thus, absent fathers) and women's increasing labour force participation (Kimmel 1996; Messner 1997). In short, the confluence of the ecological community's discovery of rapid feminization of wildlife, along with changing gender relations, suggested that the traditional man was at risk biologically and socially (Daniels 2006). Importantly, queer theorists and feminist scholars argue that this focus on changes to sexed bodies as a form of 'harm' in ecological and biomedical research on endocrine disruptors is ableist, queerphobic and heterosexist because it limits the possibilities for action against harm from synthetic pollutants, as it excludes those who do not conform to medicalized and normative definitions of sex, gender, reproduction and sexuality (see e.g. Lee and Mykitiuk 2018; Alaimo 2016; Roberts 2003; 2007; Di Chiro 2010).

Despite DDT's role as a carcinogen, neurotoxicant and endocrine disruptor, it remains a highly effective pesticide for killing mosquitoes that spread malaria. In fact, DDT is widely considered the most effective form of vector control for managing the spread of malaria and is thought to be a key reason for the near eradication of malaria in southern Africa in the late 1950s and early 1960s (Mabaso et al. 2004). When countries moved to ban DDT, there was a rapid and corresponding rise in malaria transmission that quickly reversed when DDT was reintroduced (Bouwman 2012). DDT is therefore simultaneously a means to preserve life and a profound threat to it. The continued use of DDT in regions with high rates of malaria transmission reflects calculations of risk that weigh one type of threat (cancer and endocrine disruption) against another (malaria). In short, this pesticide illuminates the contradictions inherent in a modern risk society, where human technologies meant to control one threat create new hazards distributed in unequal ways (Beck 1992). Controlling malaria with DDT increases the risk of cancer among exposed populations and not just those whose homes are sprayed with the pesticide but people living long distances from areas of application who are exposed through global flows of air, water and wildlife. These populations, such as those living in Artic regions, have little say or control over the application of DDT in the Global South yet bear a significant proportion of the risk of its continued use.

The global circulation of DDT in the environment and living organisms raises questions about what a hormone is and is not and illuminates the vulnerability of the body to toxic trespass, as well as the social and cultural anxieties around biological sex and gender relations, and disease. The continued use of DDT presents ethical and practical questions about how to protect humans and ecological systems from the deleterious effects of endocrine disruption, while accounting for the burden of disease in malarial regions. DDT reflects the risk society, where individuals and groups must navigate multiple global risks, and the navigation of risk shapes social life, particularly for cisgender women who are charged by virtue of their capacity to gestate and breastfeed as vectors of chemical transmission. DDT is a hormonal technology that has had sweeping impacts on human populations and the natural world; it remains a ubiquitous threat to health and possibly to reproductive futures for all organisms.

Notes

1 Before scientists and public health officials understood the pathways of transmission for polio they used vector control for flies to slow its spread, a misguided strategy that lasted several years. For more on this history refer to Conis (2022).

2 Not all mothers identify as cisgender women. In this entry, mother refers to an individual who bears a child or identifies as a mother.

3 The intended audience is typically cisgender women, although all individuals of reproductive age who have the capacity to become pregnant would arguably be receptive to these messages.

References

Alaimo, S. (2016), *Exposed: Environmental Politics and Pleasures in Posthuman Times*, Minneapolis: University of Minnesota Press.

Arctic Monitoring and Assessment Programme (AMAP) (2002), 'AMAP Fact Sheet: Transport of Contaminants to the Arctic, and Their Fate', Available at https://www.north-slope.org/wp-content/uploads/2022/05/contaminant-transport-and-fate.pdf (accessed 9 October 2022).

Beck, U. (1992), *Risk Society: Towards a New Modernity*, London: Sage Publications.

Beck, U. (1995), *Ecological Politics in an Age of Risk*, Cambridge: Polity Press.

Birnbaum, L. S. (2013), 'State of the Science of Endocrine Disruptors', *Environmental Health Perspectives* 121: a107.

Bouwman, H., H. Kylin, B. Sereda, and R. Bornman (2012), 'High Levels of DDT in Breast Milk: Intake, Risk, Lactation Duration, and Involvement of Gender', *Environmental Pollution* 170: 63–70.

Cadbury, D. (dir). (1994), *Assault on the Male*, BBC Media Horizon.

Cairns, K., J. Johnston, and N. MacKendrick (2013), 'Feeding the "Organic Child": Mothering Through Ethical Consumption', *Journal of Consumer Culture* 13: 97–118.

Carson, R. (2002 [1962]), *Silent Spring: 40th Anniversary Edition*, Boston: Houghton Mifflin.

Centers for Disease Control (CDC) (2021), 'Dichlorodiphenyltrichloroethane (DDT) Factsheet', Available at: https://www.cdc.gov/biomonitoring/DDT_FactSheet.html (accessed 9 October 2022).

Cohn, B. A., M. La Merrill, N. Y. Krigbaum, G. Yeh, J.-S. Park, L. Zimmermann, et al. (2015), 'DDT Exposure in Utero and Breast Cancer', *The Journal of Clinical Endocrinology & Metabolism* 100: 2865–72.

Colborn, T. and C. Clement (eds) (1992), *Chemically Induced Alterations in Sexual and Functional Development: The Wildlife/Human Connection*, vol. XXI, Princeton: Princeton Scientific Publishing Co., Inc.

Colborn, T., D. Dumanoski, and J. P. Myers (1996), *Our Stolen Future: Are we Threatening Our Fertility, Intelligence, and Survival? A Scientific Detective Story*, New York: Dutton.

Conis, E. (2022), *How to Sell a Poison: The Rise, Fall, and Toxic Return of DDT*, New York: Boldtype Books.

Cranor, C. (2011), *Legally Poisoned: How the Law Puts Us at Risk from Toxicants*, Cambridge, MA: Harvard University Press.

Daniels, C. R. (2006), *Exposing Men: The Science and Politics of Male Reproduction*, Oxford: Oxford University Press.

Di Chiro, G. (2010), 'Polluted Politics? Confronting Toxic Discourse, Sex Panic, and Eco-Normativity', in Catriona Mortimer-Sandilands and Bruce Erickson (eds), *Queer Ecologies: Sex, Nature, Politics, Desire*, 199–230, Indianapolis, IN: Indiana University Press.

Duncan, E. (1995), 'Fostering Clean Air Through Environmental Law', *New York Times*, 14 May 14, Section LI: 25.

Eskenazi, B., J. Chevrier, L. G. Rosas, H. A. Anderson, M. S. Bornman, H. Bouwman et al. (2009), 'The Pine River Statement: Human Health Consequences of DDT Use', *Environmental Health Perspectives* 117: 1359–67.

Griswold, E. (2012), 'How "Silent Spring" Ignited the Environmental Movement', *The New York Times*, 21.

Kabir, E. R., M. S. Rahman, and I. Rahman (2015), 'A Review on Endocrine Disruptors and Their Possible Impacts on Human Health', *Environmental Toxicology and Pharmacology* 40 (1): 241–58.

Kimmel, M. (1996), *Manhood in America: A Cultural History*, New York: Free Press.

Krimsky, S. (2000), *Hormonal Chaos: The Scientific and Social Origins of the Environmental Endocrine Hypothesis*, Baltimore: Johns Hopkins University Press.

Laird, B. D., A. B. Goncharov, and H. M. Chan (2013), 'Body Burden of Metals and Persistent Organic Pollutants Among Inuit in the Canadian Arctic', *Environment International* 59: 33–40.

Lappé, M. (2016), 'The Maternal Body as Environment in Autism Science', *Social Studies of Science* 46: 675–700.

Lappé, M. and R. J. Hein (2022), 'The Temporal Politics of Placenta Epigenetics: Bodies, Environments and Time', *Body & Society* 9: 49–76.

Lappé, M., R. Jeffries Hein, and H. Landecker (2019), 'Environmental Politics of Reproduction', *Annual Review of Anthropology* 48: 133–50.

Lee, R. and R. Mykitiuk (2018), 'Surviving Difference: Endocrine-Disrupting Chemicals, Intergenerational Justice and the Future of Human Reproduction', *Feminist Theory* 19 (2): 205–21.

Mabaso, M. L., B. Sharp, and C. Lengeler (2004), 'Historical Review of Malarial Control in Southern Africa with Emphasis on the use of Indoor Residual House-spraying', *Tropical Medicine & International Health* 9: 846–56.

MacKendrick, N. (2014), 'More Work for Mother: Chemical Body Burdens as a Maternal Responsibility', *Gender & Society* 28: 705–28.

MacKendrick, N. (2018), *Better Safe Than Sorry: How Consumers Navigate Exposure to Everyday Toxics*, Oakland: University of California Press.

MacKendrick, N. and K. Cairns. (2019), 'The Polluted Child and Maternal Responsibility in the US Environmental Health Movement', *Signs: Journal of Women and Culture in Society* 44: 307–32.

Malcolm, R. (2021), 'Milk's Flows: Making and Transmitting Kinship, Health, and Personhood', *Medical Humanities* 2019.

Mansfield, B. (2017), 'Folded Futurity: Epigenetic Plasticity, Temporality, and New Thresholds of Fetal Life', *Science as Culture* 26: 355–79.

Messner, M. A. (1997), *Politics of Masculinities: Men in Movements*, Lanham: AltaMira Press.

McLachlan, J. A. (2001), 'Environmental Signaling: What Embryos and Evolution Teach Us About Endocrine Disrupting Chemicals', *Endocrine Reviews* 22: 319–41.

Milnes, M. R., D. S. Bermudez, T. A. Bryan, T. M. Edwards, M. P. Gunderson, I. L. V. Larkin, et al. (2006), 'Contaminant-induced Feminization and Demasculinization of Nonmammalian Vertebrate Males in Aquatic Environments', *Environmental Research* 100: 3–17.

Roberts, C. (2003), 'Drowning in a Sea of Estrogens: Sex Hormones, Sexual Reproduction and Sex', *Sexualities* 6: 195–213.

Roberts, C. (2007), *Messengers of Sex: Hormones, Biomedicine and Feminism*, Cambridge: Cambridge University Press.

Soto, A. M. and C. Sonnenschein (2015), 'DDT, Endocrine Disruption and Breast Cancer', *Nature Reviews Endocrinology* 11: 507–8.

Valdez, N. (2018), 'The Redistribution of Reproductive Responsibility: On the Epigenetics of "Environment" in Prenatal Interventions', *Medical Anthropology Quarterly* 32: 425–42.

Valdez, N. (2021), 'The Politics of Postgenomic Reproduction: Exploring Pregnant Narratives from Within a Clinical Trial', *Science, Technology, & Human Values* 47: 1205–30.

Vandenberg, L. N., T. Colborn, T. B. Hayes, J. J. Heindel, J. D. R. Jacobs, D.-H. Lee, et al. (2012), 'Hormones and Endocrine-Disrupting Chemicals: Low-Dose Effects and Nonmonotonic Dose Responses', *Endocrine Reviews* 33: 378–455.

Wolff, M. S. (1995), 'Pesticides--How Research has Succeeded and Failed in Informing Policy: DDT and the Link with Breast Cancer', *Environmental Health Perspectives* 103 (6): 87–91.

World Health Organization (WHO) (2009), 'DDT and its Derivatives. Environmental Aspects', *Environmental Health Criteria* 83. https://apps.who.int/iris/handle/10665 /40018 (accessed 26 January 2023).

World Health Organization (WHO) (2011), 'The Use of DDT in Malaria Vector Control. A Position Statement', Available at https://apps.who.int/iris/bitstream/handle/10665 /69945/WHO_HTM_GMP_2011_eng.pdf;jsessionid=E286C9F61755D198B0CEEFE 8388BD253?sequence=1 (accessed 9 October 2022).

World Health Organization (WHO) (2015), *Human Biomonitoring: Facts and Figures (No. WHO/EURO: 2015-3209-42967-60040)*, World Health Organization. Regional Office for Europe.

6 DOPAMINE

TOM BOYLSTON

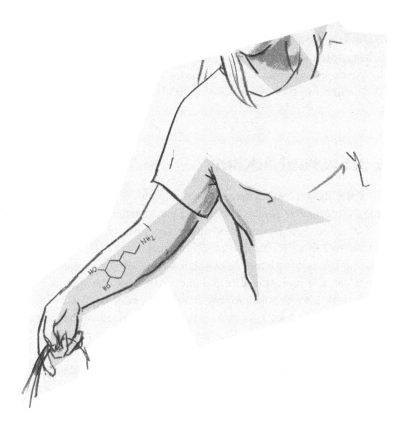

This entry tracks the recent emergence of widespread popular discourses about the neurohormone dopamine. In these discourses, dopamine is understood as the mechanism of the brain's reward system and hence as the biological mechanism of desire, habit formation and addiction. Ideas about dopamine, I suggest, play a key role in the expansion of the addiction concept to cover not just narcotics but also a range of increasingly mundane behaviours from gambling to sex to shopping, exercise and, in particular, technology use (Sedgwick 1993). Rather than seeing addiction as a danger attached to particular harmful substances, dopamine thinking casts all members of consumer society as potential addicts.

After tracing how ideas about dopamine filter from Cambridge neuroscience experiments, to the designers of video games and software platforms, and ultimately to a wider public, I ask how thinking with dopamine alters our understandings of desire and personhood. Dopamine thinking sees all behaviour as potentially addictive and so requires the subject to self-regulate – in line with neoliberal demands for self-management. However, under certain circumstances, dopamine thinking can become a way of framing critique of consumer society and of the growing influence of big tech. Dopamine thinking reduces complex human motivations to a particular kind of story about how brains learn to desire. But I hope to keep open the possibility that there might be something interesting in that reduction of desire to dopamine – or at least, something that might be helpful to some people navigating an overstimulated world.

The universal addict

Dopamine is a highly complex neurohormone, implicated in a range of processes, including learning, movement, motivation, kidney function, nausea, interest, pain, sleep and lactation. Popular dopamine discourses, however, focus narrowly on its presumptive role in anticipating rewards and forming habit loops (Eyal 2014). 'Rewards' might mean food, money, drugs or sex but also recognition, validation, points in a game, a successful dice roll and certificates of achievement. When we achieve these rewards, the narrative has it, dopamine is released: our brains recognize an action as successful and are incentivized to repeat that action. If we begin seeking a particular reward to the exclusion of other pursuits, addiction ensues.

Ideas about dopamine have been taken up by a wider public seeking to understand the increasingly complex array of attention traps that characterize contemporary life (cf. Seaver 2019). Psychiatrist Anna Lembke's popular book *Dopamine Nation: How to Find Balance in an Age of Indulgence* (Lembke 2021) exemplifies dopamine's prominence in public discourse – both as a molecule that seems to explain human desire and as part of the narrative that, in contemporary digital capitalism, we are all addicts. 'The smartphone,' Lembke writes, 'is the modern-day hypodermic needle, delivering digital dopamine 24/7 for a wired generation. If you haven't met your drug of choice yet, it's coming to a website near you.' Digital technology, for Lembke as for many other commentators, is indistinguishable from habit-forming narcotics, because each acts through the same neurochemical mechanism.

The dopamine subject is a consumer always in danger of being manipulated by behavioural design, ubiquitous software, overabundant information and cheap pleasures but equally at risk from such apparently ascetic disciplines as work or exercise, which come to be seen as having addictive potential in themselves. We are no longer thought of as addicted to particular morally problematic forms of consumption but to dopamine: to the mechanism of addiction itself. Since asceticism is as fraught as consumption, the dopamine subject must always seek balance. Avoiding problematic substances no longer suffices; avoiding technology is not a realistic option for most. You will still have a smartphone but it will come with a screentime tracker, and it will be up to you to moderate your usage.

Software and the science of reward

The past decade has seen a glut of media articles about dopamine – framed either as the key to the new science of desire or the threatening tool with which software giants have hijacked our brains. A key moment in the popularization of dopamine thinking was the Facebook ex-president Sean Parker claiming that the Facebook 'like' button had been designed to make the platform addictive by giving users 'dopamine hits' whenever they received social validation.[1] In Parker's account, Facebook's engineers had tapped into cutting-edge neuroscience to hack our brains' reward circuits. Dopamine was the key, with ideas about dopamine having been promulgated in Silicon Valley as part of the rise of the field of behavioural design. Thought leaders like B. J. Fogg, of the Stanford Behavior Design Lab, drew on the neuroscience of dopamine as part of a wider project of exploring how computers could be used to persuade people and shape their habits (Fogg 2003). The writer Nir Eyal has played a prominent part in popularizing dopamine discourse through his 2014 book *Hooked: How to Build Habit-Forming Products* – and would later pivot to advising users on how to avoid the attention traps he had helped to create (Eyal and Li-Eyal 2020).

In the field of game design, around this same period we begin to see explicit discussion of how to mobilize an understanding of dopamine in building 'Compulsion loops' – incentive structures that would keep the player coming back for more (Schüll 2012). This style of design is best known now in the controversial form of 'loot boxes' – completing an objective in a game awards you a mystery prize, which might be great or terrible. The notion is that anticipation and uncertainty make the player more likely to keep playing (or putting in money) in search of more rewards.

Evangelists such as Fogg and Eyal draw largely on the neuroscientific research of Wolfram Schultz and his team (e.g. Hollerman and Schultz 1998; Schultz 1998, 2002).[2] Schultz outlines a theory of rewards that is of obvious interest to technology designers looking to habituate people to their products: 'Rewards are crucial for individual and gene survival and support elementary processes such as drinking, eating and reproduction. This behavioural definition attributes reward function also to certain nonalimentary and nonsexual entities, including money, technical artefacts, aesthetic stimulus attributes and mental events. Rewards engage agents in such diverse behaviors as foraging and trading on stock markets' (Schultz 2010). Most anthropologists would question the claim that foraging and stock trading are similar (e.g. Ingold 1996). They could only be made equivalent through the prior exclusion of any kind of environmental context or embodied/motor learning. The neuroscientists Salamone and Correa (2012), too, are critical of reducing the complex role of dopamine in movement and motivation to a story about 'rewards'.

Indeed, while Schultz may play a part in the simplified narrative of dopamine as a reward molecule, his experimental work paints a much richer picture: 'Dopamine neurons are activated by rewarding events that are better than predicted, remain uninfluenced by events that are as good as predicted, and are depressed by events that are worse than predicted. By signaling rewards according to a prediction error, dopamine responses have the formal characteristics of a teaching signal postulated by reinforcement learning theories' (Schultz 1998). Dopamine, Schultz shows, is not simply a reward mechanism but a way of tracking prediction error – something like a novelty detector (Schultz 2016). The influence of this work in subsequent debates in cognitive science, for example, on predictive processing, is substantial (see e.g. Clark 2013); it becomes possible to think of cognition as a process of making predictions, which are then tested and constantly updated against information from the senses.

So, if dopamine is implicated in addiction (feedback loops in which we seek a particular reward at the expense of other priorities), this must be understood in a much wider context of how we learn and how we identify salience in our environment, registering moments when the 'reward' (positive or negative) from an action differs from our expectations. And yet as dopamine becomes trendy, the tendency has been to focus overwhelmingly on the simplistic narrative of dopamine as a molecule of positive reward associated with pleasure, anticipation and addiction. As Salamone and Correa (2012) argue, neuroscientists have contributed to this simplification as much as anyone.

The direct reward functions of dopamine are extremely salient in certain situations, notably in circumstances when we are susceptible to conditioning (Salamone and Correa 2012). The legitimate concern of critics of behavioural design is that, in creating a social infrastructure built on behaviourism, the tech industry teaches people to think and act in behaviourist terms: a loop between action and reward, an extremely shallow account of psychic experience, a subject responsive only to desire and aversion and incapable of ethical reflective self-discipline. Users sometimes describe themselves as living in 'Skinner boxes', operant conditioning chambers in which an animal has access to a button that gives intermittent rewards or punishments as determined by unseen experimenters. What all of this indicates is that, rather than describing how behavioural design cracked the secret of desire, we should instead ask how human social environments, in digitally mediated forms especially, are being simplified and reduced in such a way as to render reward-based motivation structures so compelling.

All history is the history of dopamine loops

The addiction-based understanding of subjectivity is taken to extremes in The Dopamine Project,[3] a website and e-book produced by a man styling himself as 'Charles Lyell'. As the original Lyell (1797–1875) demonstrated how geology shaped climate history, so the new Lyell will show how dopamine shapes human history. Synthesizing a range of neuroscientific papers and applying them to historic and contemporary events, the new Lyell wishes to demonstrate the role of dopamine addiction in all human conflict.

A classic piece of outsider theory (Eburne 2018), Lyell's reasoning is ingenious. Studies have shown the role of dopamine not only in circuits of learning, reward and reinforcement (and by extension, in addiction) but also in the affirmation of social status (e.g. Krach et al. 2010). Humans become addicted to dopamine rewards, which some obtain through drugs, but many more gain through the search for, and obsessive protection of, power, fame and status. The brilliant twist is this: natural selection has ensured that we have an innate aversion to anything that threatens our dopamine flow. And the greatest threat to the dopamine flow is knowledge about dopamine itself.

The logic is as follows: if dopamine is the universal mechanism of reinforcement learning, then the human is no longer a seeker of particular goods (food, sex, status) but merely a seeker of dopamine itself. Dopamine, like Dawkins's (2006 [1976]) Selfish Gene, is understood as a self-maximizing agent, but whereas genes spread by replication, dopamine maximizes itself through addictiveness. When we believe ourselves to be acting rationally, our primitive brains are actually aiming simply to maintain dopamine flows. If we recognized this, we would stop seeking dopamine and start acting rationally. Our primitive brains, according to Lyell, act to keep us in denial about dopamine and so preserve the dopamine flow that rational action would interrupt. Dopamine is therefore an 'anti-meme'[4] (a concept that actively inhibits its own transmission), as much involved in aversion as positive reinforcement, according to neuroscience (e.g. Bromberg-Martin et al. 2010).

For this reason, the vast majority of people, history's greatest geniuses included, instinctively repress any knowledge of dopamine and respond with hostility to anyone who confronts them with such knowledge. One gets the impression from his FAQ that Lyell has become accustomed to such hostility – he offers advice on responding to people who are 'Tired of Hearing About Dopamine'. But this explains why Lyell, by his own description 'not a smart man', could stumble upon an insight that the scientific establishment had overlooked: 'I'm sitting on one of the most significant breakthroughs of the century, as well as a straightforward explanation (dopamine-induced aversive behaviour) as to why nobody wants to know. And I can't give the information away . . . . But that hasn't kept me from trying.'

Lyell's model is instructive because it reflects – and extends ad absurdum – technology designers' understanding of desire: whatever we think we're pursuing, what we want is dopamine. In this logic, dopamine is delivered not only by objects but also social relations, which we seek in the same way we seek food. Since the object of desire is also the mechanism of desire, the result is spiralling feedback loops. The addictive qualities of social media, for example, are unsurprising, because all sociality is based on unrecognized, recursive dopamine addiction. The human being is, constitutively and ontologically, an addict. While Lyell's work is paranoid and somewhat marginal, his basic supposition of the universal addict is not so different from those of more mainstream authorities such as Lembke's *Dopamine Nation*.

Hormone heuristics

Popular appropriations of neuroscience, however, can take surprising turns. Dopamine thinking, as this volume illustrates, sits in the context of new ideas and practices about the role of hormones and neuropeptides in emotional and cognitive life. Malcolm, for example (2021), details the growing use of hormone-derived theory in developing therapies for autism; Mackenzie and Roberts (2017) have analysed the use of 'brain-based parenting' in contemporary adoption practices, in which hormonal function and the limbic system are crucially invoked.

Brain-based parenting and dopamine thinking invoke what I would call hormone heuristics. In none of these cases are hormones observed or measured, nor are hormone levels altered by pharmacological means. Instead, scientific discourses about hormones are adapted and used to think through emotionally weighted social situations (Broer et al. 2020; Pickersgill et al. 2011). Behaviours and therapies are developed with a view to altering hormonal or neurochemical balances, but at no point are hormonal levels themselves checked. We just assume that things have worked if we feel better. Rudimentary hormone heuristics are familiar from many gendered contexts – dismissing women's emotions as 'hormonal', for example, or describing a male-dominated meeting as 'full of testosterone'. But the hormone heuristics we have introduced are more complex and move far beyond gender stereotyping. Hormone ideas sometimes provide a 'sciencey' veneer to discussions of mood and behaviour, but they can also become a basis for theorizing and addressing situations in which intersubjective and environmental affective regulation is vitally important but also compromised in seemingly intractable ways.

Mackenzie and Roberts' discussion of brain-based parenting in adoption illuminates the unexpected possibilities of certain hormone-brain reductions. Adoptive parents are taught to think about their children's and their own experience through the limbic system: stress and complex trauma explained in terms of cortisol levels and the fight-or-flight response. The authors describe some hesitation regarding this biomedical framing of parenting but also argue that

> brain-based parenting can involve significant and sometimes seriously helpful shifts in parents' and children's sense of agency, moving from personhood based on psychological interiority to one that attempts to figure the brain and brain chemistry and processes as agentic without either relocating the locus of agency to the brain (as causal or determining process) or to biomedicine as the institutional-epistemic embodiment of governing expertise. (Mackenzie and Roberts 2017: 134)

They give a moving account of how a parent's response to a child having a tantrum can be helped by understanding this as an effect of things going on in the child's limbic system, beyond either of their control, but to be ridden out by providing a safe, attentive environment to allow things to slowly come to balance.

Brain-based parenting, that is, can provide welcome respite from hegemonic notions of self-mastery and shift attention from seemingly problematic individuals to building nurturing environments. Here attention to molecules and brain regions frees up space for complex empathy: 'the brain becomes a locus of action and, at the same time, gives rise to new ways of thinking about the limits on our capacity to think, talk, feel, respond or act, and suggests interestingly deep material forms of intersubjectivity and relationality' (2017: 149). In part, this new depth reflects the increasingly social and intersubjective focus of neuroscience itself (Rose and Abi-Rached 2013) – in this case, forms of attachment theory that understand affective regulation as both constitutive of selfhood and vitally dependent on the emotional feedback of social others (Schore 1994).

To ascribe stress to cortisol, love to oxytocin or desire to dopamine is both reductive and reifying. But not in the same way as, for example, equating depression to a PET scan of a depressed brain (Dumit 2003). To reduce emotions to hydrocarbons simplifies the emotion, but cumulatively it produces a notion of self that is a dynamic, internally conflicted and open-ended system, rather than a fixed, predetermined entity. If I start to take seriously my cortisol, oxytocin and dopamine levels, I may be engaging in forms of self-monitoring and self-management that align with neoliberal ethics of the 'pharmaceutical self' (Dumit 2012: 126; Jenkins 2011). But I do so by attending to my environment, my bodily sensations and my relationships with others. I experience my hormone levels as part of me but not identical to me and often, when unbalanced, at odds with my core sense of who I am.

This matters when thinking about addiction. Thinking with dopamine ascribes causation to neurochemistry but always in relation to a social environment and the influences of contexts, platforms and substances. Thus, for example, when the neurologist, author and ex-heroin user Marc Lewis argues against the disease model of addiction in favour of something more dynamic and less essentializing, he does so in the name of the contemporary neuroscience of dopamine (Lewis 2017; Berridge 2017). For Lewis, crucially, addiction is a learning process gone awry. Addiction, he argues, is not a disease but a learned pattern that becomes embedded as the brain builds new dopamine pathways, and that can be slowly unlearned by teaching the brain to form different pathways. Following Mackenzie and Roberts, thinking addiction through dopamine may open new avenues for (self-)empathy and recovery. Dopamine thinking, surprisingly, may offer an alternative to medicalization.

Reclaiming dopamine

Amid debates about whether excessive gaming or internet use ought rightly to be called addictions (e.g. Aarseth et al. 2017), it is important to remember that there are large numbers of people for whom these things are indeed associated with suffering; who would like to reduce their gaming or browsing and find themselves unable to do so; and for whom these perceived failures are associated with a wider set of social and emotional difficulties. For some of these people, dopamine thinking may open possibilities for thinking through these problems of desire and motivation.

Dopamine heuristics helped software and game developers imagine a hackable brain; neurochemistry could be altered by code infrastructures. For at least some gamers and internet users, the same theories and methods are available for their own efforts at self-management. These efforts are discussed, debated and critiqued across a series of subreddits (r/stopgaming, r/nosurf, r/productivity), in the comments of an entire subgenre of dopamine educational YouTube videos that users circulate – and in private support forums. The discourse is not hard to find.

Simplifications and errors about dopamine circulate widely but are also critiqued – most common is the idea of dopamine as the 'pleasure molecule', when in fact evidence suggests that dopamine's role in reinforcement is distinct from pleasure. Users might correct each other on the idea that only technology and drugs produce dopamine. For example, one user asks whether browsing Reddit gives you a dopamine hit, and another responds:

> Yep. So does making a sandwich. Having a shower. Talking to a friend. Completing a task at work. Your goal isn't to cut out dopamine. The problem is feedback loops, and instant gratification. You want to shun (or limit, if possible) things that give you a sense of reward with no actual reward. Things like video games, mindless surfing, or masterbation [sic].

This idea – 'the sense of reward with no actual reward' – is important. It points to an equivocation in dopamine discourse, where sometimes dopamine is seen as the true object of desire but at other times merely the mechanism for finding what is really valuable – as one user put it, 'natural social needs release dopamine.' Social validation and a sense of achievement are commonly mentioned as desirable sources of dopamine, which video games provide in attenuated, rapid-release form, hijacking more healthy circuits of recognition. This understanding runs parallel to the design of 'social loops' in social media: validation releases dopamine which leads you to share content and so on. These users – those most involved in dopamine discussions – share a common understanding with the tech developers, both about the social functions of dopamine and the hackability of the brain, but are trying to regain control of their dopamine regimes. If digital culture surrounds us with dopaminergic platforms, products and infrastructures, then the perceived solution is to figure out what are worthwhile sources of dopamine.

The contested notion of 'dopamine fasting' is a case in point. The rough idea is that your dopamine receptors become jaded from too much techno-social stimulation and need some time to 'reset' – by avoiding technology, any kind of media content, drugs, sex, masturbation and sometimes food or conversation, for twenty-four hours or longer. Some feel that this is the latest in a long line of Silicon Valley wellness fads; others say that even if dopamine fasting does not strictly alter your dopamine circuits in any significant way, it can still help people become more mindful of their habits. A Muslim user on r/productivity compares dopamine fasting to Ramadan fasting, with its focus not just on avoiding food but also on anything that might trigger unwholesome desires.

Possibilities for ethical thought, then, open up when we see dopamine not as the all-addictive object of desire but as a valuing mechanism (cf. Ecks 2022). Like other hormone heuristics, dopamine thinking can be helpful when it provides people with a means of thinking about a self that is not fully subject to the mastery of a controlling will but rather as one whose moods and desires are shaped in relation to an environment in ways we cannot fully control. To say that my dopamine has been hijacked is to ask why my will and my desire are so divergent – why I want to be creative but spend all day gaming, for example. I want to at least keep open the possibility that dopamine thinking might offer a way for people to reflect on this kind of problem without recourse to punitive discourses about failures of self-control.

For this to be possible, the narrative of the universal addict must be discarded. It is not helpful to think of ourselves as addicted to dopamine – leaving no recourse but constant self-regulation. Not only is this kind of self-management exhausting and counterproductive, it makes no space for the kind of passionate commitments that make life feel meaningful (Golub 2009). The neuroscience of dopamine is far more interesting than this, anyway – a story not of mindless reward-seeking but of how we seek salience and value (positive or negative) in a sensory environment. From a critical perspective, dopamine thinking might provide ways of describing how these processes of valuation can be hijacked, disturbed or otherwise interrupted and how they might be reclaimed.

Notes

1 https://www.axios.com/2017/12/15/sean-parker-facebook-was-designed-to-exploit -human-vulnerability-1513306782.

2 E.g. Simon Parkin, 'Has Dopamine Got Us Hooked on Tech?' *Guardian*, 4 March 2018, https://www.theguardian.com/technology/2018/mar/04/has-dopamine-got-us-hooked -on-tech-facebook-apps-addiction.

3 https://dopamineproject.org/.

4 https://www.lesswrong.com/s/3xKXGh9RXaYTYZYgZ/p/tue36NPoMY2AXs3jW.

References

Aarseth, E., A. M. Bean, H. Boonen, M. Colder Carras, M. Coulson, D. Das, J. Deleuze, E. Dunkels, J. Edman, C. J. Ferguson, M. C. Haagsma, K. Helmersson Bergmark, Z. Hussain, J. Jansz, D. Kardefelt-Winther, L. Kutner, P. Markey, R. K. L. Nielsen, N. Prause, A. Przybylski, T. Quandt, A. Schimmenti, V. Starcevic, G. Stutman, J. Van Looy, A. J. Van Rooij (2017), 'Scholars' Open Debate Paper on the World Health Organization ICD-11 Gaming Disorder Proposal', *The Journal of Behavioral Addictions* 6 (3): 267–70. https://doi.org/10.1556/2006.5.2016.088.

Berridge, K. C. (2017), 'Is Addiction a Brain Disease?', *Neuroethics* 10 (1): 29–33. doi:10.1007/s12152-016-9286-3.

Broer, T., M. Pickersgill, and S. Cunningham-Burley (2020), 'Neurobiological Limits and the Somatic Significance of Love: Caregivers' Engagements with Neuroscience in Scottish Parenting Programmes', *History of the Human Sciences* 33 (5): 85–109.

Bromberg-Martin, E. S., M. Matsumoto, and O. Hikosaka (2010), 'Dopamine in Motivational Control: Rewarding, Aversive, and Alerting', *Neuron* 68 (5): 815–34.

Clark, A. (2013), 'Whatever Next? Predictive Brains, Situated Agents, and the Future of Cognitive Science', *Behavioral and Brain Sciences* 36 (3): 181–204.

Dawkins, R. (2006 [1976]), *The Selfish Gene [30ᵗʰ Anniversary Edition]*, Oxford: Oxford University Press.

Dumit, J. (2003), 'Is It Me or My Brain? Depression and Neuroscientific Facts', *Journal of Medical Humanities* 24 (1): 35–47.

Dumit, J. (2012), *Drugs for Life: How Pharmaceutical Companies Define Our Health*, Durham: Duke University Press.

Eburne, J. (2018), *Outsider Theory: Intellectual Histories of Unorthodox Ideas*, Minneapolis: University of Minnesota Press.

Ecks, S. (2022), *Living Worth: Value and Values in Global Pharmaceutical Markets*, Durham: Duke University Press.

Eyal, N. (2014), *Hooked: How to Build Habit-Forming Products*, Canada: Penguin.

Eyal, N. and J. Li-Eyal (2020), *Indistractable: How to Control Your Attention and Choose Your Life*, London: Bloomsbury Publishing.

Fogg, B. J. (2003), *Persuasive Technology: Using Computers to Change what we Think and Do*, Burlington, MA: Morgan Kaufman.

Golub, A. (2009), *Anthropology, Internet Addiction, and Care. Savage Minds Blog.* Available at https://savageminds.org/2009/09/08/anthropology-internet-addiction-and-care/.

Hollerman, J. R. and W. Schultz (1998), 'Dopamine Neurons Report an Error in the Temporal Prediction of Reward During Learning', *Nature Neuroscience* 1 (4): 304–9. doi:10.1038/1124.

Ingold, T. (1996), 'The Optimal Forager and Economic Man', in P. Descola (ed.), *Nature and Society: Anthropological Perspectives*, 25–44, London and New York: Routledge.

Jenkins, J. (2011), 'Introduction', in J. Jenkins (ed.), *Pharmaceutical Self: The Global Shaping of Experience in an Age of Psychopharmacology*, 3–16, Santa Fe, NM: SAR Press.

Krach, S. et al. (2010), 'The Rewarding Nature of Social Interactions', *Frontiers in Behavioral Neuroscience* 4. Available at https://www.frontiersin.org/article/10.3389/fnbeh.2010.00022 (accessed 30 May 2022).

Lembke, D. A. (2021), *Dopamine Nation: Finding Balance in the Age of Indulgence*, London: Penguin.

Lewis, M. (2017), 'Addiction and the Brain: Development, Not Disease', *Neuroethics* 10 (1): 7–18.

Mackenzie, A. and C. Roberts (2017), 'Adopting Neuroscience: Parenting and Affective Indeterminacy', *Body & Society* 23 (3): 130–55.

Malcolm, R. (2021), '"There's No Constant": Oxytocin, Cortisol, and Balanced Proportionality in Hormonal Models of Autism', *Medical Anthropology* 40 (4): 375–88.

Pickersgill, M., S. Cunningham-Burley, and P. Martin (2011), 'Constituting Neurologic Subjects: Neuroscience, Subjectivity and the Mundane Significance of the Brain', *Subjectivity* 4 (3): 346–65.

Rose, N. and J. M. Abi-Rached (2013), *Neuro: The New Brain Sciences and the Management of the Mind*, Princeton: Princeton University Press.

Salamone, J. D. and M. Correa (2012), 'The Mysterious Motivational Functions of Mesolimbic Dopamine', *Neuron* 76 (3): 470–85.

Schore, A. N. (1994), *Affect Regulation and the Origin of the Self: The Neurobiology of Emotional Development*, London: Routledge.

Schüll, N. D. (2012), *Addiction by Design: Machine Gambling in Las Vegas*, Princeton: Princeton University Press.

Schultz, W. (1998), 'Predictive Reward Signal of Dopamine Neurons', *Journal of Neurophysiology* 80 (1): 1–27.

Schultz, W. (2002), 'Getting Formal with Dopamine and Reward', *Neuron* 36 (2): 241–63.

Schultz, W. (2010), 'Dopamine Signals for Reward Value and Risk: Basic and Recent Data', *Behavioral and Brain Functions* 6 (1): 24.

Schultz, W. (2016), 'Dopamine Reward Prediction Error Coding', *Dialogues in Clinical Neuroscience* 18 (1): 23–32.

Seaver, N. (2019), 'Captivating Algorithms: Recommender Systems as Traps', *Material Culture* 24 (4): 421–436.

Sedgwick, E. K. (1993), 'Epidemics of the Will', in *Tendencies*, 130–42, Durham: Duke University Press.

7 ENDOCRINE-DISRUPTING CHEMICALS (EDCs)

WIBKE STRAUBE

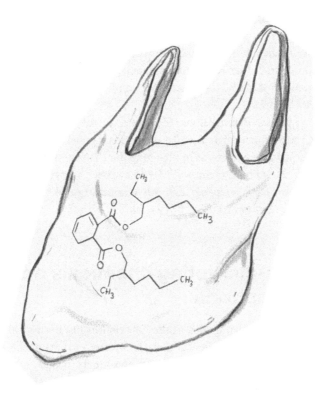

Endocrine-disrupting chemicals (EDCs) are environmental toxicants found in a wide variety of materials and items. They include pesticides (e.g. DDT, DDE), herbicides (e.g. atrazine), plasticizers (bisphenol A and other phthalates) and PCBs (Dominguez 2019), among others. Everyday household items such as non-biodegradable detergents and personal care products can contain EDCs (Khetan 2014). For instance, phthalate BPA (bisphenol A) and similar substances are widely used as softeners ('plasticizers') to create flexibility in PVC items such as plastic bags, shower curtains, cables and Tupperware containers. They are also used in liners for food cans, Teflon pans, baby bottles and a variety of cosmetics. These chemical compounds enter the food chain, for example, through plastic breakages, spurred on by heat, frost or age, off-gassing into household air, or through manufacturing effluents. They enter human and animal bodies, where they disrupt endocrine signalling pathways. Consequently, EDCs affect the well-being of aquatic, aerial and terrestrial ecosystems.

EDCs act by blocking or mimicking hormone receptors or by altering the rates of hormonal synthesis or metabolism (EPA 2022). They affect levels of oestrogen, androgen and thyroid hormones, among a range of other bodily chemical processes. The multiple molecular effects of these chemical compounds are largely unpredictable in scope (EPA 2022), yet they cause a plethora of illnesses, including lung diseases, organ failure, permanent nerve damage, chronic migraines, diabetes, ADHD, asthma and other respiratory ailments, increased cancer risk, especially breast, ovarian, prostate and testicular cancer, and disturbances in immune system functions (EPA 2022).

EDCs have gendered dimensions. They can cause infertility, premature births, a skewed 'sex ratio' in newborns as well as early-onset puberty. They can impact the genital and reproductive systems by changing the shape and function of different organs. The gendered interferences of EDCs have been sensationalized in popular media as the so-called 'sex panic' and the 'feminization' of the population (e.g. Townsend 2004; Coghlan 2005).

Endocrine-disrupting chemicals and gender dysphoria

In recent years an interesting idea in the life sciences has been gaining traction, namely that EDCs could cause gender non-conformity and are possibly responsible for the demographic increase in trans and non-binary people, especially those who seek the psychiatric diagnosis 'gender dysphoria' (APA 2022). A quote from a review in the medical science journal *Cureus* illustrates this idea; the authors observe that 'there seems to be a growing concern with regards to the relationship between endocrine disruptors and transsexuals as well as other gender minority populations' (Saleem and Rizvi 2017). While the use of the word 'transsexual' in this decontextualized form is stigmatizing, this quote shows the interest of life sciences research in investigating a possible association between EDCs and gender diversity.

The increase in the trans population is not only a topic of interest for the life sciences. It is also discussed in popular science and on social media. In those outlets, transness is sometimes framed as a form of 'modern hysteria' (Marchiano 2021) or as an 'environmental development disorder', which appears to build upon such hypotheses and concerns. In that sense, life sciences research linking EDCs and gender has a wide reach and is, most likely without intention, utilized to support the anti-trans rhetoric that has become volatile in Europe's increasingly diversity-hostile, often conservative or even far-right-dominated political ecologies.

In this entry, I would like to identify two societal ripple effects that I see emerging from the current conduct and dissemination of research on EDCs and transness in the life sciences. The first ripple effect derives from the understanding of gender non-conformity as an outcome of environmental pollution. In this, I see a risk that gender non-conformity, currently in the process of being depathologized as a 'mental disorder', could be repathologized as an 'environmental disorder'. The second ripple effect, which could be prevented through critical reflexivity and community-embedded methodologies (as I will discuss later; Vincent 2018; Henrickson et al. 2020), relates to the possibility that such research may invigorate conservative, trans-antagonistic societal discourses.

Analytically, I walk in this entry *with* and *against* gendered notions of pollution and its multiple axes that meet on the trans body, inspired and guided by the queer, trans and feminist hormone and pollution scholarship of Lynda Birke (2000), Celia Roberts (2002), Giovanna Di Chiro (2010), Mel Chen (2012), Kuura Irni (2013), Malin Ah-King and Eva Hayward (2014) and Anne Pollock (2016), among others. I align myself with the large section of feminist theory that considers sex as well as gender as socially, historically and discursively constructed (Butler 1990; Fausto-Sterling 2018). Sex and gender are interconnected and emerge as material and discursive phenomena out of a multiplicity of relations (Barad 2007). In this entry, I use the terms trans, transness, gender diversity, gender non-conformity and gender variance interchangeably.

As an environmentalist as well as a transfeminist scholar, I wish to emphasize that I consider research on petrochemical pollution, endocrine disruptors and such chemicals' impact on human, animal and planetary health important. This entry is written not to dismiss this work but with the intention of highlighting the material-discursive and ethical implications of how scientific knowledge is produced and what medical and cultural repercussions this has for the trans and non-binary community.

The emergence of gender dysphoria in the life sciences

In order to discuss emerging research on gender diversity and EDCs in the life sciences, I want to turn to the Swedish Gender Dysphoria Study [Svenska Könsdysforistudie] (SKDS) as a prominent example of research on this topic. The SKDS is located at the Department of Neuroscience at the eminent Uppsala University in Sweden. Ongoing since 2016, this study is a 'national multicentre study' conducted by psychiatrists, neurologists and endocrinologists (all consultants) in eight Swedish hospitals. Most of the involved centres host gender identity clinics where care seekers are assessed by an interdisciplinary team of professionals regarding a possible diagnosis of 'gender dysphoria' or 'transsexualism' (Axfors et al. 2021). If requested by the care seeker, these diagnoses are the foundation for access to hormone therapy, other medical interventions and changing legal gender markers. The current waiting time to start treatment is two to three years. The SKDS includes different surveys, cognitive tests and tests based on hair, saliva and baby teeth samples with the aim of detecting 'possible connections between gender dysphoria and exposure to different environmental substances in foetal stage or in early life' (SKDS n.d., text from the website translated by the author). The surveys are given to care seekers in the process of their gender evaluation process, and it would be interesting to investigate the idea of informed consent in this context of dependency and vulnerability. The study's website states that it is motivated by a wish to support trans care seekers, yet it appears to solely focus on biological factors and not account for sociocultural dimensions of transness.

The SKDS is at this point in time the only study that seeks actual data on the hypothesis of EDCs causing gender dysphoria. However, this idea had emerged in different areas of life sciences research prior to the study's inception in 2016. For instance, the short text 'Are EDCs Blurring Issues of Gender?' in *Environmental Health Perspectives* suggests: 'Scientists today are asking hard questions about potential human effects: [. . .] Can EDC exposures even be involved in the etiology of children born with ambiguous gender?' (Hood 2005). The title of the article 'Endocrine Disruptors, the Increase of Autism Spectrum Disorder and Its Comorbidity with Gender Identity Disorder – A Hypothetical Association', published in the *International Journal of Andrology*, draws parallels between EDCs and gender diversity (Bejerot, Humble and Gardner 2011), as does the earlier-mentioned *Cureus* article. A entry in the anthology *Principles of Gender-Specific Medicine* even speaks of the 'pathophysiology of transsexuality' that, according to the authors, is shaped by a combination of environmental and genetic factors (Yalamanchi, Fesseha and Dobs 2017: 91). This idea of gender non-conformity being connected to EDCs seems to stem from ongoing research endeavours in the life sciences, such as studies that have concluded that EDCs are responsible for decreased 'masculine behaviors in preschool boys' (Percy et al. 2016; see also e.g. Swan et al. 2010; Daniel et al. 2020; Evans et al. 2021). This result seems striking, considering that gendered behaviour is considered to be socioculturally acquired in many fields, for instance, within the humanities (Blaise 2014).

These examples of life sciences research display a strong reliance on eco-toxicological and molecular factors that potentially explain gender non-conformity or deviations from normative behaviour. Such explanations risk reducing layered and complex experiences of being non-binary and/or trans to a singular, molecular story (Adichie 2009). Even when such research aims to support access to care for trans people, it risks achieving the opposite, potentially producing the trans-antagonistic ripple effect of repathologizing transness as an environmental illness.

Societal impact of EDC research

A recent viral Facebook post in a vegan group illustrates how life sciences research can be utilized, even unintentionally, to back up eco-normative, conservative discourses that increase stigma and interfere with the aim of improving well-being among the trans population. In the post, an anonymous author argues that to lobby for trans and gay rights means lobbying for a capitalist, exploitative system of ecological destruction. As stated:

> The promotion of gay and trans is the promotion of sexual development disorders, caused by environmental pollutants and media and educational manipulation. . . . There is nothing natural or healthy about wanting to be the opposite from what we are born, transgender is an environmental developmental disorder that is being promoted as natural and normal. (Facebook group as quoted in Chiorando 2018)

Although the group condemned this position immediately as the individual opinion of one group member, such opinions framing transness as a form of environmental pollution are embedded in wider discourses that question the validity of gender transitioning – especially when it concerns young people. Young trans and non-binary people have in recent years been particularly targeted and their access to care increasingly jeopardized due to trans-antagonistic media representation (Indremo et al. 2022). Gender non-conformity is publicly debated as something that might not be 'real', valid or believable and could be 'contagious' (Serano 2018). It is dismissed as a 'psychic epidemic' (Marchiano 2017), a form of 'modern hysteria' (Marchiano 2021) or even classified as a 'trans epidemic', a term popularized by the author Abigail Shrier in *Irreversible Damage*, a book widely critiqued for its trans-antagonistic approach to gender diverse youth (Turban 2020; Yurcaba 2021). Other pseudo-diagnostic terms such as 'rapid-onset of gender dysphoria' (Baril and Ashley 2018; Serano 2018) are being deployed to dismiss any teenager who moves away from their assigned gender. The structures of cisnormativity embedded in these discourses result in a higher burden of depression, anxiety issues and suicidality among gender non-conforming populations (Littlejohn, Poteat and Beyrer 2019). Negative media discourses on gender non-conformity in general not only further stigmatize but also, as a recent study shows, jeopardize trans people's access to care (Indremo et al. 2022).

Recent life sciences research that interrogates transness in connection with environmental pollution risks bolstering discourses in social media and the popular press that 'chip away' (Ahmed 2016) at the legitimacy of disidentifying with and changing one's birth-assigned sex. This is what I would identify as the second ripple effect, which fundamentally undermines the potential well-being of trans and non-binary people.

Trans bodies and pollution

It is concerning that such life sciences research can enable a perspective on gender non-conformity that stigmatizes it as an environmental disorder, and that it can easily be distorted by conservative forces to support anti-trans rhetoric and dismiss gender diversity as an 'abnormality'. These two ripple effects are powerful, not only because they build on scientific knowledge production, and particularly the search for a medical answer as to why humans are gender diverse, but also because this interlinkage of pollution with gender diversity has historical roots.

Throughout the twentieth century, people who crossed gender boundaries were continuously weighed against the term 'natural' and understood as genetically 'impure' (Stryker [1994] 2006; Shotwell 2016; Straube 2020), resulting not only in social stigma but also in the 'passive eugenics' (Honkasalo 2018) of compulsory sterilization. In the early 1980s this idea of the 'unnaturalness' of gender variance resulted in its pathologization as a mental disorder through the diagnoses 'transsexualism' and 'gender identity disorder' in the *Diagnostic and Statistical Manual of Mental Disorders* (DSM) published by the American Psychological Association. Only in the DSM's recent revision has the diagnostic terminology been changed to 'gender dysphoria' in an attempt to reduce stigma and depathologize gender non-conformity. However, compulsory sterilizations of trans people as a prerequisite for changing their legal gender markers are ongoing in many European countries. Amnesty International (2014), among others, has condemned this as a human rights violation.

The current outlook in some areas of the life sciences that associate transness with pollution makes it impossible to consider gender non-conformity as a regular variation in humans rather than a disorder of some kind (e.g. Hughto, Reisner and Pachankis 2015). Furthermore, without careful consideration and positioning, this hypothetical association of pollution and gender non-conformity is in danger of reproducing an eco-normative logic about which environmental studies scholar Giovanna Di Chiro (2010) warns us: a positioning of heterosexuality and cisgender as the only natural and healthy forms of being, justified through a rhetoric of environmentalism. Such logic not only confines transness to a realm of polluted abnormality but also ignores the continuous historical existence of trans people worldwide and the emergence of a violently binary sex/gender system that emerged in connection with Christianization and colonialism (e.g. Lugones 2007; Miranda 2010). The historical contingency of linking gender minorities with pollution is based on an ultra-conservative politics of purity (Ah-King and Hayward 2014; Shotwell 2016; Ford 2020), which is in sync with the dualistic and Eurocentric idea of purity versus pollution that is always bound to the imaginary of the social and national body and informed by logics of racial purity and whiteness (Liu 2019). Gender diversity is a historical presence (Stryker 2006). It cannot be reduced to merely anthropocentric, postnatural, molecular fallout.

A suggested improvement: Ethical disclaimers

In order to appreciate the importance of EDC research while also acknowledging the risky side effects of the questions being asked for the trans community, I suggest the inclusion of an ethical disclaimer in research papers, which could provide both a sensitive framing and consideration of the potential impact of the research. The importance of including specific ethical parameters for undertaking projects implicating gender-variant populations, both in the research process and the dissemination of research outcomes, has been discussed by a range of critical thinkers (e.g. Richards et al. 2014; Vincent 2018; Bauer et al. 2019; Henrickson et al. 2020). An ethical disclaimer at the beginning of each publication could flag the researchers' intent to provide care and support to the trans community. Furthermore, feminist academic practices of 'situated knowledge' (Haraway 1988) that foreground researchers' 'reflexivity' and 'positionality' (Corlett and Mavin 2018) could inform life sciences researchers' own considerations of transparency and accountability.

Conclusion

The effects of petrochemical pollution on ecosystems as well as human bodies are unquestionable. This entry is written in support of environmental justice, and I acknowledge the importance of working towards a stronger ban on the production and application of phthalates and other EDCs. Yet it is also crucial to problematize the premise of the ongoing work in the life sciences that investigates an association between gender non-conformity and environmental chemicals.

While on the brink of being depathologized as a mental illness, the current framing of trans embodiment within the life sciences moves towards repathologizing gender non-conformity as an environmental disorder. If not carefully positioned, these studies can easily be appropriated by alt-right, populist discourses that simplify research results for an anti-trans agenda, increasing the already existing social marginalization of trans people, especially trans youth. Accompanying such studies with an ethical disclaimer that acknowledges gender diversity both as a sociocultural and *potentially* environmentally influenced form of being, and expresses the researchers' aim to improve well-being for this population, could be a first step towards addressing this risk.

Acknowledgements

I warmly thank my colleagues Kuura Irni, Lotta Kähkönen, Ida Linander, Luca Tainio, Liu Xin and Tara Mehrabi for taking the time to discuss this topic with me. Special thanks go to Andrea Ford and Lisa Raeder for their generous editorial comments. This entry is written with the support of the Kone Foundation.

References

Adichie, C. N. (2009), 'The Danger of a Single Story', Available at https://www.ted.com/talks/chimamanda_ngozi_adichie_the_danger_of_a_single_story (accessed 3 October 2022).

Ah-King, M. and E. Hayward (2014), 'Toxic Sexes. Perverting Pollution and Queering Hormone Disruption', *O-Zone: A Journal of Object-Oriented Studies* 1: 1–12.

Ahmed, S. (2016), 'An Affinity of Hammers', *Transgender Studies Quarterly* 3 (1–2): 22–34.

Amnesty International (2014), *The State Decides Who I Am: Lack of Legal Gender Recognition for Transgender People in Europe*. Available at https://www.amnesty.org/en/documents/EUR01/001/2014/en/ (accessed 30 January 2023).

APA - American Psychiatric Association (2022), *Diagnostic and Statistical Manual of Mental Disorders*, 5th edn. Available at https://doi.org/10.1176/appi.books.9780890425787.x14_Gender_Dysophoria (accessed 1 February 2023).

Axfors, C., et al. (2021), 'Preferences for Gender Affirming Treatment and Associated Factors among Transgender People in Sweden', *Sexuality Research and Social Policy*, https://doi.org/10.1007/s13178-021-00650-2.

Barad, K. (2007), *Meeting the Universe Halfway: Quantum Physics and the Entanglement of Matter and Meaning*, Durham: Duke University Press.

Baril, A. and F. Ashley (2018), 'Why "Rapid-Onset Gender Dysphoria" Is Bad Science', *The Conversation*, 22 March.

Bauer, G., et al. (2019), *CPATH Ethical Guidelines for Research Involving Transgender People & Communities*, Canada: Canadian Professional Association for Transgender Health.

Bejerot, S., M. B. Humble, and A. Gardner (2011), 'Endocrine Disruptors, the Increase of Autism Spectrum Disorder and Its Comorbidity with Gender Identity Disorder – A Hypothetical Association', *International Journal of Andrology* 34: e350.

Birke, L. (2000), 'Sitting on the Fender: Biology, Feminism, and Gender-Bending Environments', *Women's Studies International Forum* 23 (5): 587–99.

Blaise, M. (2014), 'Gender Discourses and Play', in Liz Brooker, Mindy Blaise, and Susan Edwards (eds), *Sage Handbook of Play and Learning in Early Childhood*, 115–27, London: Sage.

Butler, J. (1990), *Gender Trouble: Feminism and the Subversion of Identity*, New York: Routledge.

Chen, M. Y. (2012), *Animacies: Biopolitics, Racial Mattering, and Queer Affect*, Durham: Duke University Press.

Chiorando, M. (2018), 'Vegans Blast Vegan Facebook Group for Saying "Chemical Pollutants" Make People Gay and Transgender', *Plant Based News*, 19 July. Available at https://www.plantbasednews.org/post/vegansfacebook-group-saying-chemical-pollutants-make-people-gay-transgender (accessed 18 June 2022).

Coghlan, A. (2005), '"Gender-Bending" Chemicals Found to "Feminise" Boys', *New Scientist*, 27 May. Available at https://www.newscientist.com/article/dn7440-gender-bending-chemicals-found-to-feminise-boys/ (accessed 12 August 2022).

Corlett, S. and S. Mavin (2018), 'Reflexivity and Researcher Positionality', in C. Cassell, A. Cunliffe, and G. Grandy (eds), *The Sage Handbook of Qualitative Business and Management Research Methods*, 377–89, London: Sage.

Daniel S., et al. (2020), 'Prenatal and Early Childhood Exposure to Phthalates and Childhood Behavior at Age 7 Years', *Environment International* 143: 105894.

Di Chiro, G. (2010), 'Polluted Politics? Confronting Toxic Discourse, Sex Panic, and Eco-Normativity', in C. Mortimer-Sandilands and B. Erickson (eds), *Queer Ecologies: Sex, Nature, Politics, Desire*, 199–230, Bloomington: Indiana University Press.

Dominguez, F. (2019), 'Phthalates and Other Endocrine-Disrupting Chemicals: The 21st Century's Plague for Reproductive Health', *Fertility and Sterility* 111 (5): 885–6.

EPA – US Environmental Protection Agency (2022), 'What Is Endocrine Disruption?', Available at https://www.epa.gov/endocrine-disruption/what-endocrine-disruption #examples (accessed 13 June 2022).

Evans, S. F., et al. (2021), 'Associations between Prenatal Phthalate Exposure and Sex-Typed Play Behavior in Preschool Age Boys and Girls', *Environmental Research* 192: 110264.

Fausto-Sterling, A. (2018), 'Why Sex Is Not Binary', *New York Times*, 25 October. Available at www.nytimes.com/2018/10/25/opinion/sex-biology-binary.html (accessed 13 June 2022).

Ford, A. (2020), 'Purity Is Not the Point: Childbearing and the Impossibility of Boundaries', *Catalyst: Feminism, Theory, Technoscience*, Chemical Entanglements special issue 6 (1): 1–25.

Haraway, D. (1988), 'Situated Knowledges: The Science Question in Feminism and the Privilege of Partial Perspective', *Feminist Studies* 14: 575–99.

Henrickson, M., S. Giwa, T. Hafford-Letchfield, C. Cocker, N. J. Mulé, J. Schaub, and A. Baril (2020), 'Research Ethics with Gender and Sexually Diverse Persons', *International Journal of Environmental Research and Public Health* 17 (18): 6615.

Honkasalo, J. (2018), 'Unfit for Parenthood? Compulsory Sterilization and Transgender Reproductive Justice in Finland', *Journal of International Women's Studies* 20 (1): 40–52.

Hood, E. (2005), 'Are EDCs Blurring Issues of Gender?', *Environmental Health Perspectives* 113 (10): A670–7.

Hughto, J. M. White, S. L. Reisner, and J. E. Pachankis (2015), 'Transgender Stigma and Health', *Social Science and Medicine* 147: 222–31.

Indremo, M., et al. (2022), 'Association of Media Coverage on Transgender Health with Referrals to Child and Adolescent Gender Identity Clinics in Sweden', *JAMA Network Open* 5 (2: e2146531).

Irni, K. (2013), 'Sex, Power and Ontology: Exploring the Performativity of Hormones', *Nora – Nordic Journal of Feminist and Gender Research* 21 (1): 41–56.

Khetan, S. K. (2014), *Endocrine Disruptors in the Environment*, Hoboken: John Wiley & Sons.

Littlejohn, T., T. Poteat, and C. Beyrer (2019), 'Sexual and Gender Minorities, Public Health, and Ethics', in A. C. Mastroianni, J. P. Kahn, and N. E. Kass (eds), *The Oxford Handbook of Public Health Ethics*, 232–44, Oxford: Oxford University Press.

Liu, X. (2019), 'Nose Hair: Love It or Leave It? The Lovecidal of Bodies that Filter', *Parallax* 25 (1): 75–91.

Lugones, M. (2007), 'Heterosexualism and the Colonial/Modern Gender System', *Hypatia* 22 (1): 186–209.

Marchiano, L. (2017), 'Outbreak: On Transgender Teens and Psychic Epidemics', *Psychological Perspectives* 60 (3): 345–66.

Marchiano, L. (2021), 'Transgender Children: The Making of a Modern Hysteria', *Psychological Perspectives* 64 (3): 346–59.

Miranda, D. A. (2010), 'Extermination of the Joyas: Gendercide in Spanish California', *GLQ: A Journal of Lesbian and Gay Studies* 16 (1–2): 253–84.

Percy, Z., et al. (2016), 'Gestational Exposure to Phthalates and Gender-Related Play Behaviors in 8-Year-Old Children: An Observational Study', *Environmental Health* 15 (1): 87.

Pollock, A. (2016), 'Queering Endocrine Disruption', in Katherine Behar (ed.), *Object-Oriented Feminism*, 183–200, Minneapolis: Minnesota University Press.

Richards, C., M. Barker, P. Lenihan, and A. Lantaffi (2014), 'Who Watches the Watchmen? A Critical Perspective on the Theorization of Trans People and Clinicians', *Feminism & Psychology* 24 (2): 248–58.

Roberts, C. (2002), 'A Matter of Embodied Fact: Sex Hormones and the History of Bodies', *Feminist Theory* 3 (1): 7–26.

Saleem, F. and S. W. Rizvi (2017), 'Transgender Associations and Possible Etiology: A Literature Review', *Cureus* 9 (12): e1984.

Serano, J. (2018), 'Everything You Need to Know About Rapid Onset Gender Dysphoria', *Medium*, 22 August. Available at https://juliaserano.medium.com/everything-you-need-to-know-about-rapid-onset-gender-dysphoria-1940b8afdeba (accessed 27 October 2022).

Shotwell, A. (2016), *Against Purity. Living Ethically in Compromised Times*, Minneapolis: University of Minnesota Press.

SKDS – Svensk könsdysforistudie [Swedish Gender Dysphoria Study] (n.d.), Available at https://www.medsci.uu.se/forskning/psykiatri/projekt/psykiatrisk-epidemiologi/studier-om-konsdysfori/svenska-konsdysforistudien/ (accessed 31 January 2023).

Straube, W. (2020), 'Posthuman Ecological Intimacy, Waste, and the Trans Body in "Nånting måste gå sönder"', in D. Vakoch (ed.), *Transecology: Transgender Perspectives on Environment and Nature*, 54–78, Abingdon: Routledge.

Stryker, S. (2006 [1994]), 'My Words to Victor Frankenstein above the Village of Chamounix: Performing Transgender Rage', in S. Stryker and S. Whittle (eds), *The Transgender Studies Reader 1*, 244–56, New York: Routledge.

Stryker, S. (2006), '(De)Subjugated Knowledges: An Introduction to Transgender Studies', in S. Stryker and S. Whittle (eds), *The Transgender Studies Reader 1*, 1–18, New York: Routledge.

Swan, S. H., et al. (2010), 'Prenatal Phthalate Exposure and Reduced Masculine Play in Boys', *International Journal of Andrology* 33 (2): 259–69.

Townsend, M. (2004), 'Boys Will Be Girls – Eventually', *The Guardian*, 18 July. Available at https://www.theguardian.com/environment/2004/jul/18/food.wildlife (accessed 20 October 2022).

Turban, J. (2020), 'New Book 'Irreversible Damage' Is Full of Misinformation', *Psychology Today*, 6 December. Available at https://www.psychologytoday.com/gb/blog/political-minds/202012/new-book-irreversible-damage-is-full-misinformation (accessed 27 October 2022).

Vincent, B. W. (2018), 'Studying Trans: Recommendations for Ethical Recruitment and Collaboration with Transgender Participants in Academic Research', *Psychology and Sexuality* 9 (3): 1–15.

Yalamanchi, S., B. Fesseha, and A. Dobs (2017), 'The Transsexual Adult', in Marianne J. Legato (ed.), *Principles of Gender-Specific Medicine*, 91–105, London: Academic Press.

Yurcaba, J. (2021), 'Amazon Will Not Remove Book Advocates Say Endangers Transgender Youth', *NBC Today*, 5 May. Available at https://www.nbcnews.com/feature/nbc-out/amazon-will-not-remove-book-advocates-say-endangers-transgender-youth-n1266447 (accessed 24 October 2022).

8 FOLLICLE-STIMULATING HORMONE (FSH) AND LUTEINIZING HORMONE (LH)

RISA CROMER

Reproductive technologies that assist human conception have been essential to managing infertility for over half a century. Among them, in vitro fertilization (IVF) technology has received the lion's share of attention, especially in feminist social science scholarship (Bharadwaj and Glasner 2009; Deomampo 2016; Franklin 1997; 2007; 2013; Inhorn 1994; Kahn 2000; Roberts 2012; Thompson 2005; Wahlberg 2018; van de Wiel 2020). In this entry, I draw upon feminist science studies of hormones (Fausto-Sterling 2000; Jordan-Young and Karkazis 2019; Oudshoorn 1994; Roberts 2007; Sanabria 2016) to bring attention to the social groups and forces surrounding the development of a lesser-known reproductive technology that made the global reach and influence of infertility medicine possible: pharmaceutical drugs containing human gonadotropins. This entry considers some of the clinical, religious, nationalist, political and economic actors that organized around assisting reproduction with the landmark hormonal technology, Pergonal.

Western scientific wisdom suggests that gonadotropins are a family of hormones actively involved in the sexual development and reproductive function of vertebrate animals. In human reproduction, follicle-stimulating hormone (FSH) and luteinizing hormone (LH) are gonadotropins that play complementary roles: FSH stimulates the maturation of follicles in ovaries and the production of sperm in testes and controls the level of other hormones produced by reproductive organs, while LH supports follicular growth, egg maturation and testosterone production. Brain signals originating in the hypothalamus initiate production of FSH and LH in the anterior pituitary gland, located at the base of the brain, from where they circulate throughout the body. While there is no stable level of FSH or LH in the human body, as amounts vary between bodies and over time, 'imbalances' in FSH and LH levels are one of many contributors to infertility affecting millions of people worldwide.

Scientific researchers over the past century have actively sought to understand the workings of gonadotropins in humans as well as in other animals. Based in labs around the world, scientists pursued experiments with diverse kinds of biological materials – pregnant mare urine, live rabbits, cadaveric brain matter, to name a few – which incrementally led to identifying, extracting and purifying human-derived gonadotropins for treating infertility. The products of these scientific endeavours have become immeasurably important in fertility medicine today. For over six decades, hormonal therapeutics have provided affordable management of infertility, including to my own mother![1] An infrequently acknowledged fact is that hormonal therapeutics were elemental to the early successes of IVF (Jones et al. 1982) and have become an integral part of standard IVF regimens worldwide.[2]

This entry employs a feminist STS approach that takes us beyond scientific knowledge about gonadotropins to examine the constellation of social actors and conditions at play in stimulating excitement around assisted reproduction. In doing so, this entry disturbs conventional scientific understandings of what hormones do in the body by tracing how they are simultaneously shaped by, and in turn shape, our social worlds. In common usage, 'stimulation' means encouraging the development of, arousing interest or activity and hastening or exciting. This meaning is also latent in the etymology of the word hormone, which comes from the Greek hormaein (hor-mee-in), meaning 'to excite, to set in motion'. Conventional scientific wisdom about hormones maintains that they are chemical messengers that arouse biological activity in the body. But, as the co-editors of this volume and other feminist scholars have argued (Fausto-Sterling 2000; Jordan-Young and Karkazis 2019; Oudshoorn 1994; Roberts 2007; Sanabria 2016), hormones stimulate more than biologic activity. This entry foregrounds some of the social institutions, groups and figures that invested in assisting reproduction with hormonal technologies, from religious politics involving multiple nations across two continents to the clinical development of a pharmaceutical drug based on women's unpaid donations that generated billions of dollars in profit for private sector companies, like Serono and Merck. In these examples, we see how dynamic and disparate social groups stimulated interest in human hormones, which conditioned the possibility for gonadotropins to become treatments for infertility.

Specifically, this entry considers the production of the landmark drug Pergonal – an isolated, purified and pharmaceuticalized form of FSH and LH derived from postmenopausal women's urine. Drawing upon historical documents produced by scientists, social scientists, journalists and industry marketers, it brings into view social forces linking hormonal substances and excitement around assisting women's reproduction at a global scale. In doing so, it foregrounds what Rebecca Jordan-Young and Katrina Karkazis describe in their unauthorized biography of testosterone as 'the unexpected, [and] the forgotten' ways that human hormones come to bear various forms of social significance (2019, 5). In broadening the aperture beyond scientific narratives to tell a tale of two hormones through the production of one world-changing drug, we see how human gonadotropins were simultaneously shaped by, and in turn shaped, the global fertility industry. In tracing how Pergonal came to operate as a clinical, religious, economic and political agent, I aim to arouse curiosity about the power of hormones to stimulate activity within and beyond our bodies.

Producing Pergonal

Research on gonadotropins began in the early decades of the twentieth century. Scientists identified hormonal substances in human pituitary glands as well as in urine, first from pregnant women in 1927 and a few years later from postmenopausal women. Experimental treatments for infertility using the urine of pregnant mares and pregnant women occurred during the 1930s and 1940s, though with disappointing results. By the early 1950s, a group of international scientists self-described as 'The G-Club' began holding regular meetings in the United Kingdom, the United States and Israel to develop basic research and clinical goals for gonadotropins. They set out to create an international standard for evaluating the quality of gonadotropic preparations and to support scalable methods for producing gonadotropic treatments for clinical use.

The G-Club's discovery of research conducted soon after the Second World War by an Italian chemist working in the lab of Serono, a then small pharmaceutical company in Rome, would transform the world of assisted reproduction. In 1949, Pietro Donini and his collaborator, R. Montezemolo, published a scientific paper in an obscure journal describing their process for isolating and purifying FSH and LH from the urine of postmenopausal women. At the time, hormones derived from pregnant mare serum were the only infertility treatments available and were largely unsuccessful. Human pituitary glands were known sources for gonadotropins, but Italian law forbade extracting hormones for therapeutic use from cadaveric organs. These circumstances aroused Donini's interest in postmenopausal women's urine, known then as 'a relatively rich source of these hormones' (Bettendorf 1995a: 118). After menopause, when ovaries stop producing eggs, FSH and LH levels typically increase as the body continues to try to stimulate ovarian production. This process generates high amounts of gonadotropins in the body that are then released through the urine.

Inspired by a scientific paper on purifying hormones using permutit – a common material used to decalcify water – Donini mulled over the idea while on summer holiday of applying it to postmenopausal urine (Bettendorf 1995: 118). Upon return, he ventured into the basement of his lab's building to grab a handful of the material for initial experimenting with postmenopausal urine (The Ares-Serono Group's Corporate Scientific Publications Department 1996: 21). While working in a post-war context with constrained research conditions, Donini developed a purification process that produced the first known hormonal therapeutic containing human FSH and LH. He called the substance Pergonal, after the Italian 'per gonadi', or 'from the gonads', and noted in his paper 'the potential therapeutic usefulness of Pergonal for the therapy of human infertility' (Bettendorf 1995: 118). The Italian government approved the sale of Pergonal in 1950, but its clinical potential remained in obscurity until discovered by the G-Club nearly a decade later.

In the late 1950s, Donini received a call from Bruno Lunenfeld, who had just learned of his research. Lunenfeld was a Vienna-born, Israeli-educated medical student researching gonadotropins in Geneva; he would later become a giant in Israel's well-established reproductive medicine industry. Lunenfeld was driven throughout his career by a 'desire to find a cure for infertility' (Livneh 2002). In an interview with the Israeli newspaper *Haaretz*, he described his motivations in religious-nationalist terms: 'It was a Zionist thing. I kept thinking to myself that the Jewish people had lost so many people and that the maximum had to be done for internal immigration, in other words – to increase the number of babies born' (Livneh 2002). He embraced a view shared with him by a Rabbi that he had befriended while living in Geneva, which was that 'the greatest mitzvah [good deed] now to save the Jewish people is to deal with infertility' (Livneh 2002). For Lunenfeld, reproducing the Jewish state required the 'saving' role of science. It would also require the excitement of an Italian pharmaceutical company and the Catholic Church.[3]

A founding member of the G-Club, Lunenfeld reached out to Donini with hopes of collaborating. Pergonal appeared relatively pure, which attracted the G-Club's interest in using it as a reference material to be registered with the World Health Organization as a global standard. 'The paper excited me to the extent that I picked up the phone and made an appointment with Dr. Donini . . . [who] fetched me at the airport [in Rome] – it was love and friendship at first sight' (Bettendorf 1995b: 360). Their meeting marked the beginning of three decades of collaboration. Donini introduced Lunenfeld to the head of Serono, Pietro Bertarelli, who agreed to contribute a batch of Pergonal as an international reference material. At the same time, they began discussions about scaling up production for a clinical trial to test Pergonal's efficacy as an infertility treatment.

Donini set up a meeting for Lunenfeld to make a pitch to Serono's board of directors to support the production of Pergonal at a large scale, which would require urine from postmenopausal women. As Lunenfeld recollected, 'I, just a kid, had to stand before the board of directors and ask them to help us find 400 menopausal women that would agree to collect their urine daily. I gave my lecture, they all applauded politely and then the chairman of the board got up and said: Very nice, but we are a drug factory not a urinal factory' (Livneh 2002). A powerful board member, Guilio Pacelli, approached him afterwards to discuss the proposal further; an Italian elite and nephew of Pope Pius XII, he represented the Vatican's quarter share of the Serono drug company. After ten days of consultation with Lunenfeld, Pacelli returned to the board with a compelling addendum to the original pitch: 'My uncle, Pope Pius, has decided to help us and to ask the nuns in the old-age home to collect urine daily for a sacred cause' (Livneh 2002). The Pope's support convinced the board to approve the trial and aligned with Serono's stated desire to help 'a large number of infertile couples who seek assistance in fulfilling their dreams – a child of their own' (The Ares-Serono Group 1996: 1). While it is unclear what Pacelli meant by 'sacred cause', such as Zionist pronatalism, Catholic pronatalism, scientific saviourism or something else, the powerful potential of FSH and LH excited diverse actors – international scientists, private pharma, the Catholic Church and Israeli leaders – to collaborate in trialling a novel fertility drug.

Producing Pergonal involved the donation of hundreds of thousands of litres of urine from older Italian Catholic nuns, whose non-reproductive biological capacities became essential resources for developing the global reproductive medicine industry. Little is known about the nuns' personal motivations and experiences participating in the trial. Were their roles voluntary or obligatory, onerous or meaningful? How did they conceive of the so-called sacred cause and value their own contributions to it? The absence of historical knowledge about these women illustrates what anthropologist Sandra Bärnreuther calls the 'asymmetrical relational infrastructure . . . that animates most commodity chains and has long sustained the field of reproductive medicine' (2018: 57). The welcomed utility yet devaluation of older women's hormonal bodies for global fertility supply chains (Vertommen, Pavone and Nahman 2022) exemplifies 'the unexpected, [and] the forgotten' (Jordan-Young and Karkazis 2019: 5) forces shaping the social significances of hormones.

A commemorative book about the history of Pergonal created by Serono's then multinational conglomerate, Ares-Serono, entitled *A Tale of Two Hormones* (1996), describes the alchemical spectacle of what Lunenfeld called 'turning urine into gold' (Livneh 2002) with detailed passages about the 'cumbersome and unsavory extraction process' (The Ares-Serono Group 1996: 30). For example: 'Tanker after tanker, the menopausal urine arrived at the main entrance of the plant. [Then] it was centrifuged, filtered, and pushed through columns, and biologically tested' (The Ares-Serono Group 1996: 27). A series of photographs featuring a female scientist wearing a pink dress depicts the laboratory work, from emptying urine-filled bottles into a vat, conducting initial analyses, running the urine through small and large tanks, spinning it in a centrifuge and filtering it through kaolin – a naturally occurring clay – for further processing. These depictions emphasize the company's scientific labours and erase from view the postmenopausal suppliers of their 'gold'. Presented in the form of a children's book, pages with the company's promotional rhetoric and scientific jargon are decorated with crayon drawings of flowers and bees and accompanied by photographs of predominantly white children. The book's promotional narrative amplifies the heroic role of science in 'curing' white women's infertility: 'There were a thousand reasons not to have done it, but there was one major reason to try . . . Urine was collected – and children were born' (The Ares-Serono Group 1996: 27).

In addition to narratives about heroic science, the production of Pergonal stimulated the religious and racial politics of Zionism in which older Jewish urine donors in Israel became directly enrolled. Lunenfeld arranged additional urine collection in Israel from three Jewish nursing homes. In interviews with researchers and media about the trial, he described the unpaid donors as happy contributors to reproducing the Israeli state: 'The women donated [their urine] with pleasure, they became very happy while doing this. They were so interested that they could help make babies', he said, as reported by Sigrid Vertommen (2017: 219). An Israeli newspaper made a related remark that, despite their age and lack of reproductive capacity, older donors were 'still able to increase the size of the population' (cited in Vertommen 2017: 290). Such statements illustrate the Zionist settler demographic logic propelling Lunenfeld's clinical excitement about Pergonal's potential. He and Israeli media used these logics to align postmenopausal and infertile women in the Judaization of Israel/Palestine by supporting 'making babies' (Vertommen 2017).

In this light, it becomes clear how excitement about Pergonal's potential reached far beyond its clinical trial successes. Led by Lunenfeld, clinical trials with Pergonal took place at a Serono-funded lab based in Tel HaShomer Hospital in Israel from 1959 to 1963. After a series of failed attempts, one of Lunenfeld's patients – a 26-year-old woman with secondary amenorrhea – experienced the world's first successful delivery following treatment with Pergonal in 1962. A year later, over a dozen pregnancies had been achieved using Pergonal and, soon after, the drug was certified for clinical distribution. Israel's then prime minister Ben-Gurion was a notorious proponent of Jewish pronatalism and supporter of the Pergonal trial in Israel. According to Vertommen, his government funded a Center for Demographic Problems that launched education campaigns to 'systematically create a psychologically favorable climate, such that natality will be encouraged and stimulated' (2017: 291). Stimulating reproduction in this example describes not just the biological effect of Pergonal but also the racial-religious goals of Israel's Zionist agenda. The Center freely distributed Pergonal to infertile Jewish couples to realize this nationalist goal, described as 'a demographic project of national priority' (Vertommen 2017: 291).

Beyond the religious politics of the Israeli state, Pergonal's profit potential stimulated marketing efforts to help it gain traction in fertility medicine worldwide. Initially a market flop, Lunenfeld went on a promotional tour across Italy, giving lectures at a couple dozen clinics, hospitals and university departments. Popularity ensued, showcasing the influence of publicly funded universities in private sector business ventures, which has led to 'entrepreneurial universities' becoming key shapers of life science markets around the globe (Sunder Rajan 2006, 2017). For instance, Pergonal's popularity played an integral role in advancing Israel's burgeoning and university-supported life science industry. Global demand soared following reports of the first clinical successes in 1981 at the US-based Jones Institute, which combined Pergonal with IVF for establishing pregnancy (Jones et al. 1982). According to the Bertarelli family that owned Serono, Pergonal's success 'became the platform' for the company's 'international expansion' (Bertarelli 2022). In addition to the company's eventual purchase by Merck – a *Fortune 500* multinational pharmaceutical company with one of the largest product portfolios in sexual and reproductive medicine in global history – the Bertarelli family has invested its wealth beyond the life sciences and biotechnology to include real estate, hotels, vineyards and sailing in order to satiate its 'constant appetite for new opportunities and areas for growth' (Bertarelli 2022).

By the mid-1980s, over 100,000 postmenopausal women from around the world had supplied millions of litres of urine, and Serono was processing 30,000 litres of urine a day to keep up with demand. When meeting the growing global demand for the popular drug proved challenging, and scarce supply elicited criticism of the company's profit motives (Adelson 1995), Serono scientists sought alternative sources for the hormones. Using recombinant DNA technology emergent in the late 1970s, they began developing Gonal-F – a synthetic form of FSH made by inserting human genes derived from foetal liver cells into the genome of a Chinese hamster ovary cell line – by the billions. By the mid-1990s, this method had produced a highly purified hormone with reduced safety hazards, such as risk of disease transmission and contamination. It also altered the relational infrastructures essential to sustaining this part of the global fertility supply chain by involving a new set of actors: foetal cells, hamster ovaries, regenerative medicine scientists and infertility patients around the world. Once the main generator of sales for Serono's multi-million dollar company, the company phased out Pergonal and other urine-derived gonadotropin therapeutics in 2004. Gonal-F and related gonadotropic therapeutics containing FSH and LH remain part of the company's lucrative suite of fertility therapies in use around the world today.

Stimulating reproduction

This tale of producing two hormones and one landmark drug has drawn attention to a confluence of clinical, religious, political and economic forms of excitement around the technological assistance of human reproduction. As we saw, Lunenfeld's enthusiasm about the potential of Donini's research for advancing fertility medicine and his Zionist ideals compelled him to board a plane to Rome to forge their lucrative collaboration. His successful pitch to Serono inspired moral and financial investment in the proposed sacred cause, creating an alliance between the Vatican, private pharma, Israeli leaders and the burgeoning global fertility industry. In Israel, ambitious researchers and political leaders brought elder Jewish urine donors and Pergonal into nationalist agendas for reproducing the Jewish state. Globally, Pergonal's clinical efficacy excited diverse investors in its market potential, which strengthened relations between private pharma, university research and clinical medicine worldwide.

Taken together, transforming scientific knowledge about FSH and LH into a marketable drug for treating infertility stimulated far more than reproduction. Producing Pergonal required the excitement of diversely positioned religious authorities, national leaders, private industries and research institutions, each focused on the problems and potentials of human infertility. And still, there remain other stimulating tales about human hormones that reveal unexpected and forgotten dimensions of their power to shape our social worlds.

Notes

1 My mother was prescribed Clomid to assist with ovulation following a decade of infertility. It is an oral pill that blocks estrogen to stimulate the body's production of FSH and LH for egg production and maturation. Clomid does not contain hormones, like Pergonal, yet acts on the body to stimulate hormonal activity.

2 While IVF regimens have since changed, in the 1980s and 1990s a typical IVF regimen involved the patients injecting themselves with Pergonal over several days to mature their eggs, followed by an injection of another hormone-derived therapy – human chorionic gonadotropin – to release the eggs from the follicles, which was followed by procedures for oocyte retrieval, fertilization and transfer back into the uterus.

3 Feminist anthropologist Sandra Bärnreuther describes this as an 'unholy alliance' in the sense that the Catholic Church later opposed forms of assisted reproduction, like IVF, that human gonadotropin therapeutics made possible (2018: 45). It may be perceived as an unholy alliance in another sense based on critiques of Pope Pius XII's response to the Holocaust and the Vatican's relationship to Zionism and Palestine/Israel.

References

Adelson, A. (1995), 'Wall Street; A Fertility Drug Grows Scarce', *The New York Times*, 26 February. Available at https://www.nytimes.com/1995/02/26/business/wall-street-a-fertility-drug-grows-scarce.html.

Bärnreuther, S. (2018), 'From Urine in India to Ampoules in Europe: The Relational Infrastructure of Human Chorionic Gonadotropin', *Zeitschrift Für Ethnologie* 143 (1): 41–60.

Bertarelli (2022), 'History of Serono', Available at https://www.bertarelli.com/family/serono/.

Bettendorf, G. (1995a), 'Donini, Pietro', in G. Bettendorf (ed.), *Zur Geschichte Der Endokrinologie Und Reproduktionsmedizin: 256 Biographien Und Berichte*, 117–20, Berlin, Heidelberg: Springer.

Bettendorf, G. (1995b), 'Lunenfeld, Bruno', in G. Bettendorf (ed.), *Zur Geschichte Der Endokrinologie Und Reproduktionsmedizin: 256 Biographien Und Berichte*, 359–62, Berlin, Heidelberg: Springer.

Bharadwaj, A. and P. E. Glasner (2009), *Local Cells, Global Science: The Rise of Embryonic Stem Cell Research in India*, New York: Routledge.

Deomampo, D. (2016), *Transnational Reproduction: Race, Kinship, and Commercial Surrogacy in India*, New York: New York University Press.

Fausto-Sterling, A. (2000), *Sexing the Body: Gender Politics and the Construction of Sexuality*, New York: Basic Books.

Franklin, S. (1997), *Embodied Progress: A Cultural Account of Assisted Conception*, New York: Routledge.

Franklin, S. (2007), *Dolly Mixtures: The Remaking of Genealogy*, Durham: Duke University Press.

Franklin, S. (2013), *Biological Relatives: IVF, Stem Cells, and the Future of Kinship*, Durham: Duke University Press.

Inhorn, M. C. (1994), *Quest for Conception: Gender, Infertility, and Egyptian Medical Traditions*, Philadelphia: University of Pennsylvania Press.

Jones, H. W., G. S. Jones, M. C. Andrews, A. Acosta, C. Bundren, J. Garcia, B. Sandow, et al. (1982), 'The Program for in Vitro Fertilization at Norfolk', *Fertility and Sterility* 38 (1): 14–21.

Jordan-Young, R. M. and K. Karkazis (2019), *Testosterone: An Unauthorized Biography*, Cambridge, MA: Harvard University Press.

Kahn, S. M. (2000), *Reproducing Jews: A Cultural Account of Assisted Conception in Israel*, Durham: Duke University Press.

Livneh, N. (2002), 'The Good Father', *Haaretz*, 3 May. Available at https://www.haaretz.com/2002-05-30/ty-article/the-good-father/0000017f-dc92-d3a5-af7f-febecedc0000.

Oudshoorn, N. (1994), *Beyond the Natural Body: An Archaeology of Sex Hormones*, New York: Routledge.

Roberts, C. (2007), *Messengers of Sex: Hormones, Biomedicine, and Feminism*, New York: Cambridge University Press.

Roberts, E. F. S. (2012), *God's Laboratory: Assisted Reproduction in the Andes*, Berkeley: University of California Press.

Sanabria, E. (2016), *Plastic Bodies: Sex Hormones and Menstrual Suppression in Brazil*, Durham: Duke University Press Books.

Sunder, R. K. (2006), *Biocapital: The Constitution of Postgenomic Life*, Durham: Duke University Press.

Sunder, R. K. (2017), *Pharmocracy: Value, Politics, and Knowledge in Global Biomedicine*, Durham: Duke University Press.

The Ares-Serono Group's Corporate Scientific Publications Department (1996), *A Tale of Two Hormones: The Story of FSH and LH*, Renes, Switzerland: Imprimeries Reunies.

Thompson, C. (2005), *Making Parents: The Ontological Choreography of Reproductive Technologies*, Cambridge, MA: MIT Press.

Vertommen, S. (2017), 'From the Pergonal Project to Kadimastem: A Genealogy of Israel's Reproductive-Industrial Complex', *BioSocieties* 12 (2): 282–306.

Vertommen, S., V. Pavone, and M. Nahman (2022), 'Global Fertility Chains: An Integrative Political Economy Approach to Understanding the Reproductive Bioeconomy', *Science, Technology, & Human Values* 47 (1): 112–45.

Wahlberg, A. (2018), *Good Quality: The Routinization of Sperm Banking in China*, Oakland: University of California Press.

Wiel, L. van de (2020), *Freezing Fertility: Oocyte Cryopreservation and the Gender Politics of Aging*, New York: New York University Press.

9 GONADOTROPIN-RELEASING HORMONE ANALOGUES (GnRHa)

CRONAN CRONSHAW

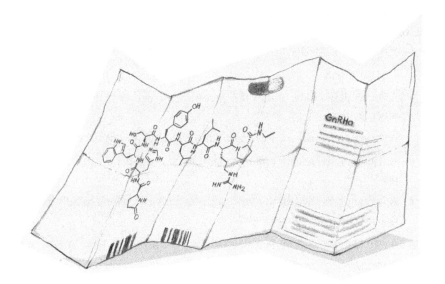

Subversive Patient Information Leaflet: GnRHa for gender dysphoria

In the UK, pharmaceutical manufacturers must supply a Patient Information Leaflet (PIL) with medication to give an overview of the product they accompany. This PIL has been created to provide an overview of gonadotropin-releasing hormone analogues (GnRHa) as a treatment for young people diagnosed with gender dysphoria. When used as an intervention for gender dysphoria, GnRHa is 'off label', meaning the product licence for GnRHa doesn't cover its use in this way.

In instances where a PIL does not relate to the prescribed use of pharmaceutical products, patients are advised to seek further information from a healthcare professional. Similarly, a PIL accompanying 'on-label' drugs usually includes a version of the message, 'You may want to talk to your doctor or pharmacist about what to expect and watch out for.' What if, instead of speaking to a medical professional, one conversed with a feminist technoscience theorist? This is the point of departure for this new-style PIL.

Gender dysphoria

Gender dysphoria is defined by the fifth edition of the *Diagnostic and Statistical Manual of Mental Disorders* (DSM-5) as distress related to a marked incongruence between experienced or expressed gender and gender assigned at birth.

Criteria for the diagnosis of gender dysphoria in children and adolescents include:

- A strong desire to be of the other gender or an insistence that one is the other gender.
- A strong preference for wearing clothes typical of the opposite gender.
- A strong preference for cross-gender roles in make-believe play or fantasy play.
- A strong preference for the toys, games or activities stereotypically used or engaged in by the other gender.
- A strong preference for playmates of the other gender.
- A strong rejection of toys, games, and activities typical of one's assigned gender.
- A strong dislike of one's sexual anatomy.
- A strong desire for the physical sex characteristics that match one's experienced gender. (Butler et al. 2018: 362)

The prescription of GnRHa is a treatment in its own right, meaning it is not exclusively employed as a precursor to further physical intervention, such as gender-affirming hormones or surgery[1] (Butler et al. 2018: 635). Rather, GnRHa can be used to provide a window for further clinical assessment while affording a young person space and time for psychotherapeutic exploration (De Vries et al. 2012).

GnRHa

GnRHa, also known as: hormone blockers, puberty blockers, blockers, puberty suppressors.

Administration: Intramuscular injection, subcutaneous injection or nasal spray.

Dose frequency: Contingent on mode of administration. Dispensation via injection can occur at one-, three- or six-month intervals. Nasal spray to be administered twice a day.

Alternative name(s): Buserelin, Casodex, Decapeptyl, Goserelin, Leuprorelin, Nafarelin, Prostap, Triptorelin, Zoladex.

GnRHa, a synthetic version of gonadotropin-releasing hormone (GnRH), is typically administered no earlier than Tanner stage 2,[2] when the first outward signs of puberty occur. GnRHa 'pauses' puberty by suppressing the production of 'sex hormones' (follicle-stimulating hormone, oestrogen and testosterone).

Puberty starts when neurons (nerve cells) in the hypothalamus (the area of the brain responsible for maintaining homeostasis) produce and release GnRH in a pulsative manner, triggering the pituitary gland (a small bean-shaped gland situated at the base of the brain) to make and release luteinizing hormone (LH) and follicle-stimulating hormone (FSH). LH and FSH act by prompting ovaries to produce oestradiol and progesterone and testicles to make testosterone.

Taking hormone blockers provides GnRH receptors (in the pituitary gland) with sustained (as opposed to pulsating) exposure to GnRHa (the synthetic version of GnRH), which causes the pituitary gland to stop producing LH and FSH, thereby halting puberty. Once exposure to GnRHa ceases, puberty will resume.

In medical and technoscientific discourses that underpin traditional PIL, hormones are framed as exclusively biological entities that function formulaically within bounded physical bodies. Hormones are simply chemicals that orchestrate different functions in the body by carrying messages through the blood to the organs, muscles and tissues: the messages hormones carry are asocial and predictable, simply instructing your body what to do and when to do it. In this view, sex hormones, as messengers of sex,[3] both express and produce sex as they stem from innate, pre-existing, genetic sex and give rise to material, secondary sex characteristics.

Contrastingly, in this PIL, the messages of GnRHa[4] and other hormones are understood to have an undeniable effect on the body, but the nature of these messages and (side) effects are treated as complexly socioculturally contingent[5] and entwined with issues of morality.[6] The reason for taking GnRHa is also considered to have an important bearing on how its (side) effects are encountered and experienced.

GnRHa isn't just used to treat gender dysphoria; it is also used to medicate several other conditions, including prostate cancer, endometriosis and precocious puberty, but the side effects will vary widely between conditions. For example, the biosocial side effects for a cisgender man, aged eighty-seven, taking GnRHa to treat prostate cancer will diverge greatly from the biosocial side effects of a seventeen-year-old diagnosed with gender dysphoria. As a consequence of taking GnRHa, the 87-year-old man will not face 'accusations of youthful uncertainty' or 'accusations of internalised homophobia', and it is doubtful that anyone will seek to accuse his (almost certainly deceased) childhood caregivers of 'poor parenting'.

Warnings and precautions

Warning: Your feelings of gender dysphoria may persist.

Gender dysphoria is only one way of understanding trans, and the way gender dysphoria enacts trans is circumspect and problematic to many people of trans experience.

Trans is sometimes framed as a 'serious medical problem' (Giordano 2008: 583), and the phrase 'born in the wrong body' (Engdahl 2014) is frequently employed as a popular shorthand for describing what it means to be trans. Relatedly, GnRHa is framed as having the potential to 'harmonize' body and mind by averting the 'natural disaster' of puberty, which 'ravages the child's body and its (gendered) integrity from within' (Sadjadi 2013: 257). However, even with GnRHa, gender dysphoria may persist because the body can never be fully possessed or controlled (see Castañeda 2015: 269, and Sadjadi 2013: 258).

Precaution: The lived body

Feelings of wrongness, experienced through the body, do not have to be interpreted as indicative of something inherently awry but might usefully be considered a biosocial phenomenon: consider the idea of the 'lived body' (Young 2005: 16 in Engdahl 2014: 269), which is socioculturally situated.

See *Side effects: Medicalization.*

See *Side effects: Gender essentialism.*

Side effects

Please note: There may be interesting tensions between desirable outcomes and unwanted ramifications, for example, the effect of having one's trans-ness (or gender dysphoria) affirmed but simultaneously medicalized, as one fulfils the diagnostic criteria necessary to acquire a desired prescription of GnRHa.

Medicalization

Medicalization is a process through which matters previously beyond the remit of medicine become understood as medical problems requiring medical treatment.

Although trans isn't always, and certainly doesn't have to be, medicalized (see Preciado 2013, for example), you may find that you are subject to medicalization because currently, access to GnRHa cannot (easily or legally) be achieved without a clinical diagnosis of gender dysphoria.

Some people find medicalization to be positive as it is often closely linked to ideas of being born trans[7] – a matter beyond one's control and, therefore, a destigmatized justification for accessing medical technologies. See *Side effects: Accusations of poor parenting: Disapproval, disdain and blame.*

Whether medicalization is experienced as a negative side effect might be affected by your existing belief systems, experiences and social positioning.

It is also worth noting that medicalization may appear as a fleeting and temporary self-induced side effect that flares up around clinicians charged with making assessments. There is a long history of trans people strategically fulfilling diagnostic criteria to achieve their required aims (e.g. access to hormones or surgery).

Trans people (and others) sometimes problematize such medicalization as a stigmatizing pathologization of difference and advocate for access to medical technologies (such as hormonal intervention) in a way that is free from institutional gatekeeping and regulation (e.g. Koyama 2003).

When medicalized and mediated through the locus of psychiatric diagnostic criteria, trans is necessarily circumscribed as binary and characterized by distress, which reifies trans in very particular, often exclusionary, ways. The notion of gender euphoria, sometimes described as 'the distinct enjoyment or satisfaction caused by the correspondence between the person's gender identity and gendered features associated with a gender other than the one assigned at birth' (Ashley and Ellis 2018: 2), emerged in trans communities as a more positive counter to gender dysphoria (characterized by distress) and a more expansive means of understanding biosocial embodiments of sex/gender (see Beischel et al. 2022 for an overview).

Essentialism

Essentialism is the belief that entities have a set of necessary characteristics that make them what they are. There are a variety of competing and overlapping forms of essentialism to which you may be subject.

The reader is advised not to question where true essence lies but to consider the effects of such material-discursive moves. It is useful to consider how essentialisms entangled with discourses related to GnRHa are used to make certain political claims and justify particular practices (while invalidating others). As the following side effects make clear, essentialist discourses can function in different ways, often towards opposing ends (e.g. gender essentialism can be used both to 'delegitimize' and 'legitimize' trans).

Trans essentialism

Implication into trans-essentialist discourses and narratives may or may not constitute an unwelcome side effect. If you subscribe to the idea of 'gendered brains' or 'trans brains' (see Bakker 2018) and/or you believe that you have been 'born trans' or 'born in the wrong body', this associated effect may be experienced as a welcome recognition of your personhood. Alternatively, you may experience the essentialism of trans as an unwanted side effect if you take seriously the idea that sex is socially and culturally produced (see Fausto-Sterling 2000). See *Warning: Your feelings of gender dysphoria may persist.* See *Side effects: Gender essentialism.*

Modes of trans essentialism tend to frame GnRHa as belonging to a package of corrective medical technologies. Whether this is experienced negatively will vary between individuals and may indeed vary for one and the same individual. See *Side effects: Medicalisation.*

The essentialism of sexuality

To essentialize sexuality is to treat it as intrinsic and fixed. This is not always experienced as a harmful side effect (indeed, some people are invested in the idea of sexuality as an essence), but sometimes, the notion of an innate and fixed sexuality is employed as a way of undermining trans young people (and adults): See *Accusations of internalized homophobia.*

Gender essentialism

Gender essentialism is the idea that gender is inborn, fixed, biologically determined and the source of differences in 'gendered' behaviour and preferences (such as liking girls' toys or enjoying wearing girls' clothes such as dresses).

You may be produced through gender essentialist discourses, mechanisms and devices (such as diagnostic criteria and assessment). Whether these occasions are perceived as a negative side effect is likely to be an individual matter. Gender essentialism, or the accusation of gender essentialism, may not be experienced negatively if you, like many others (including non-trans individuals, of course), are invested in the idea that men and women are intrinsically different, for example.

Additionally, gender essentialism may be something that is usefully operationalized while simultaneously being critiqued.[8] One may strategically endeavour to satisfy diagnostic criteria for gender dysphoria (attending a clinical assessment appointment in conventionally 'feminine clothes' when usually one prefers to wear 'masculine clothes', for example) while also (privately) finding the implicit neurosexism deeply problematic. In this scenario, the accusation of being gender essentialist or a 'dupe of gender' (Raymond 1979) will likely be an irksome side effect, especially as it may be hard to publicly voice critique of gender binarism and gender determinism without undermining one's candidature for gender-affirming care.

Denial of the present

Sometimes, trans childhood and adolescence are subsumed by and recuperated into adult narratives pertaining to identity and experience. This can happen in different ways with varying effects – for example, a gay or lesbian adult may reminisce about their childhood, saying that they are happy they weren't offered GnRHa because if so, they would have mistakenly taken a trans path,[9] or a trans adult may lay claim to trans childhood and adolescence[10] by celebrating GnRHa as neoteric means of giving all young trans people a better start in life. A consequence of these discursive moves is that a young GnRHa taker's present is denied, thereby stifling possibility.

See *Accusations of youthful uncertainty.*

Concomitant side effects often take the form of accusations:

Accusations of poor parenting: Disapproval, disdain and blame

Parents and carers who validate a trans young person's gender identity and facilitate the acquisition of GnRHa may face derision and scorn (Rahilly 2015: 342) on the basis that they have not adequately acquainted their charge with the prevailing truth regime (often referred to as the facts).

A truth regime is a 'general politics of truth . . . that is, the types of discourse [a society] accepts and makes function as true' (Foucault 2000: 131), and in the existing truth regime, there exists a 'dichotomous, sex-deterministic gender system' (Rahilly 2015: 357) in which sex and gender are naturally congruent. Trans, as a form of dissonance between sex and gender, is, therefore, a nonsensical fallacy that should not warrant access to GnRHa.

Additionally, mothers, in particular, may be held responsible for 'causing' the gender dysphoria GnRHa is intended to treat – poor parenting and erroneous hormonal regulation during gestation are sometimes cited as reasons for inculpation (Johnson and Benson 2014; Brill and Pepper 2008).

Accusations of youthful uncertainty

GnRHa, designed to halt puberty, is prescribed to adolescents, and adolescents, shy of fully formed adulthood, are deemed to be incomplete and ontologically unstable: leading to conclusions/accusations that as an adolescent's gender has not (yet) matured, an adolescent's gender cannot (yet) be known (see Castañeda 2014). See *Side effects: Denial of the present.*

Accusations of internalized homophobia

You may face the imputation that you are identifying as trans because you are unable to face up to internalized homophobia. This accusation may be articulated in a variety of ways but is likely to bear a resemblance to the following:

Propelled by self-loathing and surrounded by prejudice, lesbian and gay young people are seduced by the 'glamorous allure' of a trans identity which they believe will afford them a trouble-free heterosexual, gender-normative existence (e.g. Transgender Trend 2019).

You may find this accusation particularly grating if you are (one of many) trans people who are not heterosexual or gender-conforming (see Movement Advancement Project 2017).

See *Side Effect: Essentialism of sexuality.*

Accusation: Interfering with bodily integrity

You may face this accusation on the basis that GnRHa interferes with the sexed 'integrity' of the body that flows from chromosomes via endogenous hormones (see Raymond 1979).

This side effect can be nullified by refusing to treat the body as separate from and prior to discourse.

If the notion of prediscursive sex is suspended, the taking of GnRHa may not be understood not as an assault against the natural state of the body but as a mode of connecting with 'the body's open ended capacities' (Gill-Peterson 2014: 407) and a form of 'participation in the technical capacity of the endocrine system' (Gill-Peterson 2014: 407).

How to use the PIL

Traditionally, pharmaceutical risks are conveyed through the sections of PIL that relate to warnings, precautions and side effects. A PIL, acting as an intermediary between lab and patient-consumer, promises to be an impartial source of objective fact, and readers are tasked with diligently absorbing the information on offer to make a personal assessment of danger in relation to a fixed and singular reality. Contrastingly, this PIL encourages the reader to become engaged in 'ontological politics' (Mol 1999) by evaluating not the pros or cons of a fixed reality but the affordances and limitations of 'conditions of possibility' (Mol 1999: 75). In relation to GnRHa, this might entail considering 'how, where and by whom "the problem" of trans-puberty-requiring-GnRH-analogues is articulated' (Roberts and Cronshaw 2017: 81) – and to what effect.

Please distribute this PIL widely. Readers are encouraged to see themselves not as isolated consumers of pharmaceutical products but as citizens of realities, entangled with and invested in world-making projects.

Notes

1 Although GnRHa are sometimes presented as 'eliminating the need for further surgery' (https://www.mayoclinic.org/diseases-conditions/gender-dysphoria/in -depth/pubertal-blockers/art-20459075)/

2 The Tanner Scale (Marshall and Tanner 1969; Marshall and Tanner 1970), also known as Sexual Maturity Rating (SMR), is a classification system used to chart pubertal development.

3 See Roberts (2007) for a fascinating explication and analysis of sex hormones as messengers of sex.

4 GnRHa, as puberty suppressors, are considered to block rather than carry hormonal messages, but this is misleading. GnRHa are heavily implicated in biosocial messaging because the act of blocking is itself a message-making enterprise.

5 There is plenty to suggest that side effects and symptoms are not exclusively somatic matters. Medical anthropologist Margaret Lock (1993) found that women in Japan and women in North America experienced very different symptoms of menopause; whereas hot flushes were frequently reported as a typical symptom of menopause in America, they were seldom mentioned in Japan – a finding Lock attributed to the malleability of biology and its extricable entwinement with culture (see Roberts 2007 for an excellent overview).

6 In the UK, the provision of GnRHa as an intervention for gender dysphoria in young people has become a matter of polarized debate ever since the Tavistock's Gender Identity Development Service (GIDS) began to trial the use of GnRHa as a treatment option in 2011 (see Roberts and Cronshaw 2017).

7 Often problematically juxtaposed with choosing to be trans.

8 There is a long history of trans people strategically satisfying diagnostic criteria to access hormones and/or surgery (see Stone 1992).

9 Actor Rupert Everett, for example, told the *Sunday Times*: 'I really wanted to be a girl. Thank God the world of now wasn't then, because I'd be on hormones, and I'd be a woman. After 15 I never wanted to be a woman again' (Press Association 2016).

10 See Riley et al. (2013) for examples.

References

Ashley, F. and C. Ells (2018), 'In Favor of Covering Ethically Important Cosmetic Surgeries: Facial Feminization Surgery for Transgender People', *The American Journal of Bioethics* 18 (12): 23–5.

Bakker, J. (2018), 'Brain Structure and Function in Gender Dysphoria', in Symposium S30.3. Presented at the ECE 2018 20th European Congress of Endocrinology European Society of Endocrinology.

Beischel, W. J., S. E. M. Gauvin, and S. M. van Anders (2022) '"A Little Shiny Gender Breakthrough": Community Understandings of Gender Euphoria', *International Journal of Transgender Health* 23 (3): 1–21.

Brill, S. and R. Pepper (2008), *Transgender Child: A Handbook for Families and Professionals*, San Francisco, CA: Cleis Press.

Butler, G., N. De Graaf, B. Wren, and P. Carmichael (2018), 'Assessment and Support of Children and Adolescents with Gender Dysphoria', *Archives of Disease in Childhood* 103 (7): 631–6.

Castañeda, C. (2014), 'Childhood', *TSQ: Transgender Studies Quarterly* 1 (1–2): 59–61.

Castañeda, C. (2015), 'Developing Gender: The Medical Treatment of Transgender Young People', *Social Science & Medicine* 143 (1982): 262–70.

De Vries, A. L. C. and P. T. Cohen-Kettenis (2012), 'Clinical Management of Gender Dysphoria in Children and Adolescents: The Dutch Approach', *Journal of Homosexuality* 59 (3): 301–20.

Engdahl, U. (2014), 'Wrong Body', *TSQ: Transgender Studies Quarterly* 1 (1–2): 267–9.

Fausto-Sterling, A. (2000), *Sexing the Body: Gender Politics and the Construction of Sexuality*, 1st edn, New York: Basic Books.

Foucault, M. (2000), *Truth and Power. In Essential Works of Foucault 1954–1984*, Vol. 3, Edited by Paul Rabinow, New York: The New Press.

Gill-Peterson, J. (2014), 'The Technical Capacities of the Body: Assembling Race, Technology, and Transgender', *TSQ: Transgender Studies Quarterly* 1 (3): 402–18.

Giordano, S. (2008), 'Lives in a Chiaroscuro. Should we Suspend the Puberty of Children with Gender Identity Disorder?', *Journal of Medical Ethics* 34 (8): 580–4.

Johnson, S. L. and K. E. Benson (2014), '"It's Always the Mother's Fault": Secondary Stigma of Mothering a Transgender Child', *Journal of GLBT Family Studies* 10 (1–2): 124–44.

Koyama, E. (2003), 'The Transfeminist Manifesto', in R. Dicker and A. Piepmeier (eds), *Catching a Wave: Reclaiming Feminism for the 21st Century*, 244–62, Boston: Northeastern University Press.

Lock, M. (1993), *Encounters with Aging: Mythologies of Menopause in Japan and North America*, Berkeley and London: University of California Press.

Marshall, W. A. and J. M. Tanner (1969), 'Variations in Pattern of Pubertal Changes in Girls', *Archives of Disease in Childhood* 44 (235): 291–303.

Marshall, W. A. and J. M. Tanner (1970), 'Variations in the Pattern of Pubertal Changes in Boys', *Archives of Disease in Childhood* 45 (239): 13–23.

Mol, A. (1999), 'Ontological Politics. A Word and Some Questions', *The Sociological Review* 47 (S1): 74–89.

Movement Advancement Project, BiNetUSA, Bisexual Organizing Project, Bisexual Resource Center, National Centre for Transgender Equality (2017), 'A Closer Look: Bisexual Transgender People', Available at https://www.lgbtmap.org/file/A%20Closer%20Look%20Bisexual%20Transgender.pdf (accessed 15 June 2022).

Preciado, P. B. (2013), *Testo Junkie: Sex, Drugs and Biopolitics in the Pharmacopornographic Era*, New York: The Feminist Press.

Press Association (2016) 'Rupert Everett Warns of Dangers of Child Gender Reassignment Operations', *The Guardian*, 19 June.

Rahilly, E. P. (2015), 'The Gender Binary Meets the Gender-Variant Child: Parents' Negotiations with Childhood Gender Variance', *Gender & Society* 29 (3): 338–61.

Raymond, J. G. (1979), *The Transsexual Empire*, London: Women's Press.

Riley, E. A., L. Clemson, G. Sitharthan, and M. Diamond (2013), 'Surviving a Gender-Variant Childhood: The Views of Transgender Adults on the Needs of Gender-Variant Children and Their Parents', *Journal of Sex & Marital Therapy* 39 (3): 241–63.

Roberts, C. (2007), *Messengers of Sex: Hormones, Biomedicine and Feminism*, Cambridge: Cambridge University Press.

Roberts, C. and C. Cronshaw (2017), 'New Puberty; New Trans: Children, Pharmaceuticals and Politics', in E. Johnson (ed.), *Gendering Drugs: Feminist Studies of Pharmaceuticals*, 59–84, Cham, Switzerland: Palgrave Macmillan.

Sadjadi, S. (2013), 'The Endocrinologist's Office – Puberty Suppression: Saving Children from a Natural Disaster?', *Journal of Medical Humanities* 34 (2): 255–60.

Stone, S. (1992), 'The Empire Strikes Back: A Posttranssexual Manifesto', *Camera Obscura* 10 (2): 150–76.

Transgender Trend (2019), *Supporting Gender Diverse and Trans-Identified Students in Schools*, 3rd ed. [eBook]. Available at https://www.transgendertrend.com/wp-content/uploads/2019/08/Transgender-Trend-Resource-Pack-for-Schools3.pdf (accessed 9 July 2020).

Young, I. M. (2005), *On Female Body Experience*, New York: Oxford University Press.

10 GROWTH HORMONE

MAGDALENA RADKOWSKA-WALKOWICZ

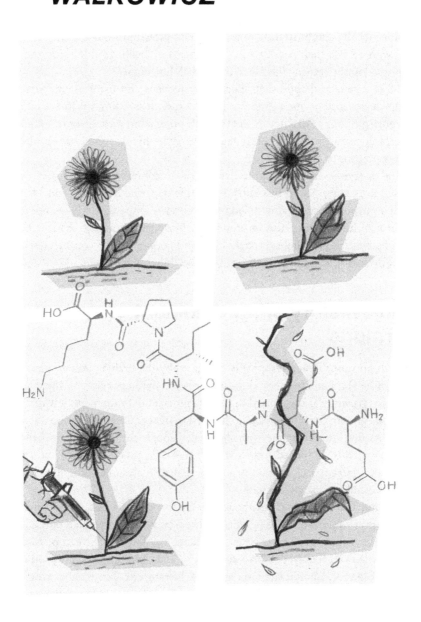

This entry presents the results of a research project on Turner syndrome (TS) conducted in 2016–19 by scholars associated with the Childhood Studies Interdisciplinary Research Team, University of Warsaw.[1] The main tools included in-depth interviews from which the above quotes come, conducted with people with TS, their parents and doctors. We also conducted the participant observations, primarily during summer camps organized by the Turner Syndrome Patients Support Society. Moreover, I, as one of the scholars of the project, observed training sessions for the administration of recombinant growth hormone (rGH) aimed at girls with TS and their parents and participated in meetings of the Coordinating Commission supervising the use of the growth hormone.

TS is a genetic disease that affects only females and involves the partial or complete absence of one of the X chromosomes. It is estimated that 1 in 2,500 newborn girls has TS. TS occurs in the whole population with the same frequency, and its appearance is not connected to lifestyle, living conditions, healthcare during pregnancy or country.

The interviews from this project reveal the uncommon power of rGH, which is used to manage TS. In this entry I describe its social meanings and ask what hidden purposes accompany its administration. I argue that rGH is not just a medical technology but also an important biosocial actor that changes bodies and possibilities, gives hope, provokes fear and both raises and conceals questions about priorities, solutions and the right of the child to knowledge.

Short history of recombinant growth hormone

Growth hormone (somatotropin) is produced by the brain's pituitary gland and governs height, bone length and muscle growth. The importance of the pituitary gland for growth was recognized in the late nineteenth century, but it wasn't until 1963 that growth hormone began to be used to treat children who were unusually short. At first, the hormone was obtained through autopsies from a cadaver's pituitary glands. It turned out, however, that this process carried the risk of transmitting Creutzfeldt-Jakob disease, a degenerative brain disorder that leads to dementia and, ultimately, death.

Around the same time, synthetic production of rGH began and pituitary-derived growth hormone was practically discontinued. 'This was not only a major breakthrough in providing a "clean" substance . . . but also created possibilities of unlimited GH supply' (Tidblad 2021: 215). Thus, in the 1980s, the production of rGH began in laboratories (Ayyar 2011), helping children with varying short stature problems to grow. Although girls with TS most often do not have growth hormone deficiency, and their pituitary glands produce it naturally, they need rGH because their bodies do not use natural growth hormone appropriately.

Turner syndrome

Physical traits characteristic of TS include short stature, low-set ears, low posterior hairline and a flat, broad chest. Women with TS can also experience various health issues, like heart or kidney problems (Sutton et al. 2005). One of the most frequent symptoms of TS is ovarian dysfunction, resulting in a late onset of puberty. Oestrogen therapy is usually introduced around the age of twelve (Gawlik et al. 2013). Only about 5 per cent of women with TS have a chance of spontaneous pregnancy (Kucharska 2019) making infertility a major concern (Sutton et al. 2005; Świątkiewicz-Mośny 2010).

TS does not affect intellectual capabilities, and only a small fraction of people with TS may suffer from some intellectual dysfunctions or learning disabilities (Hong, Kent and Kesler 2009). Nevertheless, experts have pointed out some psychological characteristics typical of patients with TS, although they do not necessarily manifest in everyone affected (Skuse 2009). These include ADHD or ADD in childhood and behaviour on the autism spectrum in adolescence and adulthood, low self-esteem as well as some emotional and social immaturity (Lagrou et al. 2003).

TS is a medical entity, described in the ICD under the number Q96 (ICD-10). Usually, it is included in the set of 'genetic diseases', a comprehensive set with imprecise boundaries. Defining TS as a disease can be problematic. Rather, it is a group of symptoms that can have certain health consequences and can lead to various diseases. In conversations with patients or their parents, we sometimes heard that it is a mistake to call TS a disease, because girls and women with the syndrome do not necessarily feel sick at all. Moreover, from a bioethical perspective, rGH treatment can be viewed as enhancement, not medical therapy (Morrison 2015; Rajtar 2019). Nevertheless, one can use the term 'disease', recognizing a broad WHO-compliant definition aligned with the social rather than biomedical model, treating health and disease as a continuum not binary opposition (Blaxter 2010). Thus, TS can be seen as part of the *medical borderlands*, where health and enhancement practices are entangled (Edmonds and Sanabria 2014; Rajtar 2019).

Hormonal therapy

A diagnosis of TS is often associated with less growth than in children without TS. Mothers of girls with TS told us that even if something in the child's behaviour or health is of concern to the parents (Maciejewska-Mroczek 2019), doctors are usually only interested if the growth of a child at preschool or early school age significantly deviates from the norm as determined by the percentile grid. The doctor would suspect a deeper health problem and refer the patient for endocrinologic examinations. This is the most common route to diagnosis for people with TS. I understand a diagnosis not only as a set of performative words spoken at a given moment but also as a broader process of negotiating the meanings of past and future experiences related to a disease or symptom complex (Nissen and Risor 2018). This is also the moment when other informed social actors (such as family members or teachers) start working on the social construction of TS (Krawczak 2019b). It should be noted, however, that today some families learn about TS prenatally, and some women were diagnosed in late adolescence or adulthood because their TS symptoms were non-specific.

If a girl is diagnosed before puberty, as is the case most often, the process of applying for funded rGH begins. The process, involving medical examinations and paperwork, lasts from several months up to over a year. The duration depends on the patient's age, the schedule of committee meetings and the diagnostic capabilities of the clinic. In fact, every Polish girl with TS who is below the third percentile on the growth chart qualifies for rGH treatment. When the hormonal medication is released, the period of daily rGH injection into the child's body begins and lasts until her puberty or even longer.[2] In the first years after diagnosis, and often also after stopping rGH therapy, the lives of people with TS and their families revolve around the issue of growth and the administration of rGH.

Inaccessibility and indispensability

On the one hand, there is an aura of inaccessibility built around rGH, while on the other, rGH is presented as an indispensable element of therapy. The figure of rGH as a hard-to-get object of desire has its historical rationality. Before 2000, rGH was not financed by the state in Poland, and its cost significantly exceeded the average earnings of Poles such that only a few patients could benefit through social fundraising or scientific programmes. Our interviewees who were not able to benefit from rGH therapy believed that their lives could have been different had they received the hormone (Reimann 2019). They attributed many of their failures to short stature. Before 2000 rGH was undoubtedly a luxury item, yet it was associated with the hope of a huge improvement in the child's quality of life and her chances for a 'normal' life in the future. 'You know, like a trip to the moon, a trip to the moon. You can't describe it in any other terms; it was simply a trip to the moon.' With these words the mother of an adult woman with TS described the moment after obtaining rGH for the treatment of her daughter.

In 1990 the Turner Syndrome Patients Support Society was established, mainly to organize financial collections enabling the purchase of rGH. At the end of 1999, rGH for people with TS was included in the list of state-funded drugs (Radkowska-Walkowicz 2019). However, before rGH is funded, a positive opinion must be issued from the Coordinating Commission supervising its use, made up of thirty-two physicians, mainly professors of medicine. They evaluate the application form with over 100 responses to questions regarding the patient's personal and medical details.

If the requirements are met, a daily routine begins for a child with TS. rGH must be stored in a fridge and injected every day in a very specific manner which is taught during training at the hospital. rGH administration is strictly controlled by doctors; once a patient is approved for funding, she will begin regular visits to the hospital (usually every three months), during which blood is collected for testing, growth and other anthropometric data are examined and additional tests are ordered if necessary. During the visit, the patient's parents must hand over empty rGH cartridges (as proof that the rGH has not been sold[3]) and can pick up new ones. Many of our interviewees pointed out the time-consuming and irrational time management during these appointments. This controlled ritual demonstrates the rGH agency. rGH affects others, time management and doctors-patients relationships. It transforms bodies, as well as increases the power of physicians, and empowers bureaucracy.

In their conversations with parents, endocrinologists emphasize in various ways how important, but also unavailable, rGH treatment is. In some narratives, obtaining a rGH refund becomes a huge success (although today almost all girls with TS do get it). Staszek, the father of nine-year-old Marysia, was very disappointed with the long period between his daughter's diagnosis and the start of therapy. Staszek could not understand what he viewed as a blockade of his daughter's treatment, which included preventing him from entering the private healthcare system:

> This is the biggest mistake we have made. And we are pissed off because if we had started earlier, when it was found out, she would have had this growth hormone administered, she would have been eight centimeters taller.[4] [. . .] And she is not because the games lasted a year. [. . .] I think that the hormone had to be administered right away, not waiting for the commission. I can afford it, I could have already paid the money.

Despite the aura of inaccessibility, rGH is also supposed to be a necessity. Although doubts regarding its use appear in the bioethical literature (arguments focus on possible side effects and whether enhancing growth is merely serving aesthetic norms; e.g. Hogle 2005; Rajtar 2019), patients are left with no choice. Agata's dad emphasizes:

> I think if we hadn't made this decision, we would have been abandoned [. . .] by the system, completely. [. . .] It's just that if we did not start treatment with growth hormone, we would be completely alone, we would come, and everyone would – I am convinced of it – prove that now, you should take care of your child yourself.

Interviewees also talked about fear of possible side effects. Among them were those mentioned by doctors (including infrequent hip, knee or other joint pain; headache; progression of spine curvature in patients with scoliosis; temporary increase in blood sugar levels) but also concerns related to the possible carcinogenic effect of rGH (on rGH safety see Backeljauw et al. 2021; Tidblad 2021). As Pola's mother said: 'She had such disturbing moles that kept growing. As I read, these girls get this hormone and everything is so stimulated that everything grows.' rGH can therefore, as another interviewee says, 'stimulate cancer cells'. However, patients' fear is ignored by most endocrinologists who do not have any other type of care to offer. 'Fear remains a private matter because it interferes with the rational necessity to implement bodily discipline. The specter of short stature scares more than the injections' (Krawczak 2019b: 134). Thus, rGH, as a biosocial actor, puts pressure on doctors to offer this treatment and diminishes the importance of other medical and psychological aspects of TS for which there is in fact no cure.

Moreover, our research shows that many endocrinologists are not prepared or do not want to talk about sexuality and motherhood with girls and their parents (Krawczak 2019). Thus, focusing on rGH helps them avoid these inconvenient topics.

What is hidden

Familiarizing girls and teenagers with the issue of short stature constitutes a significant part of the brochures and studies prepared by Polish patient organizations (Krawczak 2019b). Medical focus on rGH and the power of biomedicine, coupled with the power of patient activism that grew out of the battle for rGH, are only part of the reason that growth becomes a key issue for parents of girls with TS. rGH not only helps girls with TS to grow but also helps to hide the more complex reality of their health from them. Girls are not often informed they have a genetic disorder called TS, even after they begin their rGH therapy. Klara could not remember how she became diagnosed, 'because no one wanted to tell me'. She recalled, 'I only knew that I have to take some kind of shots and that's all I knew.'

Parents we spoke to often wondered if they should tell children with TS the truth about the diagnosis. Adult women with TS agreed that children should be informed as early as possible. Psychological research also demonstrates that not informing children about their illness may have negative effects on their psychological development (Lagrou 2017). Still many parents choose to delay sharing this information. rGH becomes an ally in this secrecy vis-à-vis children. Thus parental concerns and biomedical focus on rGH delay disclosing and discussing the problems of infertility (Krawczak 2019a), sex development and emotional and social immaturity, as well as the fact that it is a genetic condition (which is commonly thought to involve something dangerous, incurable and hereditary).

Staszek admits that he and his wife don't talk to their daughter about TS: 'We say she is not growing. We believe there is no point in [talking about TS]. Why spoil her life. It won't do her any good. She is not growing, and thanks to that hormone she will grow.'

In her research journal, recorded during summer camp for girls with TS, Anna Krawczak, one of our team researchers, described the following situation:

'Iga, tell the lady what your biggest problem is'. I was surprised because from our conversation it transpired in no way that I am interested in 'problems' or that I perceive TS as a problem. [. . .] Iga became embarrassed and hugged her mom and the question was repeated, again without the child's reply. Then the mother said 'Iga's biggest problem is her short height'. (Fieldnotes)

In her article on TS, Krawczak interpreted another of her fieldnotes:

Kasia is five years old and her most voiced problem is that she is not a famous singer, not that she is even shorter than her friends from kindergarten. However, parents need the threat of short stature to justify the daily injection regime in front of their daughters. [. . .] GH helps to deal with the main visible distinguishing feature of this condition, while not requiring the use of dangerous terms such as 'Turner syndrome', 'genetic syndrome', 'disease', 'defect'. (Krawczak 2019b:136)

The parents we spoke to associate their reluctance to talk to children with TS about their health condition with stigmatization and self-stigmatization. According to them, if the child knows about TS, she would adopt a permanent identity of a person with TS, a person suffering from a genetic disease. The parents don't want the disease to be at the centre of their daughter's life. They are convinced that talking about TS would in a way 'create' TS as a problem and create a disability. Parents' concerns about self-identification overlap with social taboos related to disability, as well as to a gender issue, since TS is associated with uncertainty about femininity and sex development and with infertility and projected lack of motherhood.

Failure to inform a child about her health condition may be considered a violation of her right to know and a refusal to recognize her subjectivity. Focus on growth and hormones, therefore, not only reveals the low position of the child in the Polish family and in the medical system but also obscures the truth about Poland's ineffective health system, which cannot cope with the complexity of conditions such as TS. As our research has shown, the lack of comprehensive medical care, especially after the transition from paediatric care to the adult care service, a complete lack of psychological support and poor gynaecological care are big problems for people with TS. Focus on rGH, then, also serves biomedical discourses that are poorly able to admit failure.

Thus, in the imagination rGH becomes a magic drug which can testify to the success of medicine, a cure that can simply be prescribed and the patient is considered properly cared for. This is why doctors often emphasize that people with TS can and should live 'normally' as long as they undergo hormone therapy. Parents also fight for this normality, and rGH offers hope for it.

However, as it turns out, this 'the biggest problem is her short height' game does not always succeed. This becomes clear in the narratives of teenagers' mothers and adult women with TS, in which the social and emotional problems of girls with TS often come to the fore. One of them said: 'When Lena started being treated with this growth hormone, I really thought that I touched the edge of heaven and that would make her a happier person. This is not true. This has not happened.' When a girl with TS grows up, mothers who previously usually agreed with the biomedical discourse begin to challenge the competence of doctors who do not recognize the extrasomatic aspects of the disease (Maciejewska-Mroczek 2019: 154). As Marta's mother said: 'it was all around such medical features. And that the child will be small, and that the child must develop these secondary sexual characteristics, and that she must take a hormone, and [. . .] that she will be short. But I, as a parent, have never, never been warned about by any other more psychological consequences.'

However most parents of girls with TS, and the daughters themselves, do not question the rationality of rGH therapy, although they note that it is burdensome, does not solve many problems and the somatic model of TS is not sufficient to describe this condition.

Conclusion

rGH helps girls with TS grow to a near-average height in the population (Kucharska 2019), making them socially invisible, and gives them hope for a satisfying, 'normal' life in the future. If we look at a rGH cartridge, however, we can see something more: the conviction about medicine's success in the fight against genetic disease, aesthetic patterns in women's height and a tribute to the percentile grid and the entire ideology of measurements in biomedicine. We should also notice several thousand punctures in a child's body and the fear of side effects. Perhaps most importantly, rGH obscures facts that different actors, for various reasons, do not want to reveal: that TS may be associated with infertility and problems with sex development, as well as with specific social and emotional difficulties, and also that 'normal' life is a relative concept that depends only to a small extent on centimetres. rGH is an ally of doctors who are unable to offer full assistance to patients and a helper of parents who are not prepared to recognize their child's right to know. rGH changes bodies and affects social interactions.

Notes

1 The research was funded by the Polish Ministry of Science and Higher Education/ National Program for the Development of Humanities (grant no.: 2bH 15 0137 83) and conducted by Magdalena Radkowska-Walkowicz (PI), Anna Krawczak, Ewa Maciejewska-Mroczek, Małgorzata Rajtar and Maria Reimann.

2 'Growth hormone therapy should be continued until a satisfactory height has been achieved, or until the bone age is above 14 years and the patient's height has increased less than 2 cm for last 12 months' (Kucharska 2012: 1643).

3 As rGH promotes muscle growth and fat loss, it is used by bodybuilders.

4 According to the medical paradigm, this probably would not have happened.

References

Ayyar, V. S. (2011), 'History of Growth Hormone Therapy', *Indian Journal of Endocrinology and Metabolism* 15 (3): 162–5.

Backeljauw, P., S. Kanumakala, S. Loche, K. O. Schwab, R. W. Pfäffle, C. Höybye, E. Lundberg, T. Battelino, B. Kriström, T. Giemza, and H. Zouater (2021), 'Safety and Effectiveness of Recombinant Human Growth Hormone in Children with Turner Syndrome: Data from the PATRO Children Study', *Hormone Research in Paediatrics* 94 (3–4): 133–43.

Blaxter, M. (2010), *Health*, Cambridge: Polity Press.

Edmonds, A. and E. Sanabria (2014), 'Medical Borderlands: Engineering the Body with Plastic Surgery and Hormonal Therapies in Brazil', *Anthropology & Medicine* 21 (2): 201–16.

Gawlik, A., A. Antosz, K. Wilk, and E. Małecka-Tendera (2013), 'Opieka medyczna w zespole Turnera – z praktycznego punktu widzenia', *Endokrynologia Pediatryczna* 12 (3[44]): 55–69.

Hogle, L. F. (2005), 'Enhancement Technologies and the Body', *Annual Review of Anthropology* 34 (1): 695–716.

Hong D., J. S. Kent, and S. Kesler (2009), 'Cognitive Profile of Turner Syndrome', *Developmental Disabilities Research Reviews* 15 (4): 270–8.

Krawczak, A. (2019a), 'Zespół Turnera. Macierzyństwo w planach', in E. Maciejewska-Mroczek, M. Radkowska-Walkowicz, and M. Reimann (eds), *Zespół Turnera. Głosy i doświadczenia*, 79–112, Warsaw: Oficyna Naukowa.

Krawczak, A. (2019b), 'Calineczki. O społecznych konstrukcjach zespołu Turnera', *Etnografia. Praktyki, Teorie, Doświadczenia* 5: 129–43.

Kucharska, A. (2012), 'Anthropometric Indices in Turner Syndrome', in V. R. Preedy (ed.), *Handbook of Anthropometry: Physical Measures of Human Form in Health and Disease*, 1635–47, New York: Springer.

Kucharska, A. (2019), 'Zespół Turnera. Aspekty medyczne', in E. Maciejewska-Mroczek, M. Radkowska-Walkowicz, and M. Reimann (eds), *Zespół Turnera. Głosy i doświadczenia*, 57–78, Warsaw: Oficyna Naukowa.

Lagrou, K. (2017), 'Psychological Aspects of Turner Syndrome', lecture at University of Warsaw, 9 October. Available at https://www.youtube.com/watch?v=QsGvHflqbQU.

Lagrou, K., C. Froidecoeur, F. Verlinde, M. Craen, J. De Schepper, I. François, and G. Massa (2003), 'Psychosocial Functioning, Self-Perception and Body Image and Their Auxologic Correlates in Growth Hormone and Oestrogen-Treated Young Adult Women with Turner Syndrome', *Hormone Research* 66 (6): 277–84.

Maciejewska-Mroczek, E. (2019), 'O (nie)pewności choroby. Narracje matek mających córki z Zespołem Turnera', in E. Maciejewska-Mroczek, M. Radkowska-Walkowicz, and M. Reimann (eds), *Zespół Turnera. Głosy i doświadczenia*, 141–70, Warsaw: Oficyna Naukowa.

Morrison, M. (2015), 'Growth Hormone, Enhancement and the Pharmaceuticalisation of Short Stature', *Social Science & Medicine* 131: 305–12.

Nissen N. and M. B. Risor (2018), *Diagnostic Fluidity. Working with Uncertainty and Mutability*, Tarragona: URV.

Radkowska-Walkowicz, M. (2019), 'The Hormone of Growth and Hope. The Case of the Turner Syndrome', *Ethnologia Polona* 40: 13–28.

Rajtar, M. (2019), 'Bioetyka i technologie wzmacniania ludzkiego ciała w kontekście doświadczeń kobiet z zespołem Turnera', in E. Maciejewska-Mroczek, M. Radkowska-Walkowicz, and M. Reimann (eds), *Zespół Turnera. Głosy i doświadczenia*, 171–97, Warsaw: Oficyna Naukowa.

Reimann, M. (2019), *Nie przywitam się z państwem na ulicy*, Wołowiec: Czarne.

Skuse, D. (2009), 'Psychological and Psychiatric Aspects of Turner Syndrome', in D. H. Gavholt (ed.), *Turner – Know Your Body! An Information Book on Turner Syndrome*, 200–17, Gothenburg: Novo Nordisk.

Sutton E., A. McInerney-Leo, C. A. Bondy, S. E. Gollust, D. King, and B. Biesecker, (2005), 'Turner Syndrome: Four Challenges Across the Lifespan', *American Journal of Medical Genetics* 139 (2): 57–66.

Świątkiewicz-Mośny, M. (2010), *Tożsamość napiętnowana. Socjologiczne stadium mechanizmów stygmatyzacji i autostygmatyzacji na przykładzie kobiet z zespołem Turnera*, Kraków: Nomos.

Tidblad, A. (2021), 'The History, Physiology and Treatment Safety of Growth Hormone', *Acta Paediatrica* 111 (2): 215–24.

11 HUMAN CHORIONIC GONADOTROPIN (hCG)

EMILY ROSS

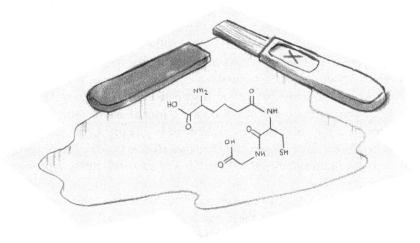

In 1973 the *Roe v. Wade* ruling established a constitutional right to abortion in the United States. In June 2022 this ruling was overturned by the US Supreme Court, a decision that has subsequently prohibited or restricted access to abortion across many states (Sidik 2022). Debates surrounding the termination of pregnancy are informed by sociocultural understandings of what a pregnancy is, when it begins and what it produces. The anticipated outcome of pregnancy, a healthy baby, is often centred in these discussions. In this entry, I consider the powerful contribution of accounts of the hormone human chorionic gonadotropin (hCG) to these widespread framings of pregnancy. I then turn to hCG in an alternative context, that of gestational trophoblastic disease (GTD). This rare condition entails abnormal changes in placental cells which require surgery and possible chemotherapy. Key to its management is regular hCG testing. Drawing on personal accounts of GTD I engage with varied meanings of hCG and consider reproductive outcomes other than a live birth. I show how the strong association between hCG and pregnancy shapes personal experiences of the condition. In centring this hormone my entry troubles foetal-centric understandings of pregnancy, which often underpin debates around reproductive rights.

hCG: The 'pregnancy hormone'

Like other contributions to this collection, my focus on hormones has been inspired by feminist theorizing on the biological. Scholarly engagement with the flows and energies of the physical body is of value to feminism's attempt to 'reconceive bodies outside of binary oppositions' (Grosz 1994: 164). Hormones in particular are pertinent sites for highlighting the entanglements of the biological and the social in bioscience. Commonly depicted as messengers of predetermined biological signals, scholars have shown that hormones do not simply express or produce biological phenomena but function within biosocial worlds that shape the ways they are represented and experienced (Roberts 2007). Scholarly attention to hormonal bodies has disrupted understandings of hormones as discrete entities with distinct effects, particularly with regard to sexual difference (Oudshoorn 1995). By considering hormones as flexible biosocial actors, their actions and functions have the potential to be understood in alternative ways, allowing for more liberating versions of biological phenomena (Roberts 2007). This entry argues that engaging meaningfully with hCG in this way can enable such perspectives on pregnancy.

As the biomarker detected by pregnancy tests within the home and the clinic, hCG is known colloquially as 'the pregnancy hormone'. According to biomedical texts hCG is first secreted by trophoblastic cells within the developing embryo in the first days of pregnancy. Trophoblastic cells form the outer layer of the early embryo, known as the trophoblast. Following implantation the trophoblast develops into a large part of the placenta, which continues to produce hCG throughout gestation (Makrigiannakis et al. 2017). The most widely cited function of hCG is the stimulation of progesterone to promote implantation and support the developing foetus (Whittaker et al. 2018; d'Hauterive et al. 2022). It has been described as 'driving' implantation and thus represented as 'critical' to establishing and sustaining a successful pregnancy (Cole 2012). More recently, studies have also reported its role in placental blood vessel formation, maternal immunotolerance of the foetus and foetal growth (Cole and Butler 2015). hCG performs important explanatory work in these scientific narratives of gestation. It is depicted as a product of the developing embryo, situated as vital to successful pregnancy and strongly associated with the development of a baby. In this entry I argue that these representations of hCG contribute to, but are also reflective of, understandings of pregnancy which privilege the foetal subject. Looking more closely at bioscientific accounts of hCG offers opportunities to interrogate these understandings. For example, dominant narratives of this hormone obscure the fact that a positive result for hCG does not signify the presence of a developing foetus but of trophoblastic (placental) tissue (Olszynko-Gryn 2014). The emphasis on its role in foetal development also detracts from the wider range of biological processes connected to hCG during this time, including to maternal immune and circulatory systems (Cole 2010). Finally, depictions of hCG as *the* pregnancy hormone obscure the wide variety of hormones involved in maintaining gestation. These are derived from maternal as well as foetal bodies and include oestrogen, progesterone and placental lactogen (hPL).

Despite these nuances, scientific narratives contribute to a strong conceptual link between the presence of hCG and a developing baby. This association endures beyond biomedicine. In the UK, widespread understandings of when someone is expecting a baby often rest on a home pregnancy test for hCG (Olszynko-Gryn 2017). This has consequences for those experiencing pregnancy. A positive result alone is sufficient to commence antenatal care and is often followed by announcements of a pregnancy to family and friends. It can prompt women to make changes to their diets and daily routines or to seek a termination. The significance of hCG to establishing a pregnancy can cause confusion or anguish, particularly in cases where hCG is detectable in reproductive events other than a healthy pregnancy. These include conceptions which initially produce hCG but which do not reach full term and experiences such as GTD, chemical pregnancies and anembryonic pregnancies, where a viable embryo does not develop (Layne 2009; Han 2014). Though it offers autonomy by allowing women to test for pregnancy privately in their own homes, feminist authors have also voiced concern that the technological assessment of this hormone has become privileged in confirming a pregnancy (Leavitt 2006). It is argued that the test has become valued over bodily signs of gestation, contributing to wider processes of the medicalization of reproduction (Jordan 1977). Much is therefore at stake in the assessment of pregnancy according to the presence of hCG, with implications for embodied experiences of pregnancy as well as the wider politics of reproduction.

I have shown that bioscientific and popular narratives of hCG shape and are shaped by understandings of pregnancy that centre the foetal subject. Scientific accounts of the hormone often foreground its role in facilitating foetal development, eliding the wider products and experiences entailed in gestation. In what follows I show how the conceptual entwinement of hCG and successful pregnancy shapes personal experiences of GTD. hCG plays an important role in diagnosing and monitoring this condition. I also show how GTD troubles dominant understandings of gestation, revealing ambiguities around what pregnancy entails and how it is defined.

Gestational trophoblastic disease and multiplicities of pregnancy

GTD encompasses several rare conditions that only arise following conception. Types of GTD include molar pregnancies whereby atypical placental cells develop alongside non-viable foetal tissue, and choriocarcinoma which is cancerous. The latter can develop many months after a live birth. GTD can be confused both clinically and experientially with a healthy pregnancy. In molar pregnancies conception occurs, but a fault in the number of maternal and/or paternal chromosomes results in the rapid replication of abnormal trophoblastic cells and no viable foetus. As hCG is secreted by the trophoblast, it is produced in high quantities and detectable on a home pregnancy test. This is despite the absence of a viable foetus or in some cases any foetal tissue at all. In addition, GTD may present symptoms that include bloating, bleeding and nausea. As such, those diagnosed may initially experience some forms of GTD as an uncomplicated pregnancy. This includes in terms of embodied experiences and anticipations for parenthood as well as biomedical procedures and antenatal appointments. They will later be told, sometimes at a routine ultrasound scan or due to persistent symptoms, that their pregnancy is not viable or may never have involved a foetal presence.

GTD therefore exposes ambiguity around definitions of pregnancy. Women's experiences, family practices and clinical work may be oriented towards a pregnancy and future baby in the absence of a foetal entity. This is in part because in biomedicalized settings, understandings of when one is pregnant are heavily tied to a positive pregnancy test. As we have seen, despite the fact that a positive result for hCG does not signify the presence of a developing foetus but of placental tissue, the conceptual entwinement of hCG with a future baby organizes practices across biomedical and wider public domains. This can have powerful effects on patient experiences and clinical practices of GTD.

To explore these experiences in more depth, I conducted a qualitative analysis of twenty online blogs written by women from the United States, the United Kingdom, Canada, Australia and Singapore experiencing molar pregnancy or choriocarcinoma (comprising posts made between January 2008 and March 2021). I carried out twelve semi-structured interviews – eight with blog authors and four with UK health professionals involved in molar pregnancy diagnosis and care (conducted between February 2021 and May 2022).[1] The patients included in this research had experienced a molar pregnancy, and two had experienced a choriocarcinoma several months after birth. Following diagnosis most patients had undergone surgery (dilation and curettage, a 'D&C') to remove the GTD tissues, and some required chemotherapy where this tissue persisted. For those with the more life-threatening choriocarcinoma, several rounds of chemotherapy were required. As the hormone produced by trophoblastic cells, the most important diagnostic marker for GTD is hCG, and all of the women in this research required regular monitoring to diagnose the condition and determine the success of treatment.

All but one patient had tested positively on a home pregnancy test prior to their diagnosis and initially experienced their condition as a healthy pregnancy. Blog posts and interviews conveyed a strong conceptual link between a positive result and a future child. As Fiona (pseudonyms are used) described in her interview:

> You get that pregnancy test that's positive and you're immediately like, awesome, we're going to have a baby. In nine months we're going to have this beautiful baby . . . so to us, we'd already started bonding with that baby.

Several women discussed marking their anticipated due date in their calendars following their pregnancy test. Gail described thinking even further into the future, imagining her 'entire life adapting to that positive'. Diana described in her blog that the mere presence of hCG as signalled by a positive result led her to imagine 'first teeth, first words, first steps'. These experiences accord with what Franklin (1991) describes as a 'teleological' account of gestation, dominant in biomedical and popular accounts. Emphasis is placed on what the foetus will become as a result of biologically determined development, with the outcome of a live birth foregrounded. This focus on a future baby overshadows wider processes and products that occur across gestation, including changes to maternal immune and circulatory systems and the formation of the placenta. Accounts that privilege the foetal subject are most often associated with its emergence through biomedical practices such as obstetric ultrasound (Taylor 1998), but these women's experiences demonstrate the symbolic power of hCG in such articulations of foetal development.

Following a positive test, many participants began to share their news with family and friends and prepare for a future baby. However, for the women in this research, symptoms or a routine ultrasound scan led to initial investigations for GTD and the identification of atypical trophoblastic tissue alongside, or in place of, foetal tissue. In many cases this tissue required surgical removal due to the risk of it becoming cancerous. The premature ending of what had initially been experienced as a healthy pregnancy was described by some women in their online blogs as a miscarriage. These online accounts detailed grief and loss as well as efforts to memorialize their pregnancy. They also described hopes for a 'rainbow baby', a term used by support groups and charities to describe a healthy baby born to parents following miscarriage, stillbirth or neonatal death (Tommy's, n.d.).

These experiences again trouble widespread sociocultural understandings of gestation, which associate pregnancy with a developing baby. Some GTD patients described very real experiences of (baby) loss, palpable even without evidence of a foetal presence. Attempting to make sense of this, one blogger distinguished baby loss from the loss of a pregnancy, describing that though she had not carried a baby 'it was still a pregnancy' and 'still a loss'. Their experiences also departed from what was described by patients as a 'regular' or 'normal' miscarriage because women diagnosed with GTD subsequently undergo hCG monitoring for a prolonged period. The ongoing presence of hCG and its regular, sometimes weekly, quantification extended their experiences of the condition. The author of one blog described that the 'happy surprise' of her pregnancy had become a 'miscarriage that wouldn't end'.

In the UK, hCG monitoring takes the form of urine and blood tests every two weeks, with these sent to one of three specialist centres via post. As staff at one centre explained, an hCG level of 5 IU/L or above is considered positive for a pregnancy. In patients with GTD, hCG levels can reach hundreds of thousands IU/L. Regular monitoring is performed to ensure that their hCG levels fall to below 5 IU/L. A rise or plateau indicates the continued presence of GTD tissue and chemotherapy may be required. Follow-up hCG testing is six months for those whose hCG normalizes after surgery, but those requiring chemotherapy are monitored for longer (Royal College of Obstetricians and Gynaecologists 2021). Annie described her experience of hCG monitoring as an exhausting 'hamster wheel'. Weekly hCG testing after chemotherapy caused anxiety when she received the urine sample kit through her letterbox and again while she waited nervously for results. In her interview Annie discussed how the strong association between hCG and successful pregnancy shaped her experiences. Despite a clinical diagnosis of GTD, for Annie the presence of hCG signalled a continuing pregnancy:

> I think because my body hadn't rejected the pregnancy, my hCG level was still elevated, was still climbing, and I'd had no bleeding, no pain, no nothing like that. I think in my head, I was like, well, it kind of isn't a miscarriage then. I haven't miscarried this pregnancy.

Joan discussed similar feelings of ambiguity:

> I know obviously I wasn't pregnant, I had a D&C, but that hormone was still there. So it was like this weird limbo where . . . you're not pregnant but your body thinks it is and you're trying to get to, like, where your body thinks it's not pregnant.

The ongoing presence of hCG following surgery troubled widespread understandings of what it means to be pregnant. To be pregnant did not necessitate a foetal presence for several of these participants. Instead, ongoing testing for hCG made pregnancy a continued corporeal reality:

> [My doctor] said things like . . . 'even though the pregnancy is no longer technically going on, the placental growth is continuing'. And her explaining, you know, like, you're still producing those hormones . . . at least was a little bit of a comfort to know . . . well, 'why do I still feel pregnant if I'm not?'

Her doctor conveyed that Gail was no longer pregnant despite continued placental growth and production of pregnancy hormones. In this case, pregnancy was clinically defined in terms of a foetal presence. This caused confusion for Gail who continued to *feel* pregnant following diagnosis and a D&C. She took comfort from the explanation that high levels of hCG were the reason for this, showing that the strong association between hCG and pregnancy could also provide reassurance at this time.

The ongoing presence of hCG not only impacted embodiment for these women but also had implications for emotional well-being. Experiences recorded in online blogs suggested that patients could become fixated on their hCG levels and the urgent need for these to fall. The fact that these were so frequently reported and regularly recorded in personal notes or online blogs meant that these readings were particularly powerful. Anticipation for their levels to drop was not only tied to women's hopes to avoid further treatment but also because they had been encouraged to delay trying to conceive again until they had completed their follow-up monitoring. This was to ensure that hCG produced during a subsequent pregnancy would not mask rising hCG levels caused by the regrowth of GTD tissues. These multiple meanings of hCG posed challenges for clinical management – specialists I interviewed acknowledged that patients often continued to try for a pregnancy before monitoring had ceased. One specialist explained that this was part of moving on from their loss or could relate to concerns about fertility and the passing of reproductive time.

These accounts have demonstrated that multiple actors entangle to produce the chemical entity we know as hCG. Pregnancy tests, bioscientific accounts, sociocultural narratives of successful gestation and embodiment entwine to render hCG as the 'pregnancy hormone', with its detection shaping medical practices and social relationships. On receiving a positive test for hCG, these research participants with wanted pregnancies reaffirmed dominant narratives of pregnancy as centring on foetal development. Carole described how she had initially viewed hCG as a 'good thing' signalling a future baby. However, engaging with hCG in an alternative context, that of disease, could also trouble these narratives; it became an 'evil thing' that Carole 'never wanted to see again'. A focus on hCG has caused us to question what a pregnancy *is*. Some participants identified themselves as having been pregnant despite the absence of a foetal entity, with these accounts emphasizing instead the role of embodied experience, hormones and placental growth. Taking this view of pregnancy, as a multiplicity of bodily and social processes, steers us away from a foetal-centric understanding. This can be useful to feminist efforts to recentre women's bodies in discussions of reproductive rights. It is also a scholarly project, contributing to work that engages with scientific knowledge to think differently about biologies, bodies and worlds (Roberts 2007).

Conclusion

A social scientific focus on hormones can demonstrate their effects beyond the biophysical, and this entry has highlighted the implications of engagement with hCG for the politics of reproduction. I have discussed the social significance of hCG and the symbolic work it performs in personal as well as bioscientific accounts. hCG can be considered an important material-semiotic actor and exemplar of how the social and the biological entwine in representations of pregnancy and pregnant bodies (Roberts 2007). As the primary diagnostic marker for pregnancy, and due in part to enduring teleological framings of foetal development, the very presence of hCG can be conceptually equated with a future baby. This can begin in the home, as those with wanted pregnancies imagine their future lives as parents following a home pregnancy test. The hormone also plays an important role in organizing clinical practice.

We have observed that the strong association between hCG and successful pregnancy shapes experiences of GTD. Its detection inspires imaginings of a future baby and experiences of confusion and loss at diagnosis. However, this condition simultaneously uncouples the presence of hCG from successful pregnancy. It disrupts linear framings of gestation which focus on the expected end point of pregnancy and have implications for antenatal care (Oaks 2001) and reproductive rights (Petchesky 1987). Instead, accounts of GTD point to the contingency of successful pregnancy following conception and highlight the multiple actors, technologies and relationships that lead to the establishment of a positive result as a pregnancy, even without the possibility of a live birth. Importantly, a focus on hCG has foregrounded the processes and products of pregnancy overlooked in foetal-centric versions of gestation, including the placenta. Highlighting the variety of entities generated by pregnancy, many of which are shared by gestating and foetal bodies, can allow for more 'generous' approaches to reproduction (Hird 2007). These acknowledge the inseparability of maternal and foetal entities, destabilizing accounts of reproduction which position them as in conflict (Martin 2010). Consideration of pregnancy beyond the foetal subject also prompts us to make room for a wide array of reproductive outcomes and to acknowledge and value the emotional and embodied work entailed in all forms of gestation, including those that end in loss (DiCaglio 2018). Further insight is required into how contemporary debates surrounding the termination of pregnancy, which often focus on the 'unborn', account for this diversity of reproductive experiences.

Engaging with hCG is thus a political project. Bioscientific articulations of this hormone represent it as 'driving' implantation and foetal growth. These echo wider sociocultural narratives of gestation which privilege foetal development, concealing the social relationships and corporeal labour sustaining pregnancy. Highlighting practices and experiences of hCG in the absence of foetal development instead foregrounds gestating bodies in the plural, maternal, foetal and placental and the flows of substance and meaning between them. This provokes openness in thinking about who or what takes responsibility for the outcome of pregnancy (Yoshizawa 2016) and about whose rights can be privileged. These questions are especially important today, in the midst of national efforts to privilege foetal bodies in ways that limit reproductive freedoms.

Note

1 Ethical approval for this research was granted by an NHS committee (21/WM/0018) and University of Sheffield departmental ethics review (037518).

References

Cole, L. A. (2010), 'Biological Functions of hCG and hCG-related Molecules', *Reproductive Biology and Endocrinology* 8 (1): 102.
Cole, L. A. (2012), 'hCG, the Wonder of Today's Science', *Reproductive Biology and Endocrinology* 10 (1): 24.
Cole, L. A. and S. A. Butler (2015), *Human Chorionic Gonadotropin (hCG)*, Amsterdam: Elsevier.
D'hauterive, S. P., R. Close, V. Gridelet, M. Mawet, M. Nisolle, and V. Geenen (2022), 'Human Chorionic Gonadotropin and Early Embryogenesis: Review', *International Journal of Molecular Sciences* 23 (3): 1380.
DiCaglio, S. (2018), 'Placental Beginnings: Reconfiguring Placental Development and Pregnancy Loss in Feminist Theory', *Feminist Theory* 20 (3): 283–98.
Grosz, E. A. (1994), *Volatile Bodies: Toward a Corporeal Feminism*, Bloomington: Indiana University Press.
Han, S. (2014), 'The Chemical Pregnancy: Technology, Mothering, and the Making of a Reproductive Experience', *Journal of the Motherhood Initiative for Research and Community Involvement* 5 (2): 42–53.
Franklin, S. (1991), 'Fetal Fascinations: New Medical Constructions of Fetal Personhood', in S. Franklin, C. Lury and J. Stacey (eds), *Off-Centre: Feminism and Cultural Studies*, 190–205, London: Routledge.
Hird, M. J. (2007), 'The Corporeal Generosity of Maternity', *Body & Society* 13 (1): 1–20.
Jordan, B. (1977), 'Part One: The Self-Diagnosis of Early Pregnancy: An Investigation of Lay Competence', *Medical Anthropology: Cross-cultural Studies in Health and Illness* 1 (2): 1–38.
Layne, L. L. (2009), 'The Home Pregnancy Test: A Feminist Technology?', *Women's Studies Quarterly* 37 (1/2): 61–79.
Leavitt, S. (2006), '"A Private Little Revolution": The Home Pregnancy Test in American Culture', *Bulletin of the History of Medicine* 80 (2): 317–45.
Makrigiannakis, A., T. Vrekoussis, E. Zoumakis, S. N. Kalantaridou, and U. Jeschke (2017), 'The Role of HCG in Implantation: A Mini-Review of Molecular and Clinical Evidence', *International Journal of Molecular Sciences*, 18 (6): 1305.
Martin, A. (2010), 'Microchimerism in the Mother(land): Blurring the Borders of Body and Nation', *Body & Society* 16 (3): 23–50.
Oaks, L. (2001), *Smoking and Pregnancy: The Politics of Fetal Protection*, New Brunswick: Rutgers University Press.
Olzynko-Gryn, J. (2014), 'The Demand for Pregnancy Testing: The Aschheim–Zondek Reaction, Diagnostic Versatility, and Laboratory Services in 1930s Britain', *Studies in*

History and Philosophy of Science Part C: Studies in History and Philosophy of Biological and Biomedical Sciences 47 (Part B): 233–47.

Olzynko-Gryn, J. (2017), 'Thin Blue Lines: Product Placement and the Drama of Pregnancy Testing in British Cinema and Television', *The British Journal for the History of Science* 50 (3): 495–520.

Oudshoorn, N. (1995), *Beyond the Natural Body: An Archeology of Sex Hormones*, London: Routledge.

Petchesky, R. P. (1987), 'Fetal Images: The Power of Visual Culture in the Politics of Reproduction', *Feminist Studies* 13 (2): 263–92.

Roberts, C. (2007), *Messengers of Sex : Hormones, Biomedicine, and Feminism*, Cambridge: Cambridge University Press.

Royal College of Obstetricians and Gynaecologists (2021), 'Management of Gestational Trophoblastic Disease', *BJOG: An International Journal of Obstetrics & Gynaecology* 128 (3): e1–e27.

Sidik, S. M. (2022), 'The Effects of Overturning Roe v. Wade in Seven Simple Charts', *Nature* 608 (7922): 254–7. https://doi.org/10.1038/d41586-022-02139-3.

Taylor, J. S. (1998), 'Image of Contradiction: Obstetrical Ultrasound in American Culture', in S. Franklin and H. Ragoné (eds), *Reproducing Reproduction: Kinship, Power and Technological Innovation*, 15–45, Philadelphia: University of Pennsylvania Press.

Tommy's (n.d.), *Rainbow Baby Information and Support*. Available at https://www.tommys.org/baby-loss-support/rainbow-baby (accessed 28 September 2022).

Whittaker, P. G., C. A. Schreiber, and M. D. Sammel (2018), 'Gestational Hormone Trajectories and Early Pregnancy Failure: A Reassessment', *Reproductive Biology and Endocrinology* 16 (1): 95.

Yoshizawa, R. S. (2016), 'Fetal–Maternal Intra-action: Politics of New Placental Biologies', *Body & Society* 22 (4): 79–105.

12 HYDROCORTISONE

IAN HARPER

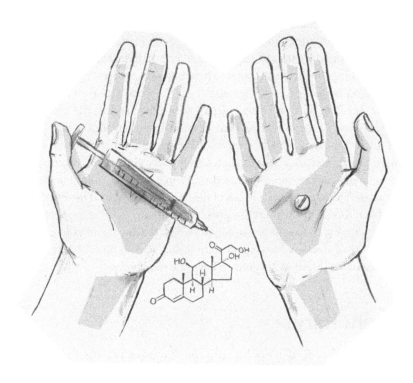

In late May 2019 I suffered a pituitary apoplexy, the medical name for a bleed into the pituitary gland located at the base of the brain. This entry takes the form of a 'neurography', a short story 'rooted in personal experience and neurological fact' (Sacks 2012: x–xi). As Sacks suggests, it is when the body breaks down that such 'pathographies' have the capacity to reveal to us aspects of body and mind that are usually hidden (Sacks 2012: 202). Presented in diary format from notes written at the time, and immediately afterwards, I recall this event to recount how medicine categorizes, atomizes and fragments. It is also a narrative of the replacement of cortisol with its synthetic derivative hydrocortisone.

29 May – 11 June (admitted 3 to 11 June)

Apoplexy

It starts with a sense of the world feeling out of sorts. Everything is just a little too bright, with a feeling of slight increased pressure above the eyes. I am unable to concentrate. I try to put the final edits to an academic paper but the meaning of what I have written evades me. All I feel like doing is lying down. And then a chronological ordering to events all become somewhat vague, as the following hours, nights and days start to telescope into each other. Over the next few days cognitively things begin to shut down. My vision is blurry. At some point I start to vomit, and it does not ease up. The headache is the worst I have ever had.

In the Accident and Emergency department triage reveals the sodium levels in my blood are dangerously low. I am given an injection, and a drip is put up – later I learn this contains hydrocortisone. Through my exhaustion and delirium, the ward I am placed on seems to stretch a long way along a central corridor and there are many patients receding into the distance. At some point I am sent for a computerized tomography (CT) scan of the brain, but I have no memory of this. I am told that this seems to point to a possible bleed into my pituitary gland. But in the fog of slipping conscious levels, cognitive diminishment and exhaustion there is just a blur of doctors, nurses and technicians, having blood taken and drips being tinkered with. An MRI confirms a pituitary apoplexy.

The pituitary

The pituitary is described in much medical literature as a 'pea-sized' gland. It sits at the base of the brain attached by a small stalk to an area called the hypothalamus. If asked to point to it I would tap my forehead between the eyes. The pituitary produces, stores and releases a range of hormones that in turn moderate other hormonal systems in the body. The gland is divided anatomically into two, an anterior and posterior. The posterior section releases the following hormones: adrenocorticotrophic hormone (ACTH); luteinizing hormone (LH) and follicle-stimulating hormone (FSH); thyroid-stimulating hormone (TSH); growth hormone-releasing hormone (GHRH); and prolactin. Each is involved in sets of so-called 'axes' effecting other organs in the body that in turn release hormones (the thyroid, the testes and ovaries, the adrenal gland on top of the kidneys). The anterior pituitary in its turn secretes vasopressin and oxytocin.

The biomedical literature tells us that the gland mediates between the brain, the nervous system and the body. It is responsible for overseeing the development and maintenance of aspects of the body's sexual characteristics, reproductive functions, growth, homeostatic mechanisms and responses to stress, internal and external. It is often granted the grandiose title of 'the master gland' or the 'leader' or 'conductor of the endocrine orchestra'. In the hierarchy of functions of current biomedical understanding of brain–body interactions, the role of the pituitary within this seems to occupy one of the more senior positions.

At stake immediately for the compromised functioning of my gland is the principle and maintenance of homeostasis, whose definition is 'a relatively stable state of equilibrium or a tendency toward such a state between the different but interdependent elements or groups of elements of an organism, population, or group' (Merriam-Webster Dictionary, n.d.). I am just about to get a practical, experiential crash course in what this means.

The fragmented body

What is unfolding in the hospital is the immediate medical and surgical consequences of a bleed into the small space where the pituitary gland is contained. There are three pressing, interrelated issues. First, because of where it is situated anatomically, particularly close to the optic nerve, it can cause acute-onset blindness from direct pressure on the nerve. This can necessitate surgical intervention. Second, because the cause of the bleed is often a tumour, or an autoimmune problem, the reasons for the bleed need to be determined and, if possible, dealt with quickly. Third, because of hormonal imbalances there can be severe unstable homeostatic complications manifesting as fluid retention problems, particularly combined with low sodium levels in the blood. Managing all three components constitutes acute medical and surgical emergencies. This understanding comes later. I am too exhausted to think and feel much of my early hospital stay as a kind of fluctuating awareness. I have this sense of a shutting down, as if my consciousness is closing in on itself.

An MRI scan makes the pituitary visible and allows for a concrete diagnosis. It means that I come under the shared care of the neurosurgeons and the endocrinologists. Immediately there is the need for access into my body. In ICU a central line is inserted. This is a catheter that is threaded through a vein in the neck to sit above the heart and allows access to the blood system for giving fluids and administering drugs. Hooked up to monitors that record my heart rate and the oxygen saturation of my blood, the process of refining the body into its anatomical and physiological state begins.

I am constantly asked about my vision. Nurses regularly check my peripheral fields as part of a general neurological check. I am having difficulty focusing on anything. But objective proof of pressure on the optic nerve is also required. I am referred to an optometrist, who produces a chart that plots my fields of vision in a circular line around a central point and against the normal distribution of visual fields. This map acts as a bridge of communication across the domain of my subjective experience – inherently untrustworthy – and the doctors' need for objective indicators and verifiable data.

Combined with this focus on vision is also a concern with conscious levels: What is your name? What is your date of birth? Where are you? What date is it today? Vision, then, and consciousness level are the two variables around which the surgeons hover, and with them the possibility of trans-sphenoidal catheters and interventions. I feel at times that they talk about my pituitary as if I weren't there in biographical and experiential form, just the embodiment of internal anatomy, pathology and exteriorized signs.

Hormonal disequilibrium

The second emergency issue is dealing with the dangerously low sodium levels in the blood and the fluid imbalances from the hormonal disequilibrium. This is the domain of the endocrinologists. Initially, my blood sodium levels are measured every few hours, combined with the close monitoring of my fluid input (drips and drink) and outputs (urine). At one point it is suggested I be catheterized to make this process of transmogrification into volumes and figures easier. This request I refuse, in part because of its sheer indignity.

I have the overwhelming sense of becoming just a series of physiological variables and numbers. What goes in and what comes out of this physical body and their precise measurements are what are enacted in this raw exercise of biomedical power. The balance of fluids, the maintaining of this and the restoring of the electrolyte composition of the blood to a normal range that make up the normative biomedical understanding of homeostatic ranges is the primary focus for the endocrinologists. The 'I', the self, the person, that unique biographical, emotional and feeling person retreats to the background of this biological entity. I have an almost hallucinogenic image of the on-call consultant sitting next to a bank of computers twiddling and adjusting banks of numbers.

And yet I play along with this objectification, this capacity to create us as a series of biological fragments, and to separate and detach these from the person, to transform us into biological, anatomical and physiological variables. I ask if I might measure my own fluid intake, to help, to give me a small sense of purpose and control, a sense of agency.

While the surgeons hover around my vision, the physicians scrutinize the serum sodium levels, concerned with low levels of serum sodium (or hyponatraemia): 'When severe hyponatraemia evolves over a period of hours, seizures, coma, permanent brain damage, respiratory arrest, brain-stem herniation and death may occur' (Biswas and Davies 2007: 375–6). When I am first admitted my sodium levels are way below the normal range: 'The lowest we have ever seen without severe neurological sequelae', says one of the many endocrinology doctors passing through the room in the early days of my admission. When I ask what this might mean in the future, I am told that there have not been any studies of the long-term impact of such a low sodium level on later cognitive functioning.

In the first few days my cognitive state is not up to following any reasoning that I may have been given as to my treatment. The biomedical terms are densely resistant to anything but advanced biomedical and endocrinological understanding. I am led into the labyrinthine pathways linking hormones and fluid balance and imploded into the body's fluid cellular flows and mechanisms that I can at best only partially understand.

I try to stay in touch with the logic of what is being enacted in my body. I learn that to raise the sodium too fast risks an osmotic imbalance between the brain and the blood serum, something that must be avoided. At one point in the night early in my stay, the nurse in charge gives me the protocols for managing hyponatraemia used in the hospital. With my difficulty reading, focusing and concentrating, I cannot make much sense of them. These are dominated by protocols for action: threshold points at which decisions needed to be made for speeding drips up, slowing them down, adding fluids with more or less sodium, administering drugs. The body becomes defined as a series of measurements linked to osmolality (the concentration of ions in fluid spaces) and the implications of this for fluid transfer across cell membranes and across differing bodily cavities, particularly across and into the brain.

Hydrocortisone

I get lost in potential causal pathways. But looming large among these is the impact of the lack of production of the hormones cortisol and vasopressin. For cortisol, the synthetic hormone hydrocortisone is used as a replacement. I am given an IV infusion for several days.

This makes me quite high. My body seems to crackle, as if all my nerve endings are frayed and coming alive. When I close my eyes, I can see lights – brilliant blue and red speckling, like a mass of dancing floaters – jiggling behind the eyelids, located somewhere back in my head. I quite enjoy sinking into the warmth of these lights and their hazing in and out. I can let these drift into a formation and then move in an imaginative journey around the internalized and medicalized landscape of my body. I imagine I am tracking the various axes around which hormones meander, in a kind of three-dimensional holographic image.

Vivid dreams and nightmares leave their traces. In one set of dreams I am paralysed and unable to move or walk – classically and widely described as sleep paralysis – and I feel that the bleed is somehow destroying some deeper autonomic processes in my being. A sense of impending doom lingers through the days and nights and throughout my admission. When I mention the vivid dreams to one of the doctors, they put it down to the high doses of hydrocortisone (rather than the trauma that I might have been going through). Saturated with dreams that mingle with my waking realities, I am left with a surreal memory of events and time in the hospital.

During my admission my sodium levels return to normal. My fluid balance and urine output are moderated with desmopressin, the synthetic form of vasopressin, and with the hydrocortisone. My blurred vision dissipates. The surgeons recede into the background, and the endocrinologists come to the fore. And I recover enough to be allowed home.

Monday 17 June

Leaving the hospital, I feel overwhelmed, vulnerable and let down by a body that has so spectacularly malfunctioned. The first thing I notice is how much the world has folded in onto itself and into my body. Outside there is too much space, and it feels too open and expansive. I feel intensely agoraphobic, with waves of panic sweeping over me. I am shocked to realize how small, introverted and retreated I have become, and in such a short period of time. Will I relearn to live again, to become, to open out, in this body so seemingly reduced and reconfigured?

Tuesday 18 June

I am exhausted much of the day. The replacement hydrocortisone tablet I take in the morning seems to kick-start my being awake. It is a form of chemical reanimation.

I read up on this synthetic compound in the sleepless nights. Hydrocortisone was discovered in the 1930s by the American Edward C. Kendell and was called, initially, Compound F. He and co-workers received the Nobel Prize for their research efforts in 1950. His initial work was involved in trying to isolate thyroxine, but he shifted to study the adrenal glands. It was the advent of the Second World War that galvanized attempts to synthesize adrenal steroids after rumours circulated that the Germans were buying and utilizing beef adrenal extract to try to prevent hypoxia in pilots (How often in the history of medicine we see war as the key trigger for medical and surgical advances!). After the war it was just the Mayo Clinic and Merck left exploring this avenue, and scaled synthesis of cortisone was achieved in 1948. It showed anti-inflammatory effects and dramatic impact on a rheumatoid arthritis sufferer (Simoni, Hill and Vaughan 2002). While the negative side effects of the drug in high dosages were soon noticed, it has remained in use for multiple conditions (NHS 2020).

Hydrocortisone is classified as a glucocorticosteroid, a steroid hormone that has metabolic and anti-inflammatory action. It is used as a replacement therapy for the natural hormone cortisol (NHS 2020). The release of cortisol revolves around an 'axis', consisting of the hypothalamus, the pituitary and the adrenal gland (the HPA axis). This axis involves the production of the adrenocorticotrophic hormone (ACTH) in the anterior pituitary that stimulates the production of cortisol from the adrenal glands. It is integrally related to the autonomic nervous system, which is subdivided into the sympathetic system (that prepares us for the classically described 'fight-or-flight' response of the body when threatened) and the parasympathetic, which has the opposite effect and relaxes us (O'Sullivan 2016: 194–7; Roberts, this volume).

The apoplexy compromised the ability of my pituitary to produce ACTH. The 'synacthen' test to determine the extent this affects the production of cortisol involved the injection of this compound into my buttock and then measuring the cortisol levels. I fail to produce enough and am recommended to continue with the hydrocortisone indefinitely.

Wednesday 19 June

I am back in hospital for the day for a 'water deprivation test', to assess my ability to concentrate my urine (as a proxy indicator for the production of the hormone vasopressin). I am now designated 'hydrocortisone dependent'. A doctor explains that the diurnal rhythms of cortisol mean that the hormone is at its highest concentrations in the morning, and it is then that I will potentially feel at my worst. They explain that there is considerable individual variation in diurnal and nocturnal production, but the treatment protocols are all developed from population studies. I will have to adapt my dosages as necessary and learn to up doses when my body is stressed.

The staff nurse tells me a story of a hydrocortisone-dependent woman who, following an accident, had an 'adrenal crisis'. She was not given her life-saving injection of hydrocortisone and died on the way to hospital. She showed me how to self-inject should it be necessary. She gives me a copy of the Pituitary Foundation's Hydrocortisone Advice for the Pituitary Patient booklet.

The booklet asks, 'When do I know that I would need an emergency injection?' You must act fast, it tells me, and within three hours in an emergency. It is strongly recommended, then, that we always keep an ampule of injectable hydrocortisone on our person. It still seems unreal that I have shifted to such absolute pharmaceutical dependence in such a short space of time. I find the future hard to imagine. Illness does that – erases certain futures yet opens up others. I am grateful to be alive and grateful to medicine's edifice for keeping me thus.

26 June

I swallow my first hydrocortisone of the day at around 6.30 am. Over the next fifteen minutes I feel the steroid starting to work: it begins with a visceral animation of the muscles of my arms and legs, like an enervation or enlivening. There is an intensification of awareness, and a sharpening of consciousness, like a lifting of a fog across my mind. My memory for words, names, people improves, and those moments where I struggle to recall the names of things fall away somewhat. My mood improves.

28 June

A month has passed since the apoplexy. I push myself to get outside and take short but lengthening walks. I sit on a low wall on the high street. I am suddenly on the verge of being overwhelmed by the business of it all. I can see how disadvantaged some groups are in this hustling space: several women with young babies, a disabled woman with a walking frame, seemingly brushed aside by the assured physical arrogance of the groups of young men, other shoppers and the privileged surety of the well.

'Room, space, expansion. Freedom – an ever-expanding physiology and world, an ever-expanding personal (and social) space – this, it came to me, with extreme clarity, this was the essence of getting better', writes Sacks upon recovering from his broken leg and associated loss of proprioception (Sacks 2012: 128). He had to learn to live whole again in the world he inhabited. His writing is bursting with insight on my post-apoplexy world: 'I found myself frightened . . . The sheer complexity and bustle of the world outside was terrifying . . . It was a tremendous relief, a liberation, to be no longer "in", but none of us, we realised, were ready to go "out"' (Sacks 2012: 138). My apoplectic afterlife is marinated in Sack's phenomenological meditations.

2 July

I walk slowly to the hospital in the morning for a repeat magnetic resonance imaging (MRI) scan. This ritual of the visualization of the inside of my skull, this making into a fixed object for medical scrutiny is the opposite of the continual sense of life's flow and metamorphosis. The need to create a fixed moment in this flow of life – a diagnostic moment, out of time and socialized space – seems the essence of advanced technologized medicine. The surgeons booked me in for this, as they want to rule out the possibility of a tumour: the blood from the bleed needs time to be reabsorbed before they will be able to develop a clearer picture. While too early still to tell from this one, subsequent scans reveal no growth.

Into November

As summer transforms to autumn, my capacity to reengage with the world increases. Yet, despite tentative attempts to expand outwards, my being in the world is still dragged back into my body, biomedically defined and delineated, made manifest through its 'dys-appearance' (Leder 1990: 66–99). Repeat MRI scans; blood tests and clinic visits; three visits to hospital with lowered sodium levels, where at each a high dose of hydrocortisone was administered via a drip. But these tail off over the coming months.

I have a follow-up appointment with the endocrine team. It is a lovely day, bright and cold, and I feel well as I walk to the hospital. I am prepared with my questions: some about fluid balance; the question of occupational health and getting back to work; a fuller explanation of the results of the tests; what is the relationship between vasopressin and oxytocin, seeing as both are produced by the posterior pituitary? Historically, as oxytocin has been categorized as a reproductive hormone (in relation to childbirth) (see Ford, this volume), this hormone's effects in men are less well known.

During the consultation I realize that there are plenty of 'partials' at work. I produce some vasopressin and some cortisol as well. I live the uncertainties of a body that talks back, that won't be entirely categorized down, that regenerates. My assumption that the impact of the apoplexy would result in permanent and irreversible destruction of pituitary tissue has not materialized.

We create narratives of our lives. An acute illness episode like this ruptures our sense of self, of time, and shifts where the future – or possible futures – may lie. Time has become reoriented in multiple ways. As I move to chronicity, a lot of the management of the conditions I have is becoming second nature and receding from moment-by-moment conscious awareness, freeing up energies that are better directed elsewhere. I have come to understand the all-consuming nature of a life being imaginatively narrowed down and disappearing into the hormonal atomization of the body.

Afterword

Since first writing this entry I have been taken off all my hormonal replacements. One future that I anticipated, that of pharmaceutical dependence on hormonal replacements for the remainder of my life, did not materialize as expected. My last synacthen test was returned normal, and I no longer require desmopressin to concentrate my urine. My hyperawareness of hidden homeostatic mechanisms through the experience of hormonal loss is returning to its subconscious state. This post-apoplexy recovery of the pituitary, so my consultant tells me, is 'not unheard of' though uncommon. While I shall hang onto my hydrocortisone tablets and injection as a psychological crutch for the time being, these are no longer biomedically required.

Acknowledgements

I am immensely grateful to all the medical personnel – doctors, nurses and auxiliary staff – who cared for me during my illness and follow-up. My family and friends, while invisible in this narrative, were of course central to my care and recovery. Thanks are also due to the participants of the workshop where I first presented this and to Andrea Ford and Celia Roberts for their feedback and encouragement to write in such a personal style.

References

Biswas, M. and J. S. Davies (2007), 'Hyponatraemia in Clinical Practice', *Postgraduate Medical Journal* 83 (980): 373–8.

Leder, D. (1990), *The Absent Body*, Chicago and London: The University of Chicago Press.

Merriam-Webster Dictionary (n.d.), 'Homeostasis', Available at https://www.merriam -webster.com/dictionary/homeostasis (accessed 5 May 2022).

NHS (2020), 'Hydrocortisone Tablets', Available at https://www.nhs.uk/medicines/ hydrocortisone-tablets/ (accessed 10 February 2023).

O'Sullivan, S. (2016), *It's All in Your Head: Stories from the Frontline of Psychosomatic Illness*, London: Vintage.

Sacks, O. (2012), *A Leg to Stand on*, London: Picador.

Simoni, R., R. Hill, and M. Vaughan (2002), 'The Isolation of Thyroxine and Cortisone: The Work of Edward C. Kendall', *The Journal of Biomedical Chemistry* 277 (21): e10.

13 MIFEPRISTONE AND MISOPROSTOL

LEAH EADES

When it comes to the 'rebellious cascades' of hormones, no volume would be complete without an entry on mifepristone and misoprostol, the so-called 'abortion pills' used to induce medication abortion. While mifepristone and misoprostol are not hormones themselves, they nonetheless trigger hormonal cascades whose effects – biochemical, sociocultural and political – can be seen both in the individual body and that of the body politic. For scholars concerned with the ways in which hormones become vehicles for scientific, ethical and political concerns, the contested arena of abortion politics and provision provides a particularly potent case study, serving as 'a sharply focused lens onto broader theoretical debates around gender and personhood, the legitimacy of scientific knowledge, neoliberalism, women's roles and rights in a liberal democracy, church-state relations, and social justice movements, among others' (Andaya and Mishtal 2017: 41).

As the other entries in this volume demonstrate, hormones are best considered not as chemical objects but as material-semiotic entities where different types of knowledges, practices and cultural imaginaries converge. In this entry, I take up the notion of cascading to trace not only the 'social lives' (Whyte, van der Geest and Hardon 2002) of mifepristone and misoprostol, as they move through the world, but also the flows set in motion by their hormonal effects and the work of the actors who seek to facilitate or inhibit these flows. In biochemical terms, a cascade effect refers to the process whereby even a very small amount of a hormone can set off a series of reactions in which the magnitude of the effect is amplified at each step (Cammack et al. 2006). In this entry, I conceptualize this cascade effect in sociocultural and political terms – as ripple effects that unfold in messy and often unforeseen ways, acquiring diverse meanings and potencies as they pass through biological and social spaces. In so doing, my goals are twofold. On the one hand, to chart how the hormonal effects of mifepristone and misoprostol come to complicate and rebel against dominant modes of knowledge production, clinical hierarchies and reproductive governance. On the other, to demonstrate how sociocultural and historical factors co-create these hormonal cascades, shaping the moral regimes and material, clinical and legal conditions through which abortion pills are accessed and experienced.

To show how the hormonal cascades set in motion by abortion pills disrupt far more than just a pregnancy, I will follow these cascades as they travel. In the first half, I follow them as they move from paper and into practice, examining how the pills' abortifacient effects are actualized and inhibited by national and supranational structures and informed by biopolitical concerns and moral regimes. In the second half, I follow abortion pills' cascades as they reverberate out into the wider world, exploring how they become terrains for reproductive governance and resistance in ways that are reshaping the political geographies of access and the political economies of expertise and authority. I conclude by making a case for further anthropological research on hormonal cascades, arguing that they are both a site rich for conceptual analysis and also – as the case of abortion demonstrates – often a matter of political urgency.

Abortion pills on paper and in practice

In the World Health Organization (WHO)'s most recent abortion care guideline, the following medication regimen is recommended:

For medical abortion at <12 weeks:

A. Recommend the use of 200 mg mifepristone administered orally, followed 1–2 days later by 800 μg misoprostol administered vaginally, sublingually or buccally.

(World Health Organization 2022: 68)

This recommendation is taken from the WHO's most recent abortion care guideline. On the surface, the regimen described appears simple enough. First, you take mifepristone, a synthetic anti-progesterone. This inhibits the action of progesterone, the hormone essential to maintaining the interior of the uterus during pregnancy, causing the uterine lining to degrade. Later, you take misoprostol, a synthetic prostaglandin (a prostaglandin is a physiologically active lipid compound with hormone-like effects). This stimulates the cervix to dilate and uterus to contract, causing the uterine lining to further break down and the uterine contents to be expelled. At this stage, the abortion is considered complete. The WHO's abortion care guideline is forward-thinking and comprehensive, based on robust analysis of clinical evidence and human rights standards. But inevitably, its recommendations can only tell a partial story; a lot is collapsed into, and condensed out of, those few short lines. While the pharmacological mechanisms of mifepristone and misoprostol may seem straightforward, competing clinical, political and moral claims intersect with economic and material conditions to shape the circumstances through which their abortifacient efficacies can be actualized. In some cases, pharmaceutical and informational flows come together, while in others they are subject to 'regulatory and moral blockages' (Hardon and Sanabria 2017: 126) that may or may not be surmountable.

Unsurprisingly, the regulation of abortion pills is a site of significant contestation, both at the national and supranational levels and within clinical settings. Mifepristone has been a contested technology since its development in the 1980s. Developed under the name RU486 by the French pharmaceutical company Roussel-Uclaf, the drug was initially withdrawn from the market in response to boycott threats by anti-abortion groups. It was only reintroduced following the intervention of both the international medical community, which claimed that the drug was an important medical advancement, and the French minister of health, who described it as 'the moral property of women' (Clarke and Montini 1993: 48). Even after this, uptake internationally was slow, with many countries taking decades to approve the drug, often hampered by protracted and highly politicized approval processes (Gynuity Health Projects 2021; see e.g. Noah 2001; Baird 2015; Campbell 2018). Due to mifepristone's role as an abortifacient, it remains unavailable in many countries, especially those where abortion is highly criminalized. In contrast, misoprostol has been able to benefit from an ability to live a 'double life', since it was initially developed and licensed as a treatment for stomach ulcers before women in Brazil seeking to illegally end their own pregnancies started to make use of its abortifacient side effects (de Zordo 2016). Since then, its off-label use has expanded to include not only medication abortion (both legal and illegal) but also a range of other reproductive health applications, including management of incomplete abortion and miscarriage, prevention and treatment of postpartum haemorrhage and induction of labour. Undeniably, misoprostol's association with illegal abortion has to some extent hindered these applications, rendering it something of 'a marginal and suspect character' (MacDonald 2021: 376; Suh 2021) in global health. Even so, its non-abortifacient indications mean it is the more readily available abortion pill in much of the world, giving it a fluidity that mifepristone does not possess that allows it to leak through regulatory and moral blockages with greater ease.

The regulatory and practical realities of mifepristone and misoprostol are reflected in the WHO's treatment of the two medications. While both drugs are included on its Model List of Essential Medicines, their use in the termination of pregnancy is qualified as only applying 'where permitted under national law and where culturally appropriate' (Perehudoff et al. 2018). In the WHO's abortion care guideline, meanwhile, it is notable that the combination regime recommended earlier is followed by two supplementary recommendations:

B. When using misoprostol alone: Recommend the use of 800 µg misoprostol administered buccally, sublingually or vaginally.

C. (NEW) Suggest the use of a combination regimen of letrozole plus misoprostol (letrozole 10 mg orally each day for 3 days followed by misoprostol 800 µg sublingually on the fourth day) as a safe and effective option.

(World Health Organization 2022: 68)

Clearly, these additional recommendations are written with contexts where mifepristone is not readily available in mind. Like misoprostol, letrozole has non-abortifacient indications (it is widely used in infertility and cancer treatments) that make it less likely to be subject to regulatory barriers. While these regimens could be considered less effective from a pharmacological perspective, for people who cannot access mifepristone, they are of course decidedly more so. As we can see, the kind of hormonal cascades that are set in motion by mifepristone and misoprostol (if, indeed, they can even be accessed in the first place) are determined from the outset by moral and political interests that shape the pharmaceutical flows and blockages through which the medications must travel.

For those who can access abortion pills, their ingestion marks not only the end of a pregnancy but also the beginning of an embodied process whose pharmacological and hormonal effects provide novel ways of understanding maternal and foetal bodies. In particular, the switch from surgical to pharmaceutical methods compels us to revisit the way we think about and conceptualize pregnancy. Unlike a surgical procedure, a woman may undergo a medication abortion without clinical supervision or even a confirmatory pregnancy test; she will likely experience cramping, bleeding and pain, similar to a heavy period or spontaneous miscarriage, stretched out over the course of several hours or days; and upon passing the pregnancy, she may encounter or handle foetal remains and other products of conception herself. Ethnographic evidence suggests that this amounts to a subjective experience that can be materially and affectively different to a surgical procedure. For example, Elaine Gale Gerber found that French women who had taken mifepristone emphasized the early and ambiguous nature of their pregnancies, seeing the foetuses as 'eggs' and themselves as 'barely' pregnant in ways that 'transcend a binary understanding of pregnancy by demonstrating a gray area between being pregnant and not' (Gerber 2002: 93). Emilia Sanabria observes a similar understanding among her Brazilian interlocuters, who differentiate between different 'degrees' (2016: 96) of abortion wherein an early medication abortion is considered more akin to menstrual regulation than the termination of a pregnancy. Such insights align with a growing body of qualitative evidence that suggests many perceive medication abortion to be more 'natural' and less like 'killing' due to its similarity to menstruation or miscarriage (Wainwright et al. 2016: 162). Yet, scholarship exploring the embodied experience of medication abortion remains relatively scarce (Purcell 2015). This relative lack of attention is surprising, especially considering feminist and anthropological scholarship's long-standing interest in maternal and foetal bodies (Martin 1987; Duden 1993; Ginsburg and Rapp 1995; Morgan and Michaels 1999; Han, Betsinger and Scott 2017). There are many potential explanations, from the methodological and ethical challenges associated with studying such questions to issues of stigma and squeamishness within academic research. Whatever the reason, it appears that in recent years an ethnographic lens has been more firmly focused on the cascading effects of abortion pills, not in the body but as they circulate within the wider world and collide with competing forms of governance and resistance. It is to this body of scholarship that we will turn to in the rest of the entry.

Abortion pills in social, clinical and political spaces

Irrespective of whether they are ingested or not, mifepristone and misoprostol act upon the world. They act upon the world as they move along supply chains, across borders and within markets; as they are discussed in the media, in whisper networks, in parliaments; as they are passed from the hands of a provider to a patient; are stockpiled, sold, dispensed and impounded. Even if they are never used to end an actual pregnancy, the abortifacient potentialities of these pills disrupt the social and moral worlds they move through, setting in motion cascades that are reshaping the politics of abortion in complex and sometimes contradictory ways. Abortion pills have come of age alongside the internet, their pharmaceutical and informational flows increasingly distributed through international networks mediated by online communication technologies. They are 'global pharmaceuticals', sites where global logics and politics 'are forced into explicitness and become a new and productive field of tension and negotiation' (Biehl 2004: 116). As abortion pills have become an increasingly important vehicle for the transmission of transnational debates, ethics and ideologies, and site for enactments of localized 'abortion wars', attempts to restrict or expand access to them have attracted the attention of both academics and activists. In this section, I track the hormonal cascades of these medications as they reverberate through social, clinical and political spaces and explore the ways in which diverse actors and forces seek to manage their abortifacient potential in ways that go beyond merely controlling access to the pills themselves. In what follows, I will consider the actors and forces that work to facilitate and inhibit these cascades, respectively.

Facilitating cascades

For abortion rights advocates, the pharmacological opportunities afforded by abortion pills provide parallel opportunities to circumvent legal restrictions and expand access out with formal healthcare systems. Under conditions of criminalization, local activists have increasingly become purveyors of abortion pills and information. In Latin America, feminist collectives have played a leading role in establishing 'abortion hotlines' and 'accompaniment' models of care for individuals seeking to self-administer misoprostol (McReynolds-Pérez 2014; Drovetta 2015; Zurbriggen, Keefe-Oates, and Gerdts 2018; Walsh 2020). A number of international non-profit organizations have also been established to supply telemedicine medication abortion services to countries where abortion is otherwise inaccessible; the most notable include Women Help Women (www .womenhelp.org), Women on Web (www.womenonweb.org) and (the United States only) Aid Access (www.aidaccess.org), all of which operate under a feminist ethos guided by a commitment to promoting access to safe abortion services and the realization of abortion rights. Under such models, the goal is twofold: not only to get the medications into women's hands but also to ensure they are effective once ingested. If taken improperly, abortion pills will not always achieve the desired result. The provision of accurate information and guidance to ensure the termination is successful, in addition to the pills themselves, is therefore crucial.

Beyond helping individual abortion seekers, such activities can also function as a symbolic challenge to established political and legal orders. While the provision of abortion pills and information in restricted settings activities often operates in a legal grey area (Singer 2019; Solheim et al. 2020), the explicit intent is often not only to circumvent local abortion laws but also to openly subvert it in a way that brings into question its very legitimacy. In Elyse Ona Singer's (2019) analysis of a Mexican feminist collective's model of abortion accompaniment, she labels such initiatives 'alegal' as opposed to 'illegal', since the activists employ human rights arguments to simultaneously critique and dismiss the authority of a legal system that denies rights to women. Looked at from this angle, the distribution of abortion pills and information in legally restricted contexts can be viewed as a form of 'transformative illegality', defined by Máiréad Enright and Emilie Cloatre as 'a world-making practice that transform[s] objects and their meanings, and create[s] new possibilities to demonstrate the incoherence of the law and the possibilities of a better system' (2018: 283). Similar efforts to harness the transformative – rather than solely abortifacient – potential of abortion pills can be seen in their adoption as 'technologies of protest'. In Brenna McCaffrey's (2022) ethnographic study of the role of abortion pills in the campaign to legalize abortion in the Republic of Ireland, she outlines how the medications became an increasingly popular prop in pro-choice direct actions. Many of these actions revolved around the public distribution and consumption of abortion pills; particularly notable campaigns involved an Abortion Pill Train, an Abortion Pill Bus and an Abortion Pill Drone. Often, the primary aim of such actions was not to directly provide abortion pills to people in need. Rather, it was to raise awareness of the fact that abortion pills were an accessible and safe option while also highlighting that the state was no longer able to prevent abortions from taking place on its shores. Such direct actions make explicit the new political geography of abortion enabled by abortion pills, whereby access is increasingly determined as much by transnational and extraterritorial actors and flows as it is by the state. As Sydney Calkin writes in her article on the topic, if we are to understand the changing political geography of abortion, 'our analysis can no longer concentrate on the state as a territorial container for abortion law, but it must take into account a more fluid and multiscalar infrastructure for abortion access outside of state-sanctioned clinic space' (2018: 23).

Inhibiting cascades

Considering the opportunities provided by abortion pills described earlier, it is hardly surprising that mifepristone and misoprostol are frequently framed in public health, advocacy and media discourses as a 'revolutionary' technology with the potential to 'change everything' about abortion (Harvey 2015; Berer and Hoggart 2018). However, there is a reason why this potential has yet to be fully realized: just as the medications provide abortion rights advocates with new opportunities to expand access, they likewise give other actors a novel tool through which to further their own agendas. The pharmacological effects of these pills can serve as both a target and a mechanism for reproductive governance, a site where 'different historical configurations of actors – such as state, religious, and international financial institutions, NGOs, and social movements – use legislative controls, economic inducements, moral injunctions, direct coercion, and ethical incitements to produce, monitor, and control reproductive behaviours and population practices' (Morgan and Roberts 2012: 243). And just like any pharmaceutical 'magic bullet', they can only go so far, constrained by their particular local, social, economic and legal context (Brandt 1985; Biehl 2007; Farmer et al. 2013). As Calkin (2018) notes, while abortion pills may be creating a new political geography of abortion, states are not passively handing over control of reproduction but rather responding with new tactics aimed at reasserting authority over their reproductive citizens and subjects. Such strategies include mounting new legislative and regulatory obstacles to prohibit or prevent pills' circulation or use outside of approved clinical spaces, increasing the surveillance and criminalization of those who provide or take the medications and legislating for abortion under restricted circumstances in order to bring the practice back under state and clinical authority. Within such logics, the hormonal cascades set in motion by these pills are constructed as something to monitor and manage – in the process, raising potentially troubling questions about the ability of the state to achieve this task.

Physicians too are also being compelled to ask such questions, as abortion pills bring underlying tensions regarding the shifting meaning of medical authority and expertise to the fore (McReynolds-Pérez 2017; Lee, Sheldon, and Macvarish 2018). Historically, pro-choice activists and physicians have often been 'uneasy allies' (Joffe, Weitz, and Stacey 2004), united by a shared goal of legal abortion but diverging over questions of medical gatekeeping. As abortion pills enable new modes of access and delivery that decrease reliance on doctors, clinicians increasingly find themselves in a situation where they must reassess their role in terms of provision and advocacy. For example, in the campaign to legalize abortion in Ireland, pro-choice doctors sought to distance themselves from their legacy as gatekeepers by envisioning themselves as 'the kind of doctor who doesn't believe doctor knows best' (Bergen 2022a). At the same time, however, their stance on the widespread illicit use of abortion pills was that clinical oversight and regulation was needed since, as one physician put it, 'it is safe medication taken in an unsafe way' (Bergen 2022b: 34). While the argument that the widespread illicit use of abortion pills required regulation was ultimately successful in helping to bring about Irish law reform, it also provided politicians with a powerful script for introducing legislation that, while considerably more liberal, remained focused on the principles of restriction, control and medical authority, to the disappointment of some activists (Calkin 2020). Such outcomes are a salient reminder that the cascades effects of abortion pills cannot always be easily predicted.

For anti-abortion activists, meanwhile, abortion pills represent a new terrain through which their tropes and arguments can be reframed and reworked. For these actors, the pills' potential for increased reproductive autonomy is framed not as an asset but as a liability that can be used to justify stricter regulation. In some cases, tactics are focused on restricting access to the pills themselves. For example, Pam Lowe (2019) has described English anti-abortion campaigners' efforts to resist a legislative change that would enable women to take abortion pills at home as opposed to in a clinic, during which they deployed the metaphor of 'backstreet abortions' (a narrative historically associated with campaigns to legalize abortion) to frame home use of abortion pills as risky and themselves as 'savers' of vulnerable women. Lowe shows that the campaign, while part of a larger shift towards risk-based framings and ostensibly secular, weaves together multiple tropes that rely on religiously informed understandings of gender and motherhood. In cases where activists cannot prevent people from accessing pills, however, their focus switches to intervening in the pharmacological process itself via the deployment of hormonal cascades of their own. 'Abortion Pill Reversal' (APR) is an unproven treatment whereby high-dosage progesterone is administered to individuals who have begun a medication abortion but now wish to continue the pregnancy (Bhatti, Nguyen and Stuart 2018). Much like the social diagnosis of 'Post Abortion Syndrome' (Kelly 2014), APR was initially developed and promoted by anti-abortion networks in the United States before being circulated internationally. In the United States, APR has been able to bypass professional dissent and diffuse into public policy via the introduction of state-level statutes that require physicians to inform patients that medication abortions are reversible (Cappello 2019). Again, the logics of APR are premised on moralistic anti-abortion tropes reworked into secularized and 'pro-women' frames (Rose 2011). While APR is promoted using the language of 'choice' and bolstered by appeals to medical notions of informed consent, the treatment is premised on the assumptions that women regret their abortions and require protection – not only from external coercion but also from themselves. Such tactics are an apt demonstration of the ways in which different knowledges, practices and cultural imaginaries converge within hormones and the cascades they produce.

Conclusion (and a coda)

In this entry, I have charted the hormonal cascades set in motion by abortion pills as they pass through biological and social worlds. In so doing, I have sought to demonstrate the richness of cascades both as a site of anthropological enquiry and as an analytical concept. By foregrounding cascades, we can untangle the ways in which biochemical processes within individual bodies have ripple effects, in sociocultural and political terms, while also being themselves shaped by sociocultural and political forces. By charting the hormonal cascades of abortion pills, I was able to elucidate the complex interplay of interconnected local and global interests that shape them. First, I showed how abortion pills' abortifacient effects are themselves actualized and inhibited by biopolitical concerns and moral regimes and explored how these effects complicate dominant ways of conceptualizing both pregnancy and abortion care. Second, I followed abortion pills' effects as they reverberated into the wider world, bringing the hormonal cascades into focus as terrains for reproductive governance and resistance in their own right.

I end this entry with a coda that highlights the political urgency of attending to such cascades. I write this just weeks after the US Supreme Court announced its decision to overturn *Roe v. Wade*. Already, the news from across the Atlantic is grim: a ten-year-old girl was reportedly denied an abortion in Ohio, there is talk of bans on abortion travel and attempts to pass a federal abortion ban, and tech companies are deleting location data around abortion clinics to protect those who attend from potential future prosecution. The ways in which this ruling will bolster efforts to roll back on sexual and reproductive rights in other parts of the world remain to be seen. Within such a context, abortion pills are likely to play a prominent role in shaping global legislative, policy and activist strategies over the upcoming years. One interesting new strategy involves efforts to get mifepristone approved as a weekly on-demand contraceptive, mobilizing the ambiguities of early pregnancy and post-coital contraception in order to circumvent regulatory and legislative restrictions on abortifacients. In a crowdfunder to raise money for clinical trials, the organizers explain: 'You could [. . .] use Mifepristone once a week to avoid getting pregnant. It also works as a morning-after pill or to end an early pregnancy. In this way, it challenges the very difference between contraception and abortion' (Women on Waves 2022). Such events are timely reminders that mifepristone and misoprostol continue to produce new 'rebellious' cascades every day. It is up to us, as scholars, to pay attention to them.

References

Andaya, E. and J. Mishtal (2017), 'The Erosion of Rights to Abortion Care in the United States: A Call for a Renewed Anthropological Engagement with the Politics of Abortion', *Medical Anthropology Quarterly* 31 (1): 40–59.
Baird, B. (2015), 'Medication Abortion in Australia: A Short History', *Reproductive Health Matters* 23 (46): 169–76.

Berer, M. and L. Hoggart (2018), 'Medical Abortion Pills have the Potential to Change Everything About Abortion', *Contraception* 97 (2): 79–81.

Bergen, S. (2022a), '"The Kind of Doctor who Doesn't Believe Doctor Knows Best": Doctors for Choice and the Medical Voice in Irish Abortion Politics, 2002–2018', *Social Science and Medicine* 297: 114817.

Bergen, S. (2022b), 'Interview with Mary Favier', *Digital Repository of Ireland, Irish Qualitative Data Archive*. doi:10.7486/DRI.p841pc88n.

Bhatti, K. Z., A. T. Nguyen, and G. S. Stuart (2018), 'Medical Abortion Reversal: Science and Politics Meet', *American Journal of Obstetrics and Gynecology* 218 (3): 315.e1–315. e6.

Biehl, J. (2004), 'The Activist State: Global Pharmaceuticals, AIDS, and Citizenship in Brazil', *Social Text* 22 (3): 105–32.

Biehl, J. (2007), *Will to Live: AIDS Therapies and the Politics of Survival*, Princeton: Princeton University Press.

Brandt, A. M. (1985), *No Magic Bullet: A Social History of Venereal Disease in the United States Since 1880*, Oxford: Oxford University Press.

Calkin, S. (2018), 'Towards a Political Geography of Abortion', *Political Geography* 69: 22–9.

Calkin, S. (2020), 'Abortion Pills in Ireland and Beyond: What can the 8th Amendment Referendum Tell Us About the Future of Self-Managed Abortion?', in K. Browne and S. Calkin (eds), *After Repeal: Rethinking Abortion Politics*, 73–89, London: Zed Books.

Cammack, R. et al. (eds) (2006), 'Cascade Sequence', in *Oxford Dictionary of Biochemistry and Molecular Biology*, 2nd edn, 101, Oxford: Oxford University Press.

Campbell, P. (2018), 'Making Sense of the Abortion Pill: A Sociotechnical Analysis of RU486 in Canada', *Health Sociology Review* 27 (2): 121–35.

Cappello, O. (2019), 'Unproven, Unethical and Dangerous: Counseling Requirements on Stopping a Medication Abortion Threaten Patients and Providers', *Guttmacher Institute*, 16 December. Available at https://www.guttmacher.org/article/2019/12/ unproven-unethical-and-dangerous-counseling-requirements-stopping-medication (accessed 30 November 2022).

Clarke, A. and T. Montini (1993), 'The Many Faces of RU486: Tales of Situated Knowledges and Technological Contestations', *Science, Technology, and Human Values* 18 (1): 42–78.

de Zordo, S. (2016), 'The Biomedicalisation of Illegal Abortion: The Double Life of Misoprostol in Brazil', *História, Ciências, Saúde-Manguinhos* 23: 19–36.

Drovetta, R. I. (2015), 'Safe Abortion Information Hotlines: An Effective Strategy for Increasing Women's Access to Safe Abortions in Latin America', *Reproductive Health Matters* 23 (45): 47–57.

Duden, B. (1993), *Disembodying Women: Perspectives on Pregnancy and the Unborn*, Cambridge, MA: Harvard University Press.

Enright, M. and E. Cloatre (2018), 'Transformative Illegality: How Condoms "Became Legal" in Ireland, 1991–1993', *Feminist Legal Studies* 26 (3): 261–84.

Farmer, P. et al. (eds) (2013), *Reimagining Global Health: An Introduction*, Berkeley: University of California Press.

Gerber, E. G. (2002), 'Deconstructing Pregnancy: RU486, Seeing 'Eggs,' and the Ambiguity of Very Early Conceptions', *Medical Anthropology Quarterly* 16 (1): 92–108.

Ginsburg, F. D. and R. Rapp (eds) (1995), *Conceiving the New World Order: The Global Politics of Reproduction*, Berkeley: University of California Press.

Gynuity Health Projects (2021) *Mifepristone Approvals*. Available at https://gynuity.org/assets/resources/biblio_ref_lst_mife_en.pdf.

Han, S., T. K. Betsinger, and A. B. Scott (2017), *The Anthropology of the Fetus: Biology, Culture, and Society*, Oxford: Berghahn Books.

Hardon, A. and E. Sanabria (2017), 'Fluid Drugs: Revisiting the Anthropology of Pharmaceuticals', *Annual Review of Anthropology*, 46 (1): 117–32.

Harvey, P. (2015), 'Medical Abortion: The Hidden Revolution', *Journal of Family Planning and Reproductive Health Care* 41 (3): 193–6.

Joffe, C. E., T. A. Weitz, and C. L. Stacey (2004), 'Uneasy Allies: Pro-choice Physicians, Feminist Health Activists and the Struggle for Abortion Rights', *Sociology of Health & Illness* 26 (6): 775–96.

Kelly, K. (2014), 'The Spread of "Post Abortion Syndrome" as Social Diagnosis', *Social Science and Medicine* 102: 18–25.

Lee, E., S. Sheldon, and J. Macvarish (2018), 'The 1967 Abortion Act Fifty Years on: Abortion, Medical Authority and the Law Revisited', *Social Science & Medicine* 212: 26–32.

Lowe, P. (2019), '(Re)imagining the "Backstreet": Anti-abortion Campaigning Against Decriminalisation in the UK', *Sociological Research Online* 24 (2): 1–15.

MacDonald, M. E. (2021), 'Misoprostol: The Social Life of a Life-Saving Drug in Global Maternal Health', *Science, Technology, & Human Values* 46 (2): 376–401.

Martin, E. (1987), *The Woman in the Body: A Cultural Analysis of Reproduction*, Boston: Beacon Press.

McCaffrey, B. (2022), *All Aboard the Abortion Pill Train: Activism, Medicine, and Reproductive Technologies in the Republic of Ireland*, PhD thesis, City University of New York.

McReynolds-Pérez, J. (2014), *Misoprostol for the Masses: The Activist-Led Proliferation of Pharmaceutical Abortion in Argentina*, PhD thesis, University of Wisconsin-Madison.

McReynolds-Pérez, J. (2017), 'No Doctors Required: Lay Activist Expertise and Pharmaceutical Abortion in Argentina', *Signs: Journal of Women in Culture & Society* 42 (2): 349–75.

Morgan, L. M. and M. W. Michaels (eds) (1999), *Fetal Subjects, Feminist Positions*, Philadelphia: University of Pennsylvania Press.

Morgan, L. M. and E. F. S. S. Roberts (2012), 'Reproductive Governance in Latin America', *Anthropology & Medicine* 19 (2): 241–54.

Noah, L. (2001), 'A Miscarriage in the Drug Approval Process: Mifepristone Embroils the FDA in Abortion Politics', *Wake Forest Law Review* 36 (3): 571–604.

Perehudoff, K. et al. (2018), 'Realising the Right to Sexual and Reproductive Health: Access to Essential Medicines for Medical Abortion as a Core Obligation', *BMC International Health and Human Rights* 18 (1): 1–7.

Purcell, C. (2015), 'The Sociology of Women's Abortion Experiences: Recent Research and Future Directions', *Sociology Compass* 9 (7): 585–96.

Rose, M. (2011), 'Pro-life, Pro-woman? Frame Extension in the American Antiabortion Movement', *Journal of Women, Politics & Policy* 32 (1): 1–27.

Sanabria, E. (2016), *Plastic Bodies: Sex Hormones and Menstrual Suppression in Brazil*, Durham and London: Duke University Press.

Singer, E. O. (2019), 'Realizing Abortion Rights at the Margins of Legality in Mexico', *Medical Anthropology: Cross-Cultural Studies in Health and Illness* 38 (2): 167–81.

Solheim, I. H. et al. (2020), 'Beyond the Law: Misoprostol and Medical Abortion in Dar es Salaam, Tanzania', *Social Science and Medicine* 245: 112676.

Suh, S. (2021), 'A Stalled Revolution? Misoprostol and the Pharmaceuticalization of Reproductive Health in Francophone Africa', *Frontiers in Sociology* 6 (April): 1–18.

Wainwright, M. et al. (2016), 'Self-management of Medical Abortion: A Qualitative Evidence Synthesis', *Reproductive Health Matters* 24 (47): 155–67.

Walsh, A. (2020), 'Feminist Networks Facilitating Access to Misoprostol in Mesoamerica', *Feminist Review* 124: 175–82.

Whyte, S. R., S. van der Geest, and A. Hardon (2002), *Social Lives of Medicines*, Cambridge: Cambridge University Press.

Women on Waves (2022), *Crowdfunder: Reclaim Your Rights! A New Post-Roe Strategy*, Available at https://www.womenonwaves.org/en/page/7730/reclaim-your-rights-a-new-strategy (accessed 5 July 2022).

World Health Organization (2022), *Abortion Care Guideline*, Geneva. Available at https://apps.who.int/iris/handle/10665/349316.

Zurbriggen, R., B. Keefe-Oates, and C. Gerdts (2018), 'Accompaniment of Second-Trimester Abortions: The Model of the Feminist Socorrista Network of Argentina', *Contraception* 97 (2): 108–15.

14 OESTROGEN

CHARLOTTE JONES AND KRISS FEARON

Over the last century, oestrogen has come to be seen as the defining female hormone. Although testicles and ovaries produce both testosterone and oestrogen, Oudshoorn (1994: 8) notes that the flawed idea that sex hormones are 'chemical messengers of femininity and masculinity' has persisted for the century since oestrogen was given its name. The word 'oestrogen' relates to the female oestrus, linking the actions of this family of hormones on the human body inextricably to female fertility and reproduction and consequently both to feminine gender conformance and the normative social timing of key life course transitions and events such as puberty, menarche, menstruation, fertility and menopause.

Hormone treatments are widely used for 'female disorders' (Löwy 1999: 520) based on the assumption that women's physical and mental health is dependent on healthy sex organs, that their bodies are 'completely controlled by hormones' (Oudshoorn 1994: 8) and that where there is a 'deficiency' of oestrogen it needs to be replaced. In this entry, we are interested in the materiality of oestrogen and its effect upon embodiment, identities and lives. While acknowledging that oestrogen is a biochemical phenomenon, we argue that it is also materialized through social interaction and within structures of power and knowledge (Roberts 2007: 19). Oestrogen does not derive from a pre-existing or inherent sex, nor does it 'produce' sex; rather, cultural and biomedical discourses of sexual difference create our understanding of oestrogen, its meaning and role. Oestrogen is thus a biosocial 'sexed' hormone, rather than a sex hormone.

Our entry draws on the experiences of women with Swyer syndrome (SS), Turner syndrome (TS) and complete and partial androgen insensitivity syndromes (CAIS/PAIS). These syndromes are linked by their medical classification as genetic conditions which lead to an oestrogen 'deficit' and share its effects, including infertility diagnosed in childhood, delayed or absent puberty and early menopause. People with these diagnoses have sexual and reproductive development which are different to medical expectations, clinically identified as disorders/differences of sex development (DSDs). A medically classified oestrogen 'deficit' may be due to unexpected ovarian development or as a result of a gonadectomy to avert the risk of gonadal malignancy. Consequently, clinicians often prescribe or impose a long-term oestrogen replacement as 'corrective'. This contrasts with trans people's use of HRT: Horak (2014) describes how 'hormone time' appropriates straight temporality (i.e. a naturalized and unquestioned heteronormative temporal organization, focused around marriage, reproduction, etc.) for more radical ends. The progressive narratives shared by trans people chronicling changes generated by HRT are oriented towards eventual self-determination, gender concordance and a joyful future (Horak 2014).

In contrast, we focus on the implications of a medically diagnosed oestrogen 'deficit' for complying with normative timing of life events such as puberty, pregnancy and menopause, arguing that the medical prescription of hormone replacements is used as a normalizing technology. We show how hormone replacements can also be stigmatizing and explore how stigmatization may be resisted, examining the strategies people with variations in sex characteristics (VSCs) deployed to achieve this and the way they work to circumvent, negotiate and reframe a sense of (mis)fitting with social timing norms. We use the term VSCs due to its translatability across a range of viewpoints and specific diagnostic labels to reflect the terminology used or preferred by participants and to highlight their medical circumstances. Some individuals prefer this terminology, or intersex, while others prefer not to use an umbrella term. We acknowledge the complexity of terminology and its political and epistemological implications (Davis 2011).

This entry draws on two research projects in the UK, led separately by the co-authors. Jones's fieldwork took place between 2013 and 2014 (Jones 2020, 2022a, 2022b). This was a small qualitative study with five women and two men with VSCs and two parents of children with VSCs. The research aimed to explore their social and medical experiences, focusing in particular on medical diagnosis and its interaction with the realization of identities and interpersonal relationships. The nine participants initially wrote about their experiences in unstructured, reflective diaries over a period of two months, then attended in-depth, one-to-one interviews in person (Jones 2022b). Fearon's fieldwork took place between 2016 and 2018 and was a qualitative study based on photo elicitation interviews with nineteen women with TS and eleven mothers of girls with TS (Fearon 2019). It examined how women with TS perceived and navigated their reproductive options and how mothers did the same on behalf of their child. These two projects and datasets have been aggregated for this entry through an extended process of discussion, reflection and co-writing through which we explored the biosocial significance of hormones – particularly oestrogen – in our work.

Expected life stages

Theories of social timing describe societal expectations that key life course events will take place at a particular age or within a particular time frame. Consequently, low levels of oestrogen may be stigmatized when the result is that social norms are not fulfilled on time, or at all. As we will show, some people repeatedly and unintentionally 'misfit' (Garland-Thompson 2011: 592) with the social timing of their peers throughout the life course, for example, through infertility diagnosed in childhood, absent menarche or early menopause (which is associated with degeneration and therefore usually deferred or avoided even within normative time frames). In turn this may have multiple implications including undermining a person's sense of gender identity (Letherby 2002) and social stigma (Becker 2000; Greil et al. 2011).

Scholarship on the embodied experiences of time illustrates how lives and bodies are interwoven with relations of power, autonomy and control, based on degrees of compliance with normative narratives of timing across the life course. Some routes are naturalized, anticipated and valorized, while others are discouraged and stigmatized (Halberstam 2005). Hence, 'chrononormativity' (Freeman 2010: 3) expresses how we are 'bound into socially meaningful embodiment through temporal regulation', where being 'early' or 'late' by comparison with peers can carry social stigma. 'Normal' development has been systematized using various methods that assess aspects of pubertal development (Baird et al. 2017) and menopause (Singer and Hunter 1999). These physical changes carry social significance: for example, menarche has been characterized as a 'status passage' (Newton 2012), bringing adult status and the beginning of a (potential) reproductive life cycle, along with the stigma of being required to manage bleeding.

Oestrogen administration may be experienced as stigmatizing due to its associations with menopause or its conflation with oral contraceptives, driven by disparaging normative narratives of timing, maturity and sexual promiscuity. In other cases, oestrogen administration is actively refused or neglected, either to tune out a diagnosis or to exercise greater agency. However this, too, has the potential to result in menopause stigma, due to the arrival of 'untimely' symptoms.

In girls with TS, the intention behind oestrogen supplementation is explicitly 'to mimic normal timing and progression of physical and social development' (Klein et al. 2018) so that girls mature in sync with their peers. Taking medication meant girls with TS could 'fit' and gain insider status by starting periods at the expected time. However, initiating puberty with medication could also raise potentially stigmatizing questions about a girl's sexual experience in settings, such as school, where girls routinely shared their experiences of menarche:

> People couldn't understand why I couldn't [have periods naturally], because I explained that I'd had to take [oestrogen] tablets. It was like, 'oh, are you on the pill? [disapproving]. You know, my mam says you're on the pill.' No, no, no, it's not like that [TSW13: woman with TS, early 50s, started the pill aged 13].

HRT, rather than the oral contraceptive pill, is a standard treatment for post-pubertal women of any age with TS, prescribed to minimize the long-term risks of early menopause, such as osteoporosis and heart problems. Its association with the menopause could produce felt stigma. For example, one participant explained that she avoided discussion of brands of tablets:

> I don't mention that I take HRT or anything . . . I don't want to use the word 'embarrassing' but it's something that you just . . . you feel a bit uncomfortable disclosing . . . I suppose because HRT is something you associate with women going through the menopause [TSW17, woman with TS, early 30s].

Attitudes to medication adherence sometimes reflected felt stigma and discomfort about the daily reminder of the diagnosis. Another participant, Paula, stopped taking HRT temporarily in her early twenties, after feeling lost and overwhelmed by her diagnosis. Paula, who has PAIS, described: 'I was kind of like – this is my little bit of control I can keep hold of, this is my bit that I can . . . I haven't got to share with anyone, I can just do it myself.' For several years, Paula lived without exogenous oestrogen and the regular medical consultations that she had been attending up until that time. By discontinuing the HRT, Paula terminated a biomedical intervention which had begun long before she became aware of her diagnosis as a teenager. When her treatment started in childhood, she notes she 'never had the choice'. In her diary, Paula recalled that the decision to attend medical appointments and take HRT was 'the only part of my life I felt in control of'.

Due to the decline in oestrogen during this interruption, Paula noted she experienced a process of 'premature' menopause between twenty and twenty-two years old. She recalled that her mother dismissed this: 'she was like, "don't be silly, you're not going through the menopause, you don't go through that until you're about fifty."' Paula's deviation from age norms created discomfort for her mother, preventing her from treating Paula's experience seriously. While her mother's denial may have been an attempt at reassurance, Paula interpreted it as further confirmation of her incongruity. Paula explained, 'your teenage daughter doesn't go through the menopause before you. [. . .] It's crackers to think.' Paula – who appeared more indifferent about her menopause – narrated her mother's reaction in terms of the linear chronology and expectations inherent in their vertical relationship, in which menopause may be associated with individual maturation (Singer and Hunter 1999) and Paula's experiences were out of sequence. Oestrogen – including its deficit and its effects – were thus positioned as relational, part of an established familial composition between mother and daughter. While Paula's rejection of hormone therapy was an attempt to regain personal control, she was tasked with other complex biosocial reactions as a result.

Relational time

The social understanding of the 'normal' body and how it develops and functions is often based on comparison. Roth (1963) argued that the life course can be perceived as a career with a forward trajectory and socially defined points of natural progression. Progress is measured by comparison with a 'reference group', usually a person's immediate peers; when children 'misfit' by falling behind their peers, this is not only stigmatized but attracts social pressure to conform, motivating parents and healthcare workers to intervene.

Due to low endogenous oestrogen, girls with TS usually take hormone supplements to initiate puberty and generally require fertility treatment to conceive. Puberty is therefore a key point at which girls misfit with their peers, through comparisons of menarche timing and discussion of future family building. Parents enacted stigma resistance by anticipating and working to minimize the potential distress caused to girls by normative conversations around fertility and contraception, for example, by providing inclusive sex education at home or ensuring that school lessons included infertility, delayed puberty and absent menstruation:

I think the conversation is always a given that everyone will go through puberty, it's a given that everybody will be able to have children. That's how I think it is, and maybe that's why they feel different, because everything is always delivered as an average-person conversation. I just wish it was more inclusive [TSM11: mother, mid-30s].

Most participants were aware of support groups for people with their specific VSC. As well as expanding the conceptualization of 'normal' bodies presented at school, these groups had a biosocial function, ensuring women and girls could meet peer comparators that more closely matched their own diagnostic experiences and share conversations that otherwise put them outside the norm for their wider peer group. These were places they could experience fitting rather than misfitting: 'I felt so much more comfortable than I ever had with people at school, with anyone else I'd met. You just feel totally different. You feel like they're totally on your wavelength, definitely' [TSW16: woman with TS, mid-20s].

However, biosocial groups also had their own social norms, including norms of accepting rather than resisting medication or surgery. If people did not fit in here either, this could result in further stigmatization. Six months prior to her interview, 32-year-old Natalie, who has CAIS, had attended her first medical consultation about CAIS since her diagnosis eleven years earlier. She described feeling under-informed and was seeking access to further information and potential medical treatment, including exogenous oestrogen, which she had not yet been given. Because of her inexperience, she felt excluded from the biosocial narrative around CAIS, which comprised HRT as part of an expected pathway and 'healthy' life trajectory (Jones 2022a) and surgery to remove gonads, due to the risk of malignancy. She explained, 'they've [other people with CAIS] all gone along with their laid-out plan: you get diagnosed, you have them [gonads] removed, you're prescribed your HRT, you live happily ever after. But they don't seem to have a plan in place for someone who doesn't want it.'

Here we have shown how the family and school can be key sites of comparison, evaluation and measurement in terms of sex development. For parents, school could also provide a significant opportunity to challenge normative expectations that might ostracize or isolate their child. We have also illustrated how VSC support and social groups can be affirmative and challenge a sense of misfitting, while also aggravating exclusion for those who do not adhere to the prevailing biomedical narratives of hormone therapy.

Uncertain futures

Scholars have found frequent promissory narratives in biomedicine, whereby medical and scientific interventions designed to overcome reproductive barriers act as 'hope technologies' (Franklin 1997). Facing an uncertain future or a difficult present, a collective hope is invested in 'the power of science and medicine' (Franklin 1997: 203) to 'deliver them from their suffering' (Rose 2007: 136). For some participants, exogenous oestrogen was part of this hope narrative. Kafer's (2013) concept of the 'curative imaginary' theorizes that decisions to medicate are often led by imaginaries of a future where the condition is 'cured' and people no longer misfit with social norms, based on a valorization of the normal, which acts as social pressure to comply with available interventions.

One participant, Sophie, explained that because of SS, her uterus was 'naturally small'. To change the uterine size, she said, 'I had loads of these hormone tablets and then they use this specific one which really helps you to have a full-size uterus. And there are reports of someone in like Estonia or somewhere, who had Swyer's, who had a baby with IVF, so you can.' Sophie's hormone time narrative (Horak 2014) is oriented towards a reproductive future. The affirmative narrative of in vitro fertilization in Estonia provided her with a sense of hope as she grappled with her prospects, and oestrogen thus granted a 'linear and teleological' source of progress towards conception (Horak 2014: 580). This successful outcome, however, relies on compliance with hormone treatment and a future imaginary in which the medicalized 'cure' is 'just around the corner, as arriving any minute now' (Kafer 2013: 44). This anticipation can also cast a shadow on the present, 'where one's life is always on hold, in limbo, waiting for the cure' (Kafer 2013: 44).

The time needed to implement reproductive choices in the context of infertility and potentially risky pregnancy also exerted pressure on women with TS to plan at a much younger age than their peers. Exogenous oestrogen was central in developing a body that could support a pregnancy, but it was only one factor. Anticipating and complying with normative expectations of motherhood could be difficult or impossible when they depended on factors beyond the women's sole control, such as having a partner. This intensified the uncertainty of future motherhood. One participant with TS described a conversation with her doctor regarding fertility intentions that took place in her early twenties, while she was an undergraduate:

She basically did the whole thing about being single: what are your plans, are you going to adopt, surrogacy, egg donation, it's going to take this long, so many years. You have to sign up to this register now if you want kids before the end of this age. You have to – actually, should have – thought about this two years ago. You should have found a partner when you were 20! Oh god! [TSW15: woman with TS, late 20s].

As Rose (2007: 148) notes, hope for biological citizens is not only wishing and anticipating, 'it postulates a certain achievable and desirable future, which requires action in the present for its realization'. Good citizens have a 'duty to be well' (Brown and Baker 2012: 20), to take up interventions that are available to them and must find their own way through the complexities of decision-making and consequences.

The biomedical demand to 'act' risks positioning a route of inaction as inadequate (see also Roen 2008). Natalie, who had not yet administered HRT, spoke of a life that might become in some way 'better' once starting exogenous oestrogen. However, despite the promised telos within the reparative AIS biomedical narrative, oestrogen and transition also caused her anticipation and unease. In her diary, she listed its possible benefits: 'having my gonads removed and being prescribed a HRT may help with my depression, may help with my personal health, May change my view on life. MAY MAY MAY. Is there a certainty??? [*sic*].' Later in the diary, Natalie asked specifically, 'What is HRT going to do to me?' In contrast to Horak's hormone time and the progressive narratives generated by HRT for trans people, Natalie wrestles with bodily autonomy, conflicted desires and expectations. As a result, she is dubious about whether the administration of HRT will provide the sense of relief, security or certainty that Horak observes for others.

Natalie was concerned about the consequences of starting HRT relatively late 'compared to a lot of the girls who started it pretty much in their teens'. She worried it could reverse some of the physical characteristics she liked about herself, such as a lack of body hair and skin unaffected by acne. The traits Natalie described are associated with pubertal development within the expected chrononormative narrative (Freeman 2010) and her explanation was retrospective, focusing on her sisters' teenage development. These characteristics were thus seen as both undesirable and untimely.

Natalie understood the potential removal of her gonads and the introduction of exogenous hormones as fundamentally transformative: 'It's like you've lived your life now, getting used to how you are now and then you've gotta start . . . it's like a new person that's gonna come out of it. But perhaps a person you don't wanna be, you don't wanna become. And that's what I'm afraid of.' Exogenous oestrogen was seen as a site of change for Natalie after a lifetime in suspense, but its inscrutability was unsettling: while it might improve facets of her life, she also feared that it might produce a sense of personal dissonance or dissociation.

We have shown how hopeful futures are constructed through biomedical narratives involving oestrogen administration. In some cases, this involved extensive pre-planning in anticipation of a future reproductive life. In cases where oestrogen had not been prescribed, its potential effects were highly anticipated, especially at an age outside of key 'transition' windows (e.g. puberty, menopause), including fears it would enact changes which were inaccurate or unwanted.

Conclusion

The experiences and attitudes of people with VSCs towards oestrogen treatment provide a lens to examine the mutual influence of biomedical conceptions of hormones and normative narratives of social timing. We focused on the compulsory nature of oestrogen as a normalizing intervention and its relationship to stigma. Oestrogen facilitates conformity with social timing at key life transitions such as puberty, avoiding the stigma of being 'early' or 'late' in development. However, people also resist stigma through other routes: by normalizing variance and developing biosocial connections. The telos of biomedical treatment is to optimize the chance of a socially desirable future that avoids obvious misfitting. Consequently, treatment is associated with imaginaries of future cure. These imaginaries can also bring uncertainty, where participants consider a future that could have been more fulfilling if the intervention had not taken place, where the intervention is only the first of many steps in realizing desires or where desires may change with time. This raises the prospect of future unfulfillment and regret, regardless of whether the intervention was used or not.

Compliance with oestrogen supplementation is construed as a socially responsible act, which provides a 'cure' for physical symptoms of oestrogen deficit. In doing so it reproduces normative, sexed expectations of social timing and development. Oestrogen is thus continuously reinscribed as a 'sexed' hormone: a biochemical phenomenon which is materialized through these temporal expectations and life stages.

References

Baird, J., I. Walker, C. Smith, and H. Inskip (2017), *Review of Methods for Determining Pubertal Status and Age of Onset of Puberty in Cohort and Longitudinal Studies*, London: CLOSER. Available at https://www.closer.ac.uk/wp-content/uploads/CLOSER -resource-Review-of-methods-for-determining-pubertal-status-and-age-of-onset-of -puberty-in-cohort-and-longitudinal-studies.pdf.

Becker, G. (2000), *The Elusive Embryo: How Women and Men Approach New Reproductive Technologies*, Berkeley: University of California Press.

Brown, B. J. and S. Baker (2012), *Responsible Citizens: Individuals, Health, and Policy Under Neoliberalism*, London: Anthem Press.

Davis, G. (2011), '"DSD is a Perfectly Fine Term": Reasserting Medical Authority Through a Shift in Intersex Terminology', *Advances in Medical Sociology*, 12: 155–82.

Fearon, K. (2019), '"Have you Ever Talked to Any Women with Turner syndrome?" Using Universal Design and Photo Elicitation Interviews in Research with Women with Mild Cognitive Impairment', *Methodological Innovations* 12: 2.

Franklin, S. (1997), *Embodied Progress: A Cultural Account of Assisted Conception*, London: Routledge.

Freeman, E. (2010), *Time Binds: Queer Temporalities, Queer Histories*, Durham: Duke University Press.

Garland-Thomson, R. (2011), 'Misfits: A Feminist Materialist Disability Concept', *Hypatia*, 26 (3): 591–609.

Greil, A., J. McQuillan, and K. Slauson-Blevins (2011), 'The Social Construction of Infertility', *Sociology Compass* 5 (8): 736–46.

Halberstam, J. J. (2005), *In a Queer Time and Place*, New York: New York University Press.

Horak, L. (2014), 'Trans on YouTube: Intimacy, Visibility, Temporality', *TSQ* 1 (4): 572–85.

Jones, C. (2020), 'Intersex, Infertility and the Future: Early Diagnoses and the Imagined Life Course', *Sociology of Health & Illness* 42 (1): 143–56.

Jones, C. (2022a), 'The Harms of Medicalisation: Intersex, Loneliness and Abandonment', *Feminist Theory* 23 (1): 39–60.

Jones, C. (2022b), '"This is What I Am and Who I Am": Exploring Authorship and Ethics in Intersex Research and Reflective Diaries', in M. Walker (ed.), *Interdisciplinary and Global Perspectives on Intersex*, , 89–105, London: Palgrave Macmillan.

Kafer, A. (2013), *Feminist, Queer, Crip*, Bloomington: Indiana University Press.

Klein, K. O., R. L. Rosenfield, R. J. Santen, A. M. Gawlik, P. F. Backeljauw, C. H. Gravholt, T. C. Sas, and N. Mauras (2018), 'Estrogen Replacement in Turner Syndrome: Literature Review and Practical Considerations', *The Journal of Clinical Endocrinology & Metabolism* 103 (5): 1790–803.

Letherby, G. (2002), 'Challenging Dominant Discourses: Identity and Change and the Experience of "Infertility" and "Involuntary Childlessness"', *Journal of Gender Studies* 11 (3): 277–88.

Löwy, I. (1999), 'Gender and Science', *Gender & History* 11 (3): 514–27.

Newton, V. L. (2012), 'Status Passage, Stigma and Menstrual Management: "Starting" and "Being on"', *Social Theory & Health* 10 (4): 392–407.

Oudshoorn, N. (1994), *Beyond the Natural Body: An Archaeology of Sex Hormones*, London: Routledge.

Roberts, C. (2007), *Messengers of Sex: Hormones, Biomedicine and Feminism*, Cambridge: Cambridge University Press.

Roen, K. (2008), '"But We Have to Do Something": Surgical "Correction" of Atypical Genitalia', *Body & Society* 14 (1): 47–66.

Rose, N. (2007), *The Politics of Life Itself: Biomedicine, Power, and Subjectivity in the Twenty-First Century*, Princeton: Princeton University Press.

Roth, J. A. (1963), *Timetables: Structuring the Passage of Time in Hospital Treatment and Other Careers*, Indianapolis: Bobbs-Merrill.

Singer, D. and D. Hunter (1999), 'The Experience of Premature Menopause: A Thematic Discourse Analysis', *Journal of Reproductive and Infant Psychology* 17 (1): 63–81.

15 OXYTOCIN

ARBEL GRINER AND RAFAELA ZORZANELLI

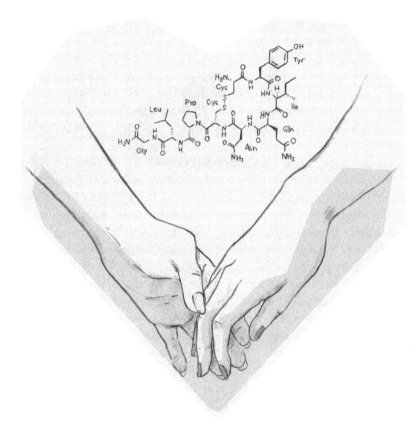

Since it was identified in the early twentieth century, oxytocin has received a lot of scientific attention. The hormone plays a significant role in uterine contractions during labour, lactation for nursing females and social behaviour and affiliation (Insel et al. 1998; Donaldson and Young 2008). It has also been found to be necessary for a series of life-dependent processes, including immune system regulation, stress coping and deoxidation (Carter 2022); pain (Rash, Aguirre-Camacho and Campbell 2014; Smith et al. 2021); nutrition (Lawson 2017; Kerem and Lawson 2021); and parenting (Tsuneoka et al. 2022).

Oxytocin paradoxes, oxytocin hype

Associated with many attachment behaviours, oxytocin has been viewed through 'rose-tinted glasses' (Yong 2012b). Some consider oxytocin as the main compound empowered with the faculty of promoting warmth, generosity, trust, confidence and other feelings, behaviours and attitudes deemed prosocial (Zak 2012). This prosocial account obscures evidence that oxytocin interacts with context-dependent variables and interindividual factors, such as gender, psychiatric conditions and personality traits (Bartz et al. 2011; Olff et al. 2013; Shamay-Tsoory and Abu-Akel 2016). Moreover, it can induce antisocial effects such as aggression, envy, relation distress and interpersonal difficulties, results which some researchers feel they must reconcile with the overarching theory of oxytocin's prosocial role (Shamay-Tsoory and Abu-Akel 2016: 2–3). The fact that not only positive effects of oxytocin are reported came to be known as the *oxytocin paradox* (Bethlehem et al. 2014).

Oxytocin's hype has yielded a large body of knowledge and debate. A search for the hormone on the *PubMed* database of scientific publications yielded as many as 30,000 results from the last two decades (Carter 2022). Sociologist and feminist scholar Victoria Pitts-Taylor points to an 'atomistic treatment' of oxytocin that runs through a large number of such studies. This atomistic view singularizes the molecule – as if it acted independently from other bodily systems and hormones – and treats its powers as deterministic (Pitts-Taylor 2016: 102). Pitts-Taylor explains that cultivating a narrative about the hormone as a supermolecule, with the capacity to solve just about any sexual, behavioural, social or romantic problem, 'not only reduces complex, multifaceted, and culturally rich concepts to neurobiology, but also obscures the many other neural systems that are thought to be involved' (ibid., 102).

We see two avenues to better understand the atomistic treatment of oxytocin. First, how it is cast as – and limited to – the promoter of prosocial behaviours. Second, the prominence and independence it has gained in explanations about prosocial behaviours, which obscures other important co-actors that usually interplay with the hormone such as vasopressin and other bodily regulatory systems.

These tendencies have led to the idea of oxytocin as 'the love hormone' (Ed Yong 2012a), or 'a biological metaphor for social attachment or "love"' (Carter 2017: 1), and something that could be prescribed for clinical and therapeutic use (Earp and Savulescu 2020). Indeed, in the neuroscience of love, which we will be exploring throughout this entry, oxytocin participates in a 'neurobiological love complex' that responds to the bodily mechanisms driving reproduction and child-rearing and that renders a person more socially or affectively prone. Furthermore, oxytocin's participation in a 'love complex' that is understood to drive attachment from 'within' has made the hormone an important piece of the literature on the *neuroenhancement of love*. In this entry, we work from our in-depth examination of bioethical literature that defends romantic relationships being chemically tweaked to induce and support 'healthy' love, bonding and romance towards the goal of normative family formation (Earp, Sandberg and Savulescu 2012). We also carefully studied the neuroscience behind these beliefs, which bioethicists use as supporting evidence for their claims. We investigate the idea that humans can be chemically re-engineered to become a morally enhanced species, a project wherein 'love' figures as a key moral tool because it allows for humans to come together, mate and, thus, guarantee survival and thriving.

We critique oxytocin's equivalence with love, how it has been used to locate love in the brain and the normative ways love is validated in the development of such therapeutic substances. Oxytocin is treated as a necessary compound in what is considered to be a healthy (and ideal) relationship, within an evolutionary logic that answers primarily to procreation and child-rearing. This situation yields a scientific object which is 'neurochemical love' – a material entanglement of chemicals directly implicated in a huge array of behaviours from survival responses to empathy. Oxytocin is the star of such scientific love, deemed to correct any deviance from the healthy path designed for love by science. Through a cascading process, oxytocin is created as something with the power to act as a cure for pathological, deviant love that escapes the evolutionary script.

The hormone of love?

For biologist Sue Carter (2022), oxytocin's 'love hormone' moniker is directly entangled with its association with reproduction – which includes social bonding, sexual behaviour, birth and maternal care. Despite the popularity of the connection between oxytocin and love, Carter (2022: 1) reminds us that '[t]he mechanisms linking love and oxytocin to each other remain both metaphorical and mysterious', and that further work is necessary in order to better understand them. Within the scientific-evolutionary framework in which studies connecting oxytocin and love are developed (Willey and Giordano 2011), love is circumscribed to processes and attitudes – to the physiology and psychology of selective behaviours and attachment (Carter 2022: 6). Selective behaviours are those practised with 'the presumed object of attachment', like allogrooming and parenting (Sue Carter 1998: 780), while attachment itself is assessed and defined by indexes such as proximity to and voluntary contact with others, stress in being separated from an individual or serenity in being around them, which are measured behaviourally and endocrinologically, through the presence and absence of different hormones and other substances (Carter 1998).

When such a strict definition of love is adopted, love can be approximated with oxytocin (Carter 2022: 6). Carter shows some elements of such approximation, indicating, for instance, that both love, in contemporary science's evolutionary understanding, and oxytocin itself evolved in more recent evolutionary times. Both can have anxiolytic and analgesic effects – rendering one calm and inhibiting fear in response to social clues – and both participate in safety promotion and trust that are essential for selective behaviour in scientific explanatory schemes. Further, science perceives love and oxytocin as 'epigenetically tuned and context dependent' and 'sexually dimorphic, among other common traits' (Carter 2022). These last two associations are key to our claim, as they *gender* both oxytocin and love, while also rendering them malleable.

Stressing commonalities between oxytocin and love does not mean, however, that they are 'the same'. Biologist and philosopher Donna Haraway reminds us that science 'has been about a search for translation, convertibility, mobility of meanings, and universality' (1988: 583); to a great extent, oxytocin's atomistic treatment facilitates this mobility of meanings. Atomizing a scientific object like oxytocin by attributing superpowers to it and giving it prominence in answering for complex phenomena like 'love' is an excellent example of approximating two objects that cannot be reduced to one another and creating between them an analogical transfer (Knorr-Cetina 1981).

Love in the brain

In order to complicate the equivalency between oxytocin and love, we now turn to the neurochemical love complex – the neural mechanisms that allow for love, as approached and conceptualized by evolutionary science, to take place (Abend 2018). The neurochemical love complex is an ideal object, in the sense that it allows for love to become standardized and amenable to scientific investigation and control in the laboratory (Latour 1999; Dror 2001; Abend 2018). In this process of making *love* an object of science, oxytocin plays a fundamental role. Along with other substances, it lends materiality to neurochemical love. Further, its rose-tinted quality also transfers moral value to scientific love. The formula is: oxytocin produces social attachment, which is a desirable effect; therefore, oxytocin-based love is desirable.

The framework that brings oxytocin, attachment and love together has been stretched to encompass *romantic love* more specifically (Fisher 1994, 2000, 2005; Acevedo et al. 2012). In relationship scenarios, oxytocin is perceived by some scientists as the substance implicated in one's self-assurance in romantic partnerships, in the reconnaissance of the physiognomy of close persons and with empathy promotion towards those seen as familiar (Wudarczyk et al. 2013; Rohden and Alzuguir 2016).

Like isolating oxytocin, isolating scientific love requires laboratory work, more specifically the deployment of a technique sociologist Gabriel Abend calls 'the production of love' (Abend 2018). Abend refers to studies in which persons are usually shown images or objects related to their loved ones while their heads are scanned in functional magnetic resonance imaging (fMRI) machines that map brain regions where oxygen-irrigated blood circulates (Fisher 2005). Between being shown one picture and the next, subjects in the fMRI machine are given tasks that aim to distract them from thinking about their loved ones. The purpose of those distractions is to deviate blood flow from brain regions associated with love; this is how researchers separate what 'love is' from what 'love is not'. In this context, oxygenated blood flow is used as a proxy for neurohormonal presence, as hormones are not actually caught in fMRI scans.

Researchers' other preferred method for creating neural correlates for love is through manipulating the brain chemistry of animal models (Insel and Shapiro 1992; Aragona and Wang 2004; Ross et al. 2009; Wang et al. 2013). Monogamy is a standard researchers rely on to understand pair-bonding, as shown in the classic research on prairie voles (Insel and Shapiro 1992; Insel et al. 1998; Aragona et al. 2003; Aragona and Wang 2004; Ross et al. 2009; Wang et al. 2013), a species whose monogamous pattern of mating, sharing territory and parenting is considered analogous to that 'formed by humans' (Aragona and Wang 2004). Most non-mammal experiments focus on 'a cluster of social behaviours, including selective affiliation, paternal care, and nest defence' (Insel, Young, and Wang 1997) that are similarly held as a contrast to polygyny and promiscuity – dismissing these as common forms of social organization in mammals as well. Researchers – including neuroscientists, biologists, endocrinologists and other experts working on connecting the human brain, feelings and the social world – stress that monogamy 'is best viewed as a social rather than a sexual strategy' (Insel, Young, and Wang 1997: 302), by means of which prosocial and pair-bonding behaviours can be probed more deeply. In the laboratory, voles' mating, bonding and parental interactions are controlled for and monitored, as neurohormones like oxytocin and vasopressin – and other substances like corticosterone and dopamine – are modulated and mapped in their brains (Aragona and Wang 2004).

On the one hand, techniques and technologies of science define the models for love studies (Carter 1998: 780); while on the other, models set limits for love as an object of inquiry. As Haraway writes, '"objects" do not preexist as such. Objects are boundary projects', and their contours 'materialize in social interaction' (1988: 595). Scientific love, in this sense, is a technological abstraction. It is a product of the lab, fabricated under conditions that necessarily detach *those who love* from contextual cues most likely indispensable to the lived experience of love as a complex human social interaction.

Romantic love in the brain is understood by contemporary neuroscience as a *complex* because it brings together three distinct systems – *lust*, *attraction* and *attachment* – forged by evolution to guarantee human reproduction and survival (Fisher: 2000). Systems, in neuroscientific jargon, are neuronal circuits that connect different parts of the brain through neurochemistry to create specific functional outputs (Shen et al. 2022). Since it is interpreted and created as reproduction- and child-rearing-centred, neurochemical love would foster procreation and affective attachment, '[r]elying on trust and belief as well as brain reward activity' that chemically produces pleasure and is linked to the limbic system (Esch and Stefano 2005: 187).

Operating from within the brain and in response to external stimuli, neurochemical lovemaking requires a lot more than oxytocin (Fisher 2000, 2005; Aragona et al. 2003; Esch and Stefano 2005). In a rough schema, neurochemical love is deemed to (1) produce and regulate *lust* by means of hormones like testosterone and oestrogen; (2) channel a dispersed sexual desire towards one specific object by generating sensations like euphoria through the circulation in the brain of substances such as noradrenaline, dopamine and serotonin; and, finally, (3) confirm such romantic choice by triggering attachment-related behaviours, or feelings of security and calmness around one specific partner, through the release of oxytocin and vasopressin (Fisher 2005; Savulescu and Sandberg 2008).

Neurochemical love, therefore, requires a cascade of hormones and neurohormones in fine interaction and coordination. Helen Fisher[1] – who since the 1980s has studied heteronormative patterns of loving from a biological anthropology perspective – implicates oxytocin in a sophisticated chemical enterprise that operates to stretch parental bonds for long enough to ensure the survival of an offspring (a four-year average) (Fisher 1994: 92). She writes that oxytocin's release in the brain, as a chemical compound of 'love', follows the augmentation of dopamine and noradrenaline levels and the lowering of serotonin levels in the ventral tegmental area (VTA) (Fisher, Aron and Brown 2006). Oxytocin's release 'corrects' the excessive state that dopamine and noradrenaline generate, which is analogous to addiction in which one craves and obsesses over a partner, thereby producing, according to Fisher, heteronormative sexual and affective preference (mating). Vasopressin, often portrayed in the scientific love schema as a male neurohormone, is understood to stimulate male loyalty to females and to the 'families' they form with them (Aragona and Wang 2004). Meanwhile, oxytocin, which is often accounted for in scientific discourse as a generator of 'feminine gender roles', is understood to regulate the entire gestational process and, beyond that, the postpartum tasks of feeding and caring for offspring (Aragona and Wang 2004).

Given these complex interactions, oxytocin's prominent role, not only in the so-called neurochemical love complex but also in the field of basic research on the connections between the hormone and social bonds, calls for cautious observation. The atomistic treatment of oxytocin becomes questionable, to say the least, pointing to two coexisting but contradictory readings stemming from the literature on the neuroscience of love. One renders oxytocin as one among many participants in the neurochemical operators of affectivity and sociality. The other –

evident in lay appropriations of the neuroscience of love as well as in the bioethics of the neuroenhancement of love – gives oxytocin prominence and stardom. This second reading attributes the quality of affection to the hormone, in a sense, allowing for the idea of pair-bond formation to extrapolate into empathy and to become enmeshed with sociality.

Technologies of social reproduction in a heteronormative order

Since scientific love – love that can be observed in a controlled laboratory environment – is fundamentally evolutionary, its underlying biological mechanisms answer primarily to procreation and child-rearing. According to the theories deployed by brain scientists, this requires heteronormative and monogamous bonds. In its 'healthy' version, then, the neurochemical love complex implies that being in love in a heteronormative relationship is a necessary condition for properly having and raising children. Therefore, child-centred conjugality, translated into neural correlates, is understood as a biological 'fix' for the irrational, extreme and unstable hormonal mode set by the chemical cocktail of the *attraction* system. As the star of child-centred conjugality, oxytocin is thrust into the position of being able to cure any deviance from the healthy path designed for love by science.

Love deemed healthy by science is free from stress and anxiety, full of confidence, visual contact, telepathy or shared thinking and empathy. It increases the repertoire of positive memories associated with the relationship, improves social attention, recognition of others, self-esteem and recollections of social situations. All of these benefits are attributed, to a great extent, to oxytocin (Wudarczyk et al. 2013: 5–10). However, the way heteronormativity, monogamy and child-centred cooperation are built into scientific models for love implies that they are no less important indexes of healthy love – even if not explicitly stated.

The heteronormative and monogamous traits of scientifically sanctioned neurochemical love have received critiques from feminist and queer science studies. Scholars have pointed to forms of kinship, affect and care that do not depend on biological descent (Hird 2004; Pitts-Taylor 2016), to the weight that cultural readings of 'nature' have on scientific theories (Haraway 1997), to the arbitrariness of monogamy as a relevant trait for studying human behaviour (Angela Willey 2016) and to the limitations imposed on biological investigation by gendered readings of hormones (Willey and Giordano 2011).

Hormones – including oxytocin, but not exclusively – are fundamental artefacts in giving materiality to and sustaining this narrative about evolutionary love. As material-semiotic elements (Haraway 1988; Roberts 2007), hormones can be thought of as connectors that approximate ideas that are not obviously or perfectly correlated. They can be taken as facilitators of analogical transfers

(Knorr-Cetina 1981), or of easy slippages, such as that between sexual pleasure and heteronormative love in the case of oxytocin (Rohden and Alzuguir 2016) or between the disposition for heteronormative romantic bonds and healthy sociality (Angela Willey 2016), in which oxytocin is also central. In this sense, beyond being fundamental to ensuring the stability of neurochemical love, oxytocin fosters the underlying value placed on heteronormativity, reproduction, child-centred and biological kinships, fixed gender roles and monogamy.

In conclusion, although neurochemical lovemaking requires an active and constant interaction of many substances, oxytocin is attributed with the 'magic' that reinforces the social order. It does the moral-material work of securing social reproduction (Hansen 2017), restating and resolving complex dynamics of cooperation by narrowing them to the nuclear family and heteronormative pair-bonding, and labour distribution, wherein an oxytocin-dependent 'organic' maternal love holds women accountable for child-rearing.

As this entry was on its way to the printer, a study was published putting into check oxytocin's role in behaviours linked with the 'love complex'. It found that, in prairie voles, 'social attachment, parturition, and parental behavior can occur' even in the absence of oxytocin receptors (Berendzen et al. 2023), perhaps opening a new entry in the narrative on oxytocin.

Note

1 See bibliography of Helen Fisher in the References section of this entry, which does not exhaust the author's publications on love and the brain.

References

Abend, G. (2018), 'The Love of Neuroscience: A Sociological Account', *Sociological Theory* 36 (1): 88–116. Available at https://doi.org/10.1177/0735275118759697.

Acevedo, B. P. et al. (2012), 'Neural Correlates of Long-term Intense Romantic Love', *Social Cognitive and Affective Neuroscience* 7 (2): 145–59. Available at https://doi.org/10.1093/scan/nsq092.

Aragona, B. J. *et al.* (2003), 'A Critical Role for Nucleus Accumbens Dopamine in Partner-Preference Formation in Male Prairie Voles', *Journal of Neuroscience* 23 (8): 3483–90. at https://doi.org/10.1523/JNEUROSCI.23-08-03483.2003.

Aragona, B. J. and Z. Wang (2004), 'The Prairie Vole (Microtus Ochrogaster): An Animal Model for Behavioral Neuroendocrine Research on Pair Bonding', *ILAR Journal* 45 (1): 35–45. Available at https://doi.org/10.1093/ilar.45.1.35.

Bartz, J. A. et al. (2011), 'Social Effects of Oxytocin in Humans: Context and Person Matter', *Trends in Cognitive Sciences* 15 (7): 301–9. Available at https://doi.org/10.1016/j.tics.2011.05.002.

Berendzen, K. M. et al. (2023), 'Oxytocin Receptor is Not Required for Social Attachment in Prairie Voles', *Neuron*. Available at https://doi.org/10.1016/j.neuron.2022.12.011.

Bethlehem, R. et al. (2014), 'The Oxytocin Paradox', *Frontiers in Behavioral Neuroscience* 8. Available at https://www.frontiersin.org/articles/10.3389/fnbeh.2014.00048 (accessed 24 October 2022).

Carter, C. S. (1998), 'Neuroendocrine Perspectives on Social Attachment and Love', *Psychoneuroendocrinology* 23 (8): 779–818, Available at: https://www.sciencedirect.com /science/article/pii/S0306453098000559 (accessed 24 October 2022).

Carter, C. S. (2017), 'The Oxytocin–Vasopressin Pathway in the Context of Love and Fear', *Frontiers in Endocrinology* 8. Available at https://www.frontiersin.org/articles/10.3389/ fendo.2017.00356 (accessed 24 October 2022).

Carter, C. S. (2022), 'Oxytocin and Love: Myths, Metaphors and Mysteries', *Comprehensive Psychoneuroendocrinology* 9: 100–7. Available at https://doi.org/10.1016/j.cpnec.2021 .100107.

Donaldson, Z. R. and L. J. Young (2008), 'Oxytocin, Vasopressin, and the Neurogenetics of Sociality', *Science* 322 (5903): 900–4. Available at https://doi.org/10.1126/science .1158668.

Dror, O. E. (2001), 'Techniques of the Brain and the Paradox of Emotions, 1880– 1930', *Science in Context* 14 (4): 643–60. Available at https://doi.org/10.1017/ S026988970100028X.

Earp, B. D., A. Sandberg, and J. Savulescu (2012), 'Natural Selection, Childrearing, and the Ethics of Marriage (and Divorce): Building a Case for the Neuroenhancement of Human Relationships', *Philosophy & Technology* 25 (4): 561–87. Available at https://doi .org/10.1007/s13347-012-0081-8.

Earp, B. D. and J. Savulescu (2020), *Love Drugs: The Chemical Future of Relationships*, 1st edn, Stanford: Redwood Press.

Esch, T. and G. B. Stefano (2005), 'The Neurobiology of Love', *Neuroendocrinology Letters* 26 (3): 18.

Fisher, H. (1994), *Anatomy of Love: A Natural History of Mating, Marriage, and Why We Stray*, New York: Ballantine Books.

Fisher, H. (2000), 'Lust, Attraction, Attachment: Biology and Evolution of the Three Primary Emotion Systems for . . . ', *Journal of Sex Education & Therapy* 25 (1): 96. Available at https://doi.org/10.1080/01614576.2000.11074334.

Fisher, H. (2005), *Why We Love: The Nature and Chemistry of Romantic Love*, 1st edn, New York: Holt Paperbacks.

Fisher, H. E., A. Aron, and L. L. Brown (2006), 'Romantic Love: A Mammalian Brain System for Mate Choice', *Philosophical Transactions of the Royal Society B: Biological Sciences* 361 (1476): 2173–86. Available at https://doi.org/10.1098/rstb.2006.1938.

Hansen, H. (2017), 'Assisted Technologies of Social Reproduction: Pharmaceutical Prosthesis for Gender, Race, and Class in the White Opioid "Crisis"', *Contemporary Drug Problems* 44 (4): 321–38. Available at https://doi.org/10.1177 /0091450917739391.

Haraway, D. (1988), 'Situated Knowledges: The Science Question in Feminism and the Privilege of Partial Perspective', *Feminist Studies* 14 (3): 575–99. Available at https://doi .org/10.2307/3178066.

Haraway, D. (1997), *Modest_Witness@Second_Millennium.FemaleMan_Meets_OncoMo use*, 1st edn, New York: Routledge.

Hird, M. J. (2004), 'Chimerism, Mosaicism and the Cultural Construction of Kinship', *Sexualities* 7 (2): 217–32. Available at https://doi.org/10.1177/1363460704042165.

Insel, T. R. et al. (1998), 'Oxytocin, Vasopressin, and the Neuroendocrine Basis of Pair Bond Formation', in H. H. Zingg, C. W. Bourque, and D. G. Bichet (eds), *Vasopressin and Oxytocin: Molecular, Cellular, and Clinical Advances*, 215–24. Boston, MA:

Springer US (Advances in Experimental Medicine and Biology). Available at https://doi.org/10.1007/978-1-4615-4871-3_28.

Insel, T. R. and L. E. Shapiro (1992), 'Oxytocin Receptor Distribution Reflects Social Organization in Monogamous and Polygamous Voles', *Proceedings of the National Academy of Sciences* 89 (13): 5981–5. Available at https://doi.org/10.1073/pnas.89.13.5981.

Insel, T. R., L. Young, and Z. Wang (1997), 'Molecular Aspects of Monogamy', *Annals of the New York Academy of Sciences* 807 (1): 302–16. Available at https://doi.org/10.1111/j.1749-6632.1997.tb51928.x.

Kerem, L. and E. A. Lawson (2021), 'The Effects of Oxytocin on Appetite Regulation, Food Intake and Metabolism in Humans', *International Journal of Molecular Sciences* 22 (14): 7737. Available at https://doi.org/10.3390/ijms22147737.

Knorr-Cetina, K. (1981), *The Manufacture of Knowledge: An Essay on the Constructivist and Contextual Nature of Science*, Oxford and New York: Pergamon Press (Pergamon International Library of Science, Technology, Engineering, and Social Studies).

Latour, B. (1999), 'Give Me a Laboratory and I Will Raise the World', in M. Biagioli (ed.), *The Science Studies Reader*, 258–75, New York: Routledge.

Lawson, E. A. (2017), 'The Effects of Oxytocin on Eating Behaviour and Metabolism in Humans', *Nature Reviews Endocrinology* 13 (12): 700–9. Available at https://doi.org/10.1038/nrendo.2017.115.

Olff, M. et al. (2013), 'The Role of Oxytocin in Social Bonding, Stress Regulation and Mental Health: An Update on the Moderating Effects of Context and Interindividual Differences', *Psychoneuroendocrinology* 38 (9): 1883–94. Available at https://doi.org/10.1016/j.psyneuen.2013.06.019.

Pitts-Taylor, V. (2016), 'Neurobiology and the Queerness of Kinship', in *The Brain's Body*, 95–118, Duke University Press (Neuroscience and Corporeal Politics). Available at https://doi.org/10.2307/j.ctv1134gg0.8.

Rash, J. A., A. Aguirre-Camacho, and T. S. Campbell (2014), 'Oxytocin and Pain: A Systematic Review and Synthesis of Findings', *The Clinical Journal of Pain* 30 (5): 453–62. Available at https://doi.org/10.1097/AJP.0b013e31829f57df.

Roberts, C. (2007), *Messengers of Sex: Hormones, Biomedicine and Feminism*, 1st edn, Cambridge; New York: Cambridge University Press.

Rohden, F. and F. V. Alzuguir (2016), 'Desvendando Sexos, Produzindo Gêneros e Medicamentos: A Promoção das Descobertas Científicas em Torno da Ocitocina', *Cadernos Pagu* [Preprint] 48. Available at https://doi.org/10.1590/18094449201600480002.

Ross, H. E. et al. (2009), 'Characterization of the Oxytocin System Regulating Affiliative Behavior in Female Prairie Voles', *Neuroscience* 162 (4): 892–903. Available at https://doi.org/10.1016/j.neuroscience.2009.05.055.

Savulescu, J. and A. Sandberg (2008), 'Neuroenhancement of Love and Marriage: The Chemicals Between Us', *Neuroethics* 1 (1): 31–44. Available at https://doi.org/10.1007/s12152-007-9002-4.

Shamay-Tsoory, S. G. and A. Abu-Akel (2016), 'The Social Salience Hypothesis of Oxytocin', *Biological Psychiatry* 79 (3): 194–202. Available at https://doi.org/10.1016/j.biopsych.2015.07.020.

Shen, Y. et al. (2022), 'The Emergence of Molecular Systems Neuroscience', *Molecular Brain* 15 (1): 7. Available at https://doi.org/10.1186/s13041-021-00885-5.

Smith, A. S. et al. (2021), 'Editorial: The Oxytocin System in Fear, Stress, Anguish, and Pain', *Frontiers in Endocrinology* 12: 737953. Available at https://doi.org/10.3389/fendo.2021.737953.

Sue Carter, C. (1998), 'Neuroendocrine Perspectives on Social Attachment and Love', *Psychoneuroendocrinology* 23 (8): 779–818. Available at https://doi.org/10.1016/S0306-4530(98)00055-9.

Tsuneoka, Y. et al. (2022), 'Oxytocin Facilitates Allomaternal Behavior Under Stress in Laboratory Mice', *Eneuro* 9 (1): ENEURO.0405–21.2022. Available at https://doi.org/10.1523/ENEURO.0405-21.2022.

Wang, H. et al. (2013), 'Histone Deacetylase Inhibitors Facilitate Partner Preference Formation in Female Prairie Voles', *Nature Neuroscience* 16 (7): 919–24. Available at https://doi.org/10.1038/nn.3420.

Willey, A. (2016), *Undoing Monogamy: The Politics of Science and the Possibilities of Biology*, Durham and London: Duke University Press.

Willey, A. and S. Giordano (2011), 'Sexual Dimorphism in Monogamy Gene Rescarch', in J. A. Fisher (ed.), *Gender and the Science of Difference: Cultural Politics of Contemporary Science and Medicine*, 108–25, New Brunswick, NJ, and London: Rutgers University Press.

Wudarczyk, O. A. et al. (2013), 'Could Intranasal Oxytocin be Used to Enhance Relationships? Research Imperatives, Clinical Policy, and Ethical Considerations', *Current Opinion in Psychiatry* 26 (5): 474–84. Available at https://doi.org/10.1097/YCO.0b013e3283642e10.

Yong, E. (2012a), 'Dark Side of the Love Hormone', *New Scientist*. Available at https://www.newscientist.com/article/mg21328512-100-dark-side-of-the-love-hormone/ (accessed 24 October 2022).

Yong, E. (2012b), 'Not a Hug Hormone – Fish Version of Oxytocin Acts as Social Spotlight', *Science*. Available at https://www.nationalgeographic.com/science/article/fish-oxytocin-isotocin-social-spotlight (accessed 23 October 2022).

Zak, P. (2012), *The Moral Molecule - The Source of Love and Prosperity*, New York: Dutton.

16 PITOCIN

ANDREA FORD

My doula bag includes fairy lights and electric candles. I throw in essential oils and a diffuser, soft cotton washcloths in rich forest green, herbal teas and a small jar of honey – the makings of a relaxing sensory experience. As a doula, a non-medical birth support person, I usually meet with clients before their births and initiate a discussion involving, among other things, curated playlists and portable speakers, favourite snacks and pillowcases that smell like home. Annika and Bryce's birth plan involved roasting a tray of potatoes the night her water broke, a high-energy snack familiar from her marathon-running days. Nicole's husband eased his antenatal anxiety by compiling an epic soundtrack of music from favourite films and video games; everyone laughed when the Jurassic Park theme song triumphantly filled the labour ward. I brought Brynna poppyseed cake and a velvety yellow rose when she texted to let me know her labour had started, a rose which she used as a reassuring object to focus on as we moved between home and hospital. In my ethnographic fieldwork on childbearing in the California Bay Area, these sensory details were not mere niceties. They were hormonal technologies, interventions in the physiology of the body.

Birthing spaces, birthing brains

In addition to training and practising as a doula to conduct my fieldwork from 2013 to 2016, I assisted at numerous childbirth education classes, professional and social activities for birth workers and gatherings of new parents, concerning myself with all aspects of local culture 'near birth'. A ubiquitous idea in the childbearing communities where I spent time is that birthing in a calm, safe-feeling environment is paramount; I encountered this theory everywhere from doula training, to birthing people explaining their homebirth rationale, to hospital nurses turning the lights down. In the United States, nearly 99 per cent of births take place in the hospital and the vast majority are overseen by obstetricians, not midwives. Yet, in recent decades many American hospitals have become less institutional in their aesthetics, featuring private rooms with birthing pools, welcoming family members and doulas and calling themselves 'Family Birthing Centers' instead of 'Labor and Delivery Wards'.

This shift is responding to home birth activism, and hybrid 'birth centres' stake out a middle ground in this debate; they are usually nearby a hospital, run by midwives and set up for comfort, privacy and a home-like feel, with abundant supplies for births but not for medical procedures like IV drugs, epidurals or surgery. American childbirth ethnography has both systematized the distinction between 'natural birth' and 'medicalized birth' (Davis-Floyd 1992) and shown how women have long made hybrids and compromises between competing models (Abel and Browner 1998). In my fieldwork, I found this difference was both taken for granted and constantly transgressed, functioning as a set of archetypes against which people could locate themselves, but which were never carried out in practice, as people navigated tensions around birth that have a distinctly American character (Ford forthcoming).

The importance of a comfortable and positive environment is hardly a new idea. It is common among communities with less medicalized approaches to birth and has featured in white, middle-class American genealogies at least since the natural birth movement of the 1970s, which began in California when lay midwives in the Bay Area were arrested for founding the first out-of-hospital birth centre (Ehrlich 1976). What is new is the emphasis on hormones as key to why this makes sense. Among the numerous factors that come into play in debates about birthplace, what I found key, and most interesting, is the idea that the body works differently in different places depending on how those places make one feel, a link which is hormonally mediated. From a hormonal perspective, then, the physiological success of labour is dependent on place-based affect.

Often, these hormonal narratives merged with popular neuroscience. 'There's a hormone cocktail in birth that switches moms from left to right brain thinking,' said Kristen, a childbirth educator with the American programme 'Birthing from Within' teaching a class in San Francisco. 'It's about activating that deep brain stem area, the amygdala, not the prefrontal cortex.' Neuroscience holds the prefrontal cortex responsible for cognition; it's the 'thinking brain'. By contrast, the brain stem is responsible for systemic and motor function and the amygdala for emotions and memory. During fieldwork I frequently heard references to the amygdala and brain stem as the 'reptilian brain' because it is older, evolutionarily speaking. Kristen presumed we had heard that analytic, logical, instrumental thought comes from the left brain hemisphere and creative, emotional, intuitive thought from the right. Although the distinctions between right and left brain and 'thinking brain' and 'reptilian brain' don't necessarily map onto each other, Kristen was recruiting the authoritative language of science to teach us which kinds of knowledge are relevant for birth. For her and many others I encountered, accessing emotional and intuitive knowing is crucial, as is keeping the reptilian brain at ease (see Odent 2019; Davis-Floyd 2018). Oxytocin, popularly known as 'the love hormone', is understood as key to both processes.

Oxytocin was developing a bit of a cult following in the communities where I spent time. A doula I met at a retreat taught her own childbirth preparation course called 'Birth Chemistry'; its logo featured a molecular diagram of oxytocin with a heart at its centre. I saw necklaces fashioned to represent the same molecule, and a popular science book came out called *Oxytocin: The Biological Guide to Motherhood* (Uvnäs-Moberg 2016). Countless birth blogs extoll oxytocin's virtues, and it features in cartoons and memes. But the reason oxytocin has become so prominent has to do largely with its synthetic cousin, which, as the story often goes, is also its nemesis and antithesis: the drug Pitocin (sometimes called Syntocinon). Consider an emblematic post on the natural birth website Mommypotamus.com, which shows an illustration of a brain, the left half of which is a black and white line drawing and the right half a psychedelic rainbow dripping outside the lines.[1] The title of the post is 'Pitocin vs. Oxytocin: 5 Important Ways They're Different'. The implication is that the left half of the image is one's brain on 'Pit', and the right half is one's brain on 'Oxy' (as the two were sometimes called).

Pitocin has been used regularly in hospital-managed childbirth for over fifty years. Oxytocin's uterine-contracting properties were discovered by a British pharmacologist in 1909 (the word 'oxytocin' was coined from the Greek for 'quick birth'). In 1953, oxytocin became the first polypeptide hormone to be sequenced and, two years later, synthesized; the lead scientist, Vincent du Vigneaud, was awarded the Nobel Prize (Den Hertog, De Groot and Van Dongen 2001). Pitocin-induced or augmented contractions are supposed to be stronger and more effective, and the drug is used to speed up 'slow' labours and induce labour when babies are 'late'. Pitocin is usually given alongside an epidural, which relieves the sensations of labour by numbing the birthing person from the waist down. According to the durable medical metaphor of women's bodies as machines in need of external management (Martin 2001), super strong contractions and super strong pain relief are a great combination.

Yet this story has been contested for decades by activists pushing against medically managed birth. While such pushback has long been politically and ideologically motivated (Kline 2016), its latest iteration also features hormones and biology. Basically, in a story I encountered throughout fieldwork, endogenous oxytocin was understood as part of a hormonal cascade, supporting a view of birth as a responsive process instead of a mechanical problem, and often narrated in terms of the body's wisdom and wise design. The cascade metaphor was used to encompass experiential qualities such as stress or pleasure and advocate for their relevance on a molecular level. By contrast, Pitocin was not only not part of a beneficial cascade but caused a cascade of its own: a cascade of interventions.[2]

Competing cascades

The list of oxytocin's capacities and responsibilities, as I encountered them in speaking with people and browsing online forums, includes causing uterine contractions, providing pain relief, initiating lactation and stimulating bonding between birthing person and infant. It is also associated with cuddling, affection and orgasm. Pitocin very effectively stimulates uterine contractions, but although its chemical signature is identical to oxytocin's, it doesn't carry any of the other functions. Pitocin is administered intravenously and stays only in the bloodstream; by contrast, oxytocin (produced in the hypothalamus) goes into the bloodstream and the brain. In the brain, it triggers beta-endorphin release that calms pain (endorphins are sometimes called 'endogenous morphine') and stimulates the release of other hormones that help soften the cervix. Oxytocin is produced in pulses or waves, giving the birthing person, uterine muscles and foetus breaks between contractions. Its levels usually spike just before the pushing phase of labour, triggering a 'foetal ejection reflex' that involves epinephrine and norepinephrine, the 'excitement hormones'. By contrast with oxytocin's fluctuations, Pitocin is administered continuously, although its intensity can be adjusted by a medical professional. After the birth, oxytocin helps the uterus expel the placenta and contract its blood vessels, so they stop bleeding (an intramuscular shot of Pitocin is commonly given after an unmedicated labour to boost this haemorrhage prevention). I heard people speculate that before modern medicine, the oxytocin released by breastfeeding would have saved mothers' lives by preventing postpartum haemorrhage.

Also often articulated in evolutionary terms and in relation to the 'reptilian brain', stress and fear were understood to block the oxytocin cascade through the 'fight, flight or freeze' response involving cortisol and adrenaline. If there is danger present, one can't relax and 'surrender' to birth (a common turn of phrase). Physicians well known within the natural birth community, like Sarah Buckley and Michel Odent, extol this view. Odent famously advocates that women give birth in a dark room with only another woman quietly knitting in the corner (Shanley and Odent 2012 – I have thought about adding an unfinished knitting project to my doula bag, but I'm a terrible knitter and my attempts would soothe no one!). Among doulas I knew, going to the hospital was itself seen as a disruptive and stressful intervention, if sometimes a necessary one. Buckley rhapsodizes about the ecstatic birth possible when hormones are allowed to take oneself out of one's normal state (literally 'ex-stasis') (Buckley 2010). This perspective is making its way into authoritative medical literature, considering birth a 'neuro-psycho-social event' in which endogenous oxytocin cascades are key not only to physiology but also the birthing person's (and foetus's) psychological experience. A PlosOne paper of which Buckley is among the eleven authors suggests that the 'spontaneous altered state of consciousness, that some women experience, may well be a hallmark of physiological childbirth in humans' (Olza et al. 2020: 1).

A common argument related to this physiological view of childbirth asserts that medical interventions cause the problems they then claim to fix, a 'cascade of interventions' story that usually features Pitocin as the villain. Because contractions caused by Pitocin are more painful, they prompt labouring people to request epidural pain relief. Because the birthing person cannot then easily stand or walk (and must be continuously monitored and often have a catheter), they must lie on a hospital bed. This sedentariness can stall labour, and lying down makes it more difficult for the baby to pass through the pelvis. In a non-medical approach – for example, in my doula training – movement is a key 'coping mechanism' and recommended practice for managing pain and progressing labour. Because labour has slowed, Pitocin is increased. Although the birthing person cannot feel the now hyperstrong contractions, the foetus can, leading to foetal 'distress' – changes in heart rate indicating lack of oxygen. Such 'hypoxia' makes delivery seem urgent, which may lead to an emergency caesarean. Labours with Pitocin and epidurals are more likely to be deemed 'failure to progress' (which some protest is merely 'failure to wait'), another cause for caesarean. Pitocin can thus be said to drive the American caesarean 'epidemic' (Morris 2016), with rates at around 33 per cent as opposed to the World Health Organization's recommended maximum of 10 per cent.

Crafting the birthing environment, then, involves both moderating stress and fear-related hormones and managing access to Pitocin, both of which interrupt the 'good' hormone cascade needed for birth. Desirable place-based affects are not simply a matter of having relaxing music or someone familiar nearby but are inextricably entwined with the technological apparatus at hand and regimes of protocol, liability and insurance. Consider a nurse doing a Pitocin induction because the amniotic sac ruptured and hospital protocol states that labour must be induced after twenty-four hours because of infection risk: although the nurse may be kind and informative or brusque and controlling, which will shape how the patient feels and which hormone cascades they are subject to, in another sense the policy itself is a third actor in the room. Infrastructures shape birthplace accessibility, as most people in the United States choose a hospital or provider based on their insurance plan, and most insurance does not cover home births. The fact that a birthplace has ready access to Pitocin and other medical procedures can itself produce feelings of safety or threat, depending on who you talk to. Hospital promotion of interventions can be unpleasant for people who intend to birth without them, ranging from nervous annoyance to coercion and violation. On the other hand, cultural pressure to birth 'naturally' can produce its own copious anxiety! Many people feel more relaxed with such technologies at hand 'if needed', which is the basis for the common idea that hospitals are the 'safest' place to give birth.

Uncertainties and complications

Hormones mediate the emotional, social, infrastructural and material facets of birth environments. Yet attending to hormone cascades can cause a tangle of uncertainty about cause and effect. Did the 'natural' oxytocin response fail or did conditions prohibit it from ever being achieved? Maybe the birthing person's fear stopped their oxytocin from working. Maybe the pressure to make progress created anxiety that halted progress, or perhaps labour induction saved the baby's life because staying in the womb was risky. Maybe the birthing person was exhausted and wanted rest more than they wanted a vaginal birth, or perhaps the epidural provided rest that gave them strength to push the baby out vaginally. Maybe the drugs during labour prevented their milk from coming in or perhaps their baby would have had trouble latching onto the breast even without any interventions. Then again, that optimal window for bonding and latching may have been lost forever in the operating room.

Like any drug, Pitocin is a tool that can be used in various ways towards various ends, and many factors complicate achieving its 'ideal' use. Since at least the 1980s, obstetrics research has critiqued and refined Pitocin use (e.g. Brindley and Sokol 1988), but 'best practice' recommendations don't always align with actual practices as many providers continue to operate on tradition or outdated training. Also, at least in the stories I encountered in birth communities (spanning medical and non-medical spaces), there was conflicting information about whether and how Pitocin overrides the physiological oxytocin response. Oxytocin production is controlled by a positive feedback mechanism where release of the hormone stimulates more of its own release,[3] and there is reason to think Pitocin blocks or dulls the oxytocin receptors, interrupting the feedback loop (Gottlieb 2019). If an advanced stage of labour is reached prior to Pitocin use, the 'natural' cascade may have had a chance to build momentum; on the other hand, judiciously modest amounts of Pitocin might provide a boost without setting off a cascade.

It is also unclear what effects the foetus may suffer during labour. Some say that because endogenous oxytocin creates systemic effects, it also reaches the foetus, relieving pain and helping them stay calm (medical expertise over the past century has largely discounted foetal and infant ability to feel pain; Chamberlain 1998). Whether the baby will have drugs in their bloodstream after birth, and whether this matters, is unclear and contentious. Perhaps the epidural narcotics will cause them to be dull or agitated. Perhaps they won't have experienced the preparatory effects of oxytocin or adrenaline. If neither the baby nor the birthing person have had the 'hormone cocktail' that stimulates bonding and breastfeeding, perhaps these activities might be challenging, which might contribute to maternal postpartum depression (Bell, Erickson and Carter 2014; Gu et al. 2016) and infant failure to thrive (see the Association for Pre- and Perinatal Psychology and Health (APPPAH), founded in the Bay Area).

Further complicating things, Pitocin's use and abuse echoes histories of prestige and abjection in accessing medical spaces and tools. Access to pain relief during labour has been (and continues to be) denied to people of colour on the basis of racist beliefs that they are 'hardier' and less sensitive to pain (Scott and Davis 2021). Obstetrics and gynaecology were shaped by the idea that wealthy white women are 'overcivilized', 'fragile' and 'hysterical' while non-European women were coded as 'savages' and closer to animals on racist evolutionary hierarchies (Briggs 2000). African American communities that had been excluded from hospital care viewed accessing it in the later twentieth century as a success, albeit one that changed the nature of bodies and communities (Fraser 1998). On the other hand, Black doulas I knew, and others who were not from white middle-class backgrounds, emphasized their connection to traditional knowledge and indigenous wisdom; a few quipped that medical knowledge integrating hormonal, affective understandings of physiology had simply finally caught up to what people knew already!

The white, middle-class feminism of the natural birth movement pushed against patronizing obstetrics by embracing birth's intensity and 'reclaiming' a version of animal power. Yet a few decades earlier, advocating for medical pain relief was a key first-wave feminist cause, pushing against a misogynistic Christian heritage interpreting labour pain as Eve's curse for women to bear (Gonzalez 2013). In the

US context of private medical insurance, there can be vast differences between crowded public hospitals where Pitocin is sometimes used to speed up labours and vacate beds and 'Family Birthing Centers' with jacuzzies. When I volunteered at a Catholic home for childbearing women in difficult circumstances, the middle-classness of positive associations with 'home' was thrown into relief; people tended to want to go to the hospital as soon as possible and stay as long as possible, where they felt attended to and in charge in a different way. Social stratifications and political histories complicate what counts as a 'comfortable environment'.

Making the 'natural' body

Bodies are not blank canvases but are always already constituted through habits of being and knowing. As Emilia Sanabria (2016) shows in her work on the hormonal body in Brazil, it is inadequate (though common) to evaluate the politics of intervention via a false dichotomy between technological 'interventions' and natural 'non-interventions'. Thus, as happens in the birthing spaces where I spent time, the 'natural' body must be cultivated and acted upon, as well (Oudshoorn 1994). The Oxytocin-as-hero, Pitocin-as-villain and Pitocin-as-saviour stories are not only simplified but part of broader cultural projects to understand bodies and bodily experience in certain ways.

Navigating the tangle of influences, interpretations and uncertainties around birth has become a new rite of passage, particularly for aspirational-class American childbearing people. As I describe elsewhere (Ford 2020), this requires gathering scientific information and getting in touch with one's desires, preferences and fears, then proactively shaping one's birth experience by unleashing the 'primordial' body and 'gut instinct' alongside a rational, informed strategy for optimized decision-making. Hormones are implicit in many aspects of this process. Through cultivating not only their external environment but also their internal capacities, birthing people might maximize their oxytocin cascade and, in turn, their birth 'outcomes' variously defined. To some extent, hormones are considered involuntary biological responses, yet one can learn which hormonal responses are beneficial and rationally train oneself, through 'mindfulness' or something similar, to be more or less open to their effects. Ideas about properly cultivated birthing sensibilities posit hormones as both a site of innate response and a medium for self-cultivation (see also Roberts, Malcolm and Boylston in this volume).

Far from simply being imposter oxytocin, a less talented and meddlesome sibling, Pitocin is part of this multifaceted, slippery, ever-evolving constellation of meanings attached to bodily experiences of childbirth. It is part of the cultural apparatus that enables some birthing people to shape their techno-natural hormonal self and (attempt to) craft a personally optimal experience, while forcing others into cursory and institutionally convenient care. It sometimes seemed to me like a useful scapegoat to explain why bodies 'failed' to perform as expected, yet could also serve as an anchor for those who appreciate a sense of technological control.

The stories told about Pitocin are spooled into bigger cultural projects, such as obstetrician Michel Odent's postulation that widespread Pitocin use (alongside epidurals and caesareans, which all disrupt the oxytocin cascade) negatively affects the perinatal 'primal health period' and 'primal adaptive system' during which an endocrine, immune and nervous system 'template' of health is set (1986). He connects Pitocin to contemporary rises in non-communicable diseases that have been linked with oxytocin processing, such as autism and anorexia (2010), as well as antisocial behaviour that he glosses as 'the (in)ability to love', pushing the hormonal bridge between biology and the social to an extreme (2007; see also Krol et al. 2019; and Malcolm and Griner and Zorzanelli in this volume). Researchers are calling for investigations into these developmental and epigenetic effects (Sakala, Romano and Buckley 2016) as well as better research into childbirth trauma and the role of endogenous and synthetic oxytocin in preventing and treating post-traumatic stress disorder (Witteveen et al. 2020).

The science of hormones and the bodily imaginary it makes possible increasingly bridges not only the biological and social but also concerned birth actors of diverse backgrounds and allegiances. Scientific and evidentiary rationales merge with political emphasis on the importance of birthing people's experience and respectful care provision. Much like 'evidence' itself (Ford 2019; Akrich et al. 2014), hormones can mean different things to different actors while allowing them to access the same authoritative language, which then serves as a platform for effecting change. Hormones are biomedically recognized, measurable, material substances, yet are entwined with experiential energies like 'stress' or 'pleasure'. Talk of hormones carries the scientific authority associated with objectivity, while narratives of birthing bodies increasingly emphasize how hormones are involved in creating and responding to subjective experiences. Birth activism is a provocative example of how cultural, biological, social and environmental understandings of hormones are becoming (re)integrated into ways of knowing bodies and practicing care.

Acknowledgements

With special thanks to Celia Roberts, Lisa Raeder, Hannah Chazin and Meghan Morris for discussing this piece with me. This research was funded in part by the Wellcome Trust (grant number 209519/Z/17/Z).

Notes

1 https://web.archive.org/web/20220427141633/https://mommypotamus.com/pitocin -oxytocin/. The earliest comments on the page are from 2014. Accessed 27 April 2022.
2 This webpage is an excellent example: https://web.archive.org/web/20220521212222/ https://www.mamanatural.com/epidural-side-effects/.
3 https://www.yourhormones.info/hormones/oxytocin/.

References

Abel, E. and C. Browner (1998), 'Selective Compliance with Biomedical Authority and the Uses of Experiential Knowledge', in M. Lock and P. Kaufert (eds), *Pragmatic Women and Body Politics*, 310–26, Cambridge: Cambridge University.

Akrich, M., L. Máire, C. Roberts, and J. Arriscado Nunes (2014), 'Practising Childbirth Activism: A Politics of Evidence', *BioSocieties* 9 (2): 129–52.

Bell, A. F., E. N. Erickson, and C. S. Carter (2014), 'Beyond Labor: The Role of Natural and Synthetic Oxytocin in the Transition to Motherhood', *Journal of Midwifery & Women's Health* 59 (1): 35–42.

Briggs, L. (2000), 'The Race of Hysteria: "Overcivilization" and the "Savage" Woman in Late Nineteenth-Century Obstetrics and Gynecology', *American Quarterly* 52 (2): 246–73.

Brindley, B. A. and R. J. Sokol (1988), 'Induction and Augmentation of Labor: Basis and Methods for Current Practice', *Obstetrical & Gynecological Survey* 43 (12): 730–43.

Buckley, S. (2010), *Ecstatic Birth: Nature's Hormonal Blueprint for Labor*. Available at https://sarahbuckley.com/wp-content/uploads/2014/02/Ecstatic-birth-ebook-w.pdf.

Chamberlain, D. (1998), '"Babies Don't Feel Pain": A Century of Denial in Medicine', in R. Davis-Floyd and J. Dumit (eds), *Cyborg Babies: From Techno-Sex to Techno-Tots*, 168–92, New York: Routledge.

Davis-Floyd, R. (1992), *Birth as an American Rite of Passage*, Berkeley: University of California.

Davis-Floyd, R. (2018), *Ways of Knowing About Birth: Mothers, Midwives, Medicine, & Birth Activism*, Long Grove: Waveland.

Ehrlich, K. H. (1976), 'The Santa Cruz Birth Center Today', *Birth and the Family Journal* 3 (3): 119–26.

Ford, A. (2019), 'Advocating for Evidence in Birth: Proving Cause, Effecting Outcomes, and Making the Case for "Curers"', *Medicine Anthropology Theory* 6 (2): 25–48.

Ford, A. (2020), 'Birthing From Within: Nature, Technology, and Self-Making in Silicon Valley Childbearing', *Cultural Anthropology* 35 (4): 602–30.

Ford, A. (forthcoming), *Near Birth: The Doula Phenomenon and American Values*, University of California Press.

Fraser, G. J. (1998), *African American Midwifery in the South*, Cambridge, MA: Harvard University Press.

Gonzalez, M. and I. Lusztig (2013), 'The Birth of Motherhood', *The New Inquiry*. Available at https://thenewinquiry.com/the-birth-of-motherhood/.

Gottlieb, M. M. (2019), 'A Mathematical Model Relating Pitocin Use During Labor With Offspring Autism Development in Terms of Oxytocin Receptor Desensitization in the Fetal Brain', *Computational and Mathematical Methods in Medicine* 2019: 8276715.

Gu, V., N. Feeley, I. Gold, B. Hayton, and S Robins (2016), 'Intrapartum Synthetic Oxytocin and Its Effects on Maternal Well-being At 2 Months Postpartum', *Birth* 43 (1): 28–35.

den Hertog, C. E. C., A. N. J. A. de Groot, and P. W. J van Dongen (2001), 'History and Use of Oxytocics', *European Journal of Obstetrics & Gynecology and Reproductive Biology* 94 (1): 8–12.

Kline, W. (2016), 'The Little Manual That Started a Revolution: How Hippie Midwifery Became Mainstream', in D. Kaiser and P. McCray (eds), *Groovy Science: Knowledge, Innovation, and American Counterculture*, Chicago: The University of Chicago Press.

Krol, K. M., R. G. Moulder, T. S. Lillard, T. Grossmann, and J. J. Connelly (2019), 'Epigenetic Dynamics in Infancy and the Impact of Maternal Engagement', *Science Advances* 5 (10): eaay0680.

Martin, E. (2001), *The Woman in the Body: A Cultural Analysis of Reproduction*, Boston: Beacon Press.

Morris, T. (2016), *Cut it Out: The C-Section Epidemic in America*, New York: New York University Press.

Odent, M. (1986), *Primal Health: A Blueprint for Our Survival*, Sussex: Clairview.

Odent, M. (2007), 'Antisocial Behaviours from a Primal Health Research Perspective', *Midwifery Today* 81: 12.

Odent, M. (2010), 'Autism and Anorexia Nervosa: Two Facets of the Same Disease?', *Med Hypotheses* 75 (1): 79–81.

Odent, M. (2019), 'Physiological Birth Preparation', *Journal of Prenatal & Perinatal Psychology & Health* 33 (3): 1–6.

Olza, I., K. Uvnas-Moberg, A. Ekström-Bergström, P. Leahy-Warren, S. I. Karlsdottir, M. Nieuwenhuijze, S. Villarmea, E. Hadjigeorgiou, M. Kazmierczak, and A. Spyridou (2020), 'Birth as a Neuro-Psycho-social Event: An Integrative Model of Maternal Experiences and Their Relation to Neurohormonal Events During Childbirth', *PlosOne* 15 (7): e0230992.

Oudshoorn, N. (1994), *Beyond the Natural Body: An Archaeology of Sex Hormones*, London: Routledge.

Sakala, C., A. M. Romano, and S. J. Buckley (2016), 'Hormonal Physiology of Childbearing, an Essential Framework for Maternal-Newborn Nursing', *Journal of Obstetric, Gynecologic, & Neonatal Nursing* 45 (2): 264–75.

Sanabria, E. (2016), *Plastic Bodies: Sex Hormones and Menstrual Suppression in Brazil*, Durham: Duke University Press.

Scott, K. A. and D-A. Davis (2021), 'Obstetric Racism: Naming and Identifying a Way Out of Black Women's Adverse Medical Experiences', *American Anthropologist* 123 (3): 681–4.

Shanley, L. K. and M. Odent (2012), *Unassisted Childbirth*, Santa Barbara: Praeger.

Uvnäs-Moberg, K. (2016), *Oxytocin: The Biological Guide to Motherhood*, Amarillo: Praeclarus Press.

Witteveen, A. B., C. A. I. Stramrood, J. Henrichs, J. C. Flanagan, M. G. van Pampus, and M. Olff (2020), 'The Oxytocinergic System in PTSD Following Traumatic Childbirth', *Archives of Women's Mental Health* 23 (3): 317–29.

17 PROGESTERONE

NAYANTARA SHEORAN APPLETON

*   *   *

Taiaki Tūmua

Biochemistry. a hormone, $C_{21}H_{30}O_2$

Pharmacology. a commercial form of this compound, obtained from the corpus luteum of pregnant sows or synthesized: used for multiple purposes ranging from gender-affirming therapy to building muscle mass.

Also known in the English language as:

Progesterone

Biochemistry. a hormone, $C_{21}H_{30}O_2$, that prepares the uterus for the fertilized ovum and maintains pregnancy.

Pharmacology. a commercial form of this compound, obtained from the corpus luteum of pregnant sows or synthesized: used in the treatment of dysfunctional uterine bleeding, dysmenorrhea, threatened or recurrent abortion, etc.

Source: Collins Dictionary

Etymology (English). a name given to a class of hormones capable of preparing the endometrium to receive the fertilized ovum; the term combines 'pro-' in the sense of 'before' and 'in behalf of' with a derivative of the Latin *gestare,* 'to bear'. The active principal originally extracted from the corpora lutea of sows was called 'progestin' by A. W. Comer and W. M. Allen in 1929. Later, this was refined as progesterone to indicate both its action and its steroid structure.

*   *   *

This entry makes the case that we need a new language, a new word and new understandings for progesterone (among other biological matter) – to unmoor it from etymology where it was designated a 'female' hormone for reproductive purposes. The gendered language of science has long been questioned (Martin 1991) and in *Testosterone Rex*, Cordelia Fine makes visible the problematic science of 'gendering' a hormone in particular (Fine 2017). The naming and categorization bears not only the imprint of the hormone but rather also the biases and limits of imagination of the researchers doing this work at the moment of 'discovery'.

Language matters.

Language shapes.

Language restricts and also makes possible.

From the early structuralist roots of semiotic and linguistic theory to what I call a femo-queer possibility, language is power. I use femo-queer as a term to identify queer-aligning feminists and/or progressive feminist-aligning queer folx. Far from theorized thus far, it is a term that has allowed me to teach and engage with students through a politics that is in opposition to the politics of trans-exclusionary radical feminists (TERFs). It is words, language, doing political work. For bell hooks, 'Like desire, language disrupts, refuses to be contained within boundaries' (hooks 1994: 167). Language for new possibilities also lives in borderlands, and Gloria Anzaldúa reminds us of multiple languages she spoke as a way to speak back to particular oppressions:

> I will no longer be made to feel ashamed of existing. I will have my voice: Indian, Spanish, white. I will have my serpent's tongue – my woman's voice, my sexual voice, my poet's voice. I will overcome the tradition of silence. (Anzaldúa 2007: 81)

Language makes possible overcoming traditions – of silence and, as I show later, of science. Multiple languages, working multiply across scales, resist a singularity and make possible rhizomatic understandings of biological matter.

Inspired by Hélène Cixous's feminist work on the body (Cixous et al. 1976), Deboleena Roy encourages a critical science by feminists to think about language on and about the scientific object:

> Part of the feminist practice of creating a breach and causing fissures, ruptures and transformations to our scientific knowledge of the body requires that feminists invent a language that is subversive. This is indeed a formidable task in the case of developing a language for a new history of biology, one that incorporates critical feminist inquiries into the actual matters of the biological body. It is formidable because it necessitates questioning biological 'truths' that have been established by the authority of scientific law and reasoning. (Roy 2007)

In this, one of her earlier writings, Roy asks to undertake this 'formidable' task of not only finding new language for biological matter but also using that new language to continually revisit that biological matter.

It was thus one of my first research undertakings to see what progesterone is called in different languages – starting with languages familiar to me. I found that this hormone, in different locations and linguistic traditions in Hindi, is essentially progesterone spelled differently or in a different script. However, in looking up medical dictionaries in Te Reo Māori, the language of the people of Aotearoa New Zealand where I live as manuhiri (guest/immigrant), I found that the word is not a derivative of 'pro' or 'gestate'. Rather, it is Taiaki Tūmua.

Taiaki Tūmua and a vocabulary for the future

Taiaki Tūmua
1. (noun) progesterone
(*Source*: Te Aka, Māori Dictionary)

It is vital to make clear here that I am just an early learner of te reo, having only moved to Aotearoa in 2015. I am manuhiri – a guest in Aotearoa as a first-generation immigrant. I am neither a te reo expert nor a linguist. I am not claiming the language or the work it does but instead sharing with a wider audience a word that I have had to learn as I do research in Aotearoa. This writing is funded by a research project titled 'Social lives of Sex Hormones: (Re)imagining Our Bodies, Ourselves in Aotearoa New Zealand'. I am working on the social lives of hormones, I have to know what they are called in languages outside of English. I want to – I *need* to – use the words that help me understand this biological material as unmoored for its histories of 'gestate'.

Taiaki Tūmua is not related to gestation or pregnancy etymologically speaking. This is *not* a footnote but rather an important part of the politics of imagining a future science vocabulary. Finding words that tell stories of biological material that are not hinged on singular origin stories of/from white, cis, endosex, elite men (and women) working in laboratories means making space for multiplicity.

As I am writing this short glossary entry on Taiaki Tūmua, colleagues in Aotearoa have published a paper on how Māori and Pacific postgraduate students in science, technology, engineering and math (STEM) are not only under-represented, but also when they are 'included' in the sciences in New Zealand universities they are made to suffer 'institutional habits' that limit them and their contributions. They write:

> Institutional habits are the actions and responses that are ingrained into our university systems that are not endemic but have become 'naturalised' over time and hence made invisible. These institutional habits generate excess labour for Indigenous people and enforce exclusion of Indigenous knowledge in universities (Acton et al. 2017; Ruwhiu 2014). Importantly, our collaborators also articulated how institutional habits drive behaviours around research funding. (McAllister et al. 2022)

The very title of this paper, 'seen but unheard', is a stark reminder of how words, utterances and languages of Indigenous communities are unheard within the sciences. It is clear from this research that even in 2022, when included, Indigenous scholars do not get a chance to shape the spaces or the sciences within which they are working – instead, they are made to feel marginal and exhausted at all turns. If there is any hope of future-facing progressive scientific knowledge, the contemporary (not historically settled) task is manyfold. First, to include more diversity in the spaces where scientific knowledge is generated (i.e. change the spaces). Second, to change scientific knowledge itself by paying attention to the material of scientific inquiry. And third (not finally), to change the language with which we explore to allow for a generative multiplicity[1] in our knowledges of facts.

More than reproduction

Previously, I have written about feminist commons with technoscientific futures (Appleton 2017b) as a space where we again make 'common' scientific knowledge and build multiply from that space but with a particular attention to contemporary and progressive possibilities. In that reworking not only of the biological matter but also our semiotic sense of it, we pay particular attention to ensuring a 'strong objectivity' (Harding 1992b, 1992a, 1995) lest we repeat the original problematic. The current understanding of hormones (among other biology) is vastly different from what was 'discovered' in the early 1900s. And while previously I have written about the 'unintended logics' and consequences of hormones (Appleton 2019), I now revisit that 'unintended' as a reflection on the language that teaches us about the 'intended' use of particular hormones. Our language and the words we use for most biological materials are still hinged on the original word used at moment of discovery, ignoring the fact that such language can limit not only what we know but also what we are willing to spend energy towards knowing.

For reasons of space and design, I outline only two areas of emerging research that 'unsettle'[2] the way we have been writing about Taiaki Tūmua. I cannot map out entire debates in each of these fields but instead draw on review articles that outline the debates that have shaped their respective fields. It is vital to note that Taiaki Tūmua does a *lot* in the human body from developing muscle mass, impacting metabolism and influencing experiences of menopause, to shaping our very physical and emotional desires. However, it has also incorrectly been assumed to do other things that it does not. Two key areas that require us to decouple Taiaki Tūmua from the female reproductive system and gestation are its role in the central nervous system (CNS) and gender-affirming hormone therapy (GAHT).

In a 2019 review article for *Frontiers of Neuroscience*, Juan Carlos González-Orozco and Ignacio Camacho-Arroyo highlight the fact that both males and females synthesize Taiaki Tūmua. This review draws from an extensive range of studies to highlight that Taiaki Tūmua plays a vital role in the CNS for all humans and that such actions are present through the life course. Taiaki Tūmua regulates non-reproductive functions, including neuroprotection, neuromodulation, myelination, neurogenesis, neuronal plasticity, and mood (Schumacher et al. 2004). Therefore, given that progesterone is synthesized, metabolized and exerts its actions in the CNS, it is referred to as a 'neurosteroid' (González-Orozco and Camacho-Arroyo 2019).

Emerging research shows that use of progesterone/Taiaki Tūmua in GAHT for transwomen and non-binary people is assumed to help in breast maturation, prevention of bone loss and to convey benefits for cardiovascular health; however, these claims have largely been extrapolated from cisgender women's bodies. More research on these key parameters has been called for (Milionis et al. 2022). The use of Taiaki Tūmua for GAHT by transwomen has largely been influenced by the historical ideas around how this hormone works in cis women's bodies because of its historical attachment as a 'women's hormone.' In a 2022 review article[3] in *Endocrine Practice*, Patel et al. show that its use for GAHT for trans women leads to reduced HDL levels and increased thromboembolism, and further, that assumed benefits to breast development or quality of life were in fact inconclusive (Patel et al. 2022). They similarly call for further research on the assumed versus real benefits of using Taiaki Tūmua in GAHT for transwomen.

The two listings above are but the few places where Taiaki Tūmua does/undoes outside of the 'gestational' space that deemed it a 'female hormone' in a lab in the

1920s. Taiaki Tūmua is a hormone in all bodies but also needs to be examined differently in different bodies (e.g. in transwomen's bodies). Celia Roberts, in some of her pathbreaking work on feminist engagements with sex hormones, asked feminists of science to find a 'middle way', where the biological is not rejected or ignored in attempts to recast hormones as social beings (Roberts 2000). The (limited) research outlined above is from scientists who are willing to see the roles and functions of Taiaki Tūmua beyond the 'female sex hormone' function of managing and maintaining a pregnancy.

Porous skins, hormonal balances and environmental change

If we take Roberts's call for the 'middle way' seriously (i.e. paying attention to the biological matter alongside the social – including language), we then also have to account for the huge impact of environmental shifts on both the biological and social. Taiaki Tūmua will not be immune to the climatic change and its direct impact on its concentrations in our body – however, how it reacts needs sustained analysis, from both the natural and social sciences.

There is now a well-established consensus on prenatal, perinatal and environmental impacts on hormonal levels alongside the hormonal shifts as the body ages. It is clear that our biology, our biological body, is never settled – if anything, it is constantly evolving. It is rendered plastic by the fluctuations and manipulations of our hormonal regimes (Sanabria 2016). This is magnified when examining the hormonal body and its constant fluidity (daily, weekly, monthly and yearly) – especially considering environmental shifts. Human bodies, alongside those of non-humans, are constantly exposed and submerged in chemical regimens (Hardon 2021; Hardon et al. 2013; Murphy 2008, 2017; Wylie 2018). Social scientists have shown how anxieties around shifting biologies (human and non-human) because of such chemical exposures are described in natural science scholarship as out of control or heterosexual-reproduction-run-amuck (Ah-King and Hayward 2014; Lappé et al. 2019; Pollock 2016).

Currently, within the natural sciences there is a great concern about amphibian and fish reproduction which is impacted by gestagens (which are comprised of both endogenous progestogens and synthetic progestins) found in water because of paper mill, wastewater and animal agricultural facilities (Frankel et al. 2016; Orlando and Ellestad 2014). Further research shows, however, that the presence of progestins – progesterone (P4) and drospirenone (DRS) – also impacts the circadian rhythms of zebrafish (Zhao et al. 2015). Although the focus thus far has typically been on the impact of Taiaki Tūmua (and other gestagens) on reproduction, Zhao et al. (2015), in seeing the impact on circadian rhythms, suggest further studies that examine the impact of these on other physiological processes. While we know that increased Taiaki Tūmua levels will lead to changes in reproduction – both in human and non-humans – there is a renewed call to examine the impact of environmental progestins on more than reproduction. As the studies listed in the previous section show, Taiaki Tūmua is more than just a gestational hormone and thus, circulating in our 'environments' alongside other influences (stress, movement, poverty, nutrition, etc.), it will shape all our bodies beyond reproduction. Humans, animals and plants alike are exposed to synthesized chemicals that influence us – our biology and our social worlds.

Taiaki Tūmua is in our waterways, food chains and in our medicine cabinets – and it is shaping us. Locating 'responsibility' for hormonal states 'out of control', then, becomes complicated, as they exceed any given person's control and require thinking about responsibility for illness and wellness in social and ecological terms. While there is an emerging 'wellness' field of 'hormonal balancing' (Appleton 2022), this is seated in politics of self-responsibilization and Not In My Back Yard (NIMBY) sensibilities that apportion blame elsewhere and afford rich bodies agency in avoiding toxicity. These politics are couched in a 'pull yourself up by your bootstraps' middle-class white sensibility – where the suggestion seems to be that a global-level environment shift can be managed by eating kale and micro-greens!

I am reminded of a conversation with Mani Mitchell, a friend and colleague, who has been at the forefront of intersex rights and justice for decades. Chatting about environmental degradation, they said:

> I know it's really bad with these toxins, but they also have been fretting about intersex children because of these toxic exposures. There will be more of us, and that can't be a bad thing, can it Nayan?

Mani is perhaps onto something. While absolutely worried about the climate crisis, Mani is careful to also consider the reality of living through this crisis without blaming the victims. Environmental change is shaping all biology – including reproductive. There is emerging research that endocrine-disrupting chemical exposures in foetal development stages are leading to an increased prevalence of variation and atypical sexual development in human children (Rich et al. 2016). And while this may be a point of anxiety in some spaces, it is perhaps an opportunity within feminist and queer studies of science to renew their commitment to changing the language of science. Our task is multifold – to recognize that our extractive capitalistic/colonial systems are changing all our biologies and then also make space in society for these changed biologies (intersex lives being one example).

This current interdisciplinary volume works to extend and perhaps render redundant the historic boundaries of hormonal sciences. For my own writing, I draw on critical science studies scholars who talk and talk back to 'Science' (or

Western science) to change languages of anxiety around non-binary and non-heteronormative lives made visible in and through our hormonal shifts. This call is also to recognize that the language(s) used for certain hormones are limiting their own analysis – that is, Taiaki Tūmua being seen often as a 'female hormone' because of its English name progesterone (attaching it to gestation). This book and scholars working on both the science and sociality of hormones must rebuild a scientific common with new language and new positionalities.

Conclusion: Language of/for new possibilities

In 2020, the *Journal of Molecular Endocrinology* published a special issue celebrating ninety years of the discovery of progesterone. The special issue titled 'Ninety Years of Progesterone: The "Other" Ovarian Hormone'. Yes, Taiaki Tūmua is produced in the ovaries, but if a body has adrenal glands and testes, it is produced there as well. In recentring the ovaries as a site of production of Taiaki Tūmua, the endocrinologists do this biological material disservice. It is the other ovarian hormone, but it is also a testicular and adrenal hormone. For social scientists of science, we have to ensure that our *language* for change of science and scientific spaces is also heard among the scientists. Ideally, when we come to celebrate 100 years of Taiaki Tūmua (progesterone – English), the special issue can be retitled '100 Years of Taiaki Tūmua: The Possibilities!'

When thinking about hormonal theory, we cannot ignore the *work words do* – alongside the work of the hormones themselves. To theorize, we need new languages – this glossary is one such way. We need to change the language of science and hormones if we want to highlight how language has limited the way we think about these scientific artefacts. In attempting to reimagine progesterone as a scientific artefact, biological material and social actor, we will at some point need a new word. A new language to decouple it from being a sex hormone in 'women's' body to enable reproduction. This work of decoupling a 'sex hormone' from its essentialist and reductive reading is well underway with Roberts's work on oestrogen (Roberts 2003, 2007) and Fine's on testosterone (Fine 2017). It is in moving beyond the initially articulated 'work' 'sex hormones' did that we can see that the possibilities are limitless – and scientists and social scientist will have to work together to re-articulate these multifaceted biological matter.

And to do this with laughter, humility and honesty. As Roy writes:

What has made me laugh as a feminist scientist, and what has allowed me to bring humor to my political project, has been the realization that each and every biological experiment I conducted in the lab was in fact an experiment in uncertainty, an experiment in transforming uncertainty into materiality. There is much room for feminist philosophies of subjectivity and theories of embodiment to guide these transformations from uncertainty to materiality. (Roy 2007)

We cannot ignore the fact that Taiaki Tūmua is a hormonal *matter* that needs a reanalysis. Calling progesterone by another name will not change its cellular structure or what it does in the body. However, in calling it something that decouples it from reproduction will compel us to collectively think about hormones as biology that transgresses bodily systems and functions and even the boundary of our skin. A new language for Taiaki Tūmua and all it does in human and non-human bodies will account for its history in reproductive sciences but also a future that recognizes environmental seepages and a new scientific body that is porous in both material and immaterial ways.

Notes

1 Multiplicity, as Michelle Murphy shows us, is incredibly complex. While on the one hand our evidence shows a multiplicity of chemical exposures, it also limits the legal standings with which communities can litigate problematic corporations – because they use 'multiplicity' to shift or evade responsibility to 'other' exposures (Murphy 2006, 2008).

2 'Unsettling' here is informed by the politics of different/previous unsettling(s) (Tarlo 2003; Murphy 2015; Appleton 2017a).

3 They draw on ten studies for this review, which also highlights the limited amount of research on GAHT in the medical sciences.

References

Acton, R., P. Salter, M. Lenoy, and R. (Bob) Stevenson (2017), 'Conversations on Cultural Sustainability: Stimuli for Embedding Indigenous Knowledges and Ways of Being into Curriculum', *Higher Education Research & Development* 36 (7): 1311–25. Available at https://doi.org/10.1080/07294360.2017.1325852

Ah-King, M. and E. Hayward (2014), 'Perverting Pollution and Queering Hormone Disruption', *O-Zone: A Journal of Object-Oriented Studies* 1: 1–12.

Anzaldúa, G. (2007), *Borderlands: The New Mestiza = La Frontera*, 3rd edn, San Francisco, CA: Aunt Lute Books.

Appleton, N. S. (2017a), 'Unsettling the (presumed) Settled: Contents and Discontents of Contraception in Aotearoa New Zealand', *Health, Culture and Society* 9: 90–6. Available at https://doi.org/10.5195/hcs.2017.243.

Appleton, N. S. (2017b), 'Feminist Commons and Techno-Scientific Futures', *Commoning Ethnography* 1 (1): 142–51. Available at https://doi.org/10.26686/ce.v1i1.4120.

Appleton, N. S. (2019), 'Unintended Logics—Hormones', *Cultural Anthropology Blog*, 7 August. Available at https://culanth.org/fieldsights/1513-unintended-logics.

Appleton, N. S. (2022), 'Contraceptive Futures? The Hormonal Body, Populationism and Reproductive Justice in the Face of Climate Change', in V. Boydell and K. Dow (eds), *Technologies of Reproduction Across the Lifecourse*, 109–29, Bingley: Emerald Publishing Limited.

Cixous, H., K. Cohen, and P. Cohen (1976), 'The Laugh of the Medusa', *Signs* 1 (4): 875–93.

Fine, C. (2017), *Testosterone Rex: Unmaking the Myths of Our Gendered Minds*, Icon Books Ltd.

Frankel, T. E., M. T. Meyer, D. W. Kolpin, A. B. Gillis, D. A. Alvarez, and E. F. Orlando (2016), 'Exposure to the Contraceptive Progestin, Gestodene, Alters Reproductive Behavior, Arrests Egg Deposition, and Masculinizes Development in the Fathead Minnow (Pimephales Promelas)', *Environmental Science & Technology* 50 (11): 5991–9.

González-Orozco, J. C. and I. Camacho-Arroyo (2019), 'Progesterone Actions During Central Nervous System Development', *Frontiers in Neuroscience* 13. Available at https://www.frontiersin.org/articles/10.3389/fnins.2019.00503.

Harding, S. (1992a) 'After the Neutrality Ideal: Science, Politics, and "strong Objectivity"', *Social Research* 59 (3): 567–87.

Harding, S. (1992b), 'Rethinking Standpoint Epistemology: What is "strong Objectivity?"', *The Centennial Review* 36 (3): 437–70.

Harding, S. (1995) '"Strong Objectivity": A Response to the new Objectivity Question', *Synthese* 104 (3): 331–49.

Hardon, A. (2021), 'Chemical Futures', in A. Hardon (ed.), *Chemical Youth: Navigating Uncertainty in Search of the Good Life*, 281–310, Springer International Publishing.

Hardon, A., N. I. Idrus, and T. D. Hymans (2013), 'Chemical Sexualities: The use of Pharmaceutical and Cosmetic Products by Youth in South Sulawesi, Indonesia', *Reproductive Health Matters* 21 (41): 214–24.

hooks, b. (1994) 'Language: Teaching New Worlds/New Words', *Teaching to Transgress: Education as the Practice of Freedom*, 167–75, London: Routledge.

Lappé, M., R. Jeffries Hein, and H. Landecker (2019), 'Environmental Politics of Reproduction', *Annual Review of Anthropology* 48 (1): 133–50. Available at https://doi.org/10.1146/annurev-anthro-102218-011346.

Martin, E. (1991) 'The Egg and the Sperm: How Science Has Constructed a Romance Based on Stereotypical Male-Female Roles', *Signs* 16 (3): 485–501.

McAllister (Te Aitanga a Māhaki), T., Naepi (Naitasiri/Palagi), S., Walker (Whakatōhea), L., Gillon (Ngāti Awa, N., Ngāiterangi), Ashlea, Clark (Ngāpuhi), P., Lambert (Ngāti Mutunga, N. T.), Emma, McCambridge, A. B., Thoms (Ngāi Tahu -Ngāti Kurī, N. T.), Channell, Housiaux (Ātiawa ki Whakarongotai, N. T., Ngāti Raukawa, Te Atihaunui a Pāpārangi), Jordan, Ehau-Taumaunu (Ngāti Uepōhatu, N. P., Te Ātiawa, Te Whānau-ā-Apanui), Hanareia, Waikauri Connell (Atihaunui a Pāpārangi, N. T., Tūwharetoa), Charlotte Joy, Keenan (Te Atiawa, T., Rawiri, Thomas) (Ngāti Mutunga o Wharekauri, T. Ā., Ngāi Tohora, Rapuwai), Kristie-Lee, Maslen-Miller (Samoan), A., Tupaea (Ngāti Koata, N. T., Ngāti Kuia, Te Aitanga a Māhaki, Ngāti Mūtunga), Morgan, Mauriohooho (Ngāti Raukawa ki Wharepuhunga, N. T., Ngāti Maniapoto, Waikato), Kate, Puli'uvea, C., Rapata (Kāi Tahu), H., Nicholas (Ngā Pū Toru -'Avaiki Nui), S. A., . . . Alipia, T. (2022), 'Seen but Unheard: Navigating Turbulent Waters as Māori and Pacific Postgraduate Students in STEM', *Journal of the Royal Society of New Zealand* 1–19. Available at https://doi.org/10.1080/03036758.2022.2097710.

Milionis, C., I. Ilias, and E. Koukkou (2022), 'Progesterone in Gender-affirming Therapy of Trans Women', *World Journal of Biological Chemistry* 13 (3): 66–71. Available at https://doi.org/10.4331/wjbc.v13.i3.66.

Murphy, M. (2006), *Sick Building Syndrome and the Problem of Uncertainty: Environmental Politics, Technoscience, and Women Workers*, Durham: Duke University Press. Available at https://doi.org/10.1215/9780822387831.

Murphy, M. (2008), 'Chemical Regimes of Living', *Environmental History* 13 (4): 695–703.

Murphy, M. (2015), 'Unsettling Care: Troubling Transnational Itineraries of Care in Feminist Health Practices', *Social Studies of Science* 45 (5): 717–37. Available at https://doi.org/10.1177/0306312715589136.

Murphy, M. (2017) 'Alterlife and Decolonial Chemical Relations', *Cultural Anthropology* 32 (4): 494–503. Available at https://doi.org/10.14506/ca32.4.02.

Orlando, E. F. and L. E. Ellestad (2014), 'Sources, Concentrations, and Exposure Effects of Environmental Gestagens on Fish and Other Aquatic Wildlife, With an Emphasis on Reproduction', *General and Comparative Endocrinology* 203: 241–9. Available at https://doi.org/10.1016/j.ygcen.2014.03.038

Patel, K. T., S. Adeel, J. R. Miragaya, and V. Tangpricha (2022), 'Progestogen Use in Gender Affirming Hormone Therapy: A Systematic Review', *Endocrine Practice* 28 (12): 1244–52. Available at https://doi.org/10.1016/j.eprac.2022.08.012.

Pollock, A. (2016), 'Queering Endocrine Disruption', in K. Behar (ed.), *Object-Oriented Feminism*, 183–99, Minneapolis: University of Minnesota Press.

Rich, A. L., L. M. Phipps, S. Tiwari, H. Rudraraju, and P. O. Dokpesi (2016), 'The Increasing Prevalence in Intersex Variation from Toxicological Dysregulation in Fetal Reproductive Tissue Differentiation and Development by Endocrine-Disrupting Chemicals', *Environmental Health Insights* 10: 163–71. Available at https://doi.org/10.4137/EHI.S39825.

Roberts, C. (2000), 'Biological Behavior? Hormones, Psychology, and Sex', *NWSA Journal* 12 (3): 1–20.

Roberts, C. (2003) 'Drowning in a sea of Estrogens: Sex Hormones, Sexual Reproduction and sex', *Sexualities* 6 (2): 195–213.

Roberts, C. (2007), *Messengers of Sex: Hormones, Biomedicine and Feminism*, Cambridge: Cambridge University Press.

Roy, D. (2007), 'Somatic Matters: Becoming Molecular in Molecular Biology', *Rhizomes: Cultural Studies in Emerging Knowledge* 14. Available at http://www.rhizomes.net/issue14/roy/roy.html.

Ruwhiu, D. (2014), 'Voices That Matter: Speaking Up for the "Indigenous" in Business Education', in R. Westwood, G. Jack, F. R. Khan, and M. Frenkel (eds.), *Core-Periphery Relations and Organisation Studies*, 185–203, Palgrave Macmillan UK. Available at https://doi.org/10.1057/9781137309051_9.

Sanabria, E. (2016) *Plastic Bodies: Sex Hormones and Menstrual Suppression in Brazil*, Durham: Duke University Press.

Schumacher, M., R. Guennoun, F. Robert, C. Carelli, N. Gago, A. Ghoumari, M. C. Gonzalez Deniselle, S. L. Gonzalez, C. Ibanez, F. Labombarda, H. Coirini, E.-E. Baulieu, and A. F. De Nicola (2004), 'Local Synthesis and Dual Actions of Progesterone in the Nervous System: Neuroprotection and Myelination', *Growth Hormone & IGF Research* 14: 18–33. https://doi.org/10.1016/j.ghir.2004.03.007.

Tarlo, E. (2003), *Unsettling Memories: Narratives of the Emergency in Delhi*, Berkeley: University of California Press.

Wylie, S. A. (2018), *Fractivism: Corporate Bodies and Chemical Bonds*, Illustrated edn, Durham: Duke University Press.

Zhao, Y., S. Castiglioni, and K. Fent (2015), 'Environmental Progestins Progesterone and Drospirenone Alter the Circadian Rhythm Network in Zebrafish (Danio Rerio)', *Environmental Science & Technology* 49 (16): 10155–64. Available at https://doi.org/10.1021/acs.est.5b02226.

18 PROGESTOGENS

MARIANA RIOS SANDOVAL

A group of people wander in the Belleville Parc, nested in the historically working class but rapidly gentrifying 20eme arrondissement of Paris. The group is led by Elena, a young photographer turned herbalist. She is in her early thirties. The rest of the group is composed of five or six people, including an anthropologist taking notes in her mobile phone. Elena meanders. We follow. Every now and then she stops to introduce us to a tree, a bush or a flower, like someone introducing an old friend. We listen to her intently, trying to tune out the background of persistent traffic noise and the occasional ambulance or police siren. Elena leans over a flat bush of nettle. This plant of dark green leaves with pointy edges causes a burning sensation to the skin but is edible when cooked and can be used in mother tincture to counter benign enlargement of the prostate. Nettle accumulates heavy metals in its body, as it can grow in heavily polluted soil. 'Nettle is a resistant. There is a sexy aspect to it', says Elena. We meet other plants, some used to treat period pain or postpartum depression or to support breastfeeding. Towards the end of the guided walk Elena stops near a specimen she claims is one of her favourites.

Achille millefolium, commonly known as yarrow, is composed of many tiny white inflorescences and can be easily missed among the tall grass if one is not paying attention. Despite its discreet appearance, Elena vouches for Achille's fantastic properties for women and all people with uteruses. She explains that this is a plant with progestogenic effects, making it key in treating period pain, pre-menstrual syndrome and endometriosis, all conditions for which biomedical knowledge falls short (Griffith 2019; Hudson 2022; Seear 2009; Wright 2019).

Elena is part of a collective of feminist herbalists who educate others on how to rely on plants to care for sexual and reproductive health. Their collective, Rosae canine, named after a wild rose commonly found in Europe, organizes guided walks around city parks and sidewalks to raise awareness of the fact that nature also exists in urban contexts, and that plants are not only decorative but can also engage in all sorts of partnerships, including healing ones. One of the ways the collective does this is by teaching others how to use plants to heal bodies by supporting and restoring hormonal balance, partly through the action of phytohormones, hormone-like chemicals produced by the plant. These botanical walks serve as an entry point for discussing broader issues having to do with gender, power and expertise in caring for bodies.

Compounds featured in this entry fall into the biomedical category of progestogens because of their shared ability to bind to progesterone receptors in the body, regardless of their origin. Progestogens are an eclectic family of molecules. Progesterone, the main progestogen produced in animal bodies, including those of humans, participates in hormonal pathways regulating processes that make reproduction possible: oestrous and menstrual cycles, spermiogenesis, pregnancy, birth and lactation. There are nevertheless many other progestogens of plant, laboratory or industrial origin that, by binding to progesterone receptors, can join in hormonal communications with both intended and unforeseen effects. I will focus on the progestogenic action of a very heterogeneous, even disparate group of compounds, because this shared ability matters in a particular context: self-gynaecological practices, like the ones promoted by Elena's collective. Such practices have flourished in the aftermath of what is commonly known as the '*crise de la pilule*' (crisis of the contraceptive pill) in France: a growing disaffection for the contraceptive method that has been the bedrock of French family planning for more than seventy years. The move away from the pill has given way to a more heterogeneous contraceptive landscape, a little less reliant on synthetic hormones but, most critically, one where common understandings of what hormones are and do are changing in significant ways.

Progestins and the French contraceptive norm

Progestins are a synthetic version of progesterone. They are also the active principle in the contraceptive pill. Nowadays at least a dozen progestins exist in the market, each having a slightly different molecular structure. Depending on these structural variations, and on the dosage, progestins can prevent pregnancy by inhibiting ovulation, blocking the penetration of sperm by thickening the cervical mucus or causing endometrial changes that prevent implantation (Bitzer 2015). Progestins are familiar molecules to women in France. Most women interact with them unknowingly, by taking their *pilule* every day. However, since the 2012 'pill scare', which will be discussed later in this entry, contraceptive pills' composition, progestin-only or combined with oestrogen, is commonly featured in newspapers and a broad range of magazines (Bordenet and Gittus 2014; Riche 2013). One in two women of reproductive age uses *la pilule* as a contraceptive method (Roux et al. 2017). Among women under thirty years old, the proportion of oral contraception users is even higher, reaching 70 or even 80 per cent depending on the age group (Bajos et al. 2012). Other hormonal methods such as the implant, patch and the vaginal ring are available to women through public health insurance since the early 2000s. Their use varies widely depending on age groups and ethnic origin and globally represents around 5 per cent of the total contraceptive users (Roux et al. 2017).

Oral hormonal contraception enjoys a prominent status in France. Its legalization in 1967 was an emblematic victory for the local birth control and feminist movements and constitutes one of the main societal changes experienced in the twentieth century, which allowed women to have better control of whether and when to have children (Pavard 2012). In the decades since its legalization, the pill became the core element of the French contraceptive norm, deeply engrained in political, medical and social institutions. The management of women's fertility with the aid of synthetic hormones, mainly progestins, stabilized as a default, reliable biomedical technology and a structuring element of heteronormative sexuality and reproduction.

While in other Western countries such as the United States or the Netherlands local feminist movements raised concerns about synthetic hormones' potential health consequences for women, in France feminists and doctors did not generally express concern around this issue, creating a more favourable environment for using hormones to manage female reproductive bodies (Löwy and Weisz 2005). Nathalie Bajos (2012) describes the French contraceptive landscape as a 'fixed contraceptive model' that has remained fairly stable since the late 1970s, a model whereby women begin taking the pill at the beginning of sexual activity, condoms are limited to new or casual sexual relationships and intrauterine devices (IUDs) with or without hormones are only used once couples do not wish to have more children. This model speaks to the relevance of the pill, and therefore progestins, as the contraceptive norm. However, this description does not capture other ways in which progestins are entangled with the management of women's bodies and lives, beyond fertility.

While doing ethnographic research on the negotiation of feminist and environmental concerns in contraceptive practices, I observed that many of my research participants had started taking *la pilule* well before they intended to begin having sexual relations, sometimes even a full year. Oral contraceptives were prescribed to treat period pain or acne. The use of progestins often extends to the perimenopausal years as well, in the form of hormone replacement therapy (HRT). Finally, infertility, whether male or female, is usually treated on the female partner's body through assisted reproduction technologies, which also involve progestins (Löwy 2009).

Given the important place that *la pilule* occupies in France, socially and medically, and the regular attacks on both contraception and abortion from conservative and religious groups, social sciences were reluctant to engage in a critical analysis of the contraceptive norm. A new generation of feminist scholars has begun to dissect this 'pilulocentric' model, in the words of Alexandra Roux (2022), who has taken a close look at the history of how the contraceptive pill became a medically and socially accepted technology. Cécile Thomé and Mylène Rouzaud-Cornabas (2017) show how contraceptive work has become the responsibility of women, who must also manage the possible side effects of taking hormones, a kind of labour that remains, for the most part, invisible. Through a careful analysis of medical practitioners' discourses, Cécile Ventola (2014) evidences how privileging contraceptive hormones that act on female bodies over other methods of birth control involving male partners, such as condoms or withdrawal, has reinforced traditional gender roles, including the idea that only women are interested in and concerned by contraception.

La crise de la pilule: Unsettling the place of progestins and the contraceptive norm

The popularity of the pill rose steadily from the 1970s until the early 2000s, after which the number of users of this kind of contraception has been declining slowly but steadily, a change that is often referred to as *la crise de la pilule* (the crisis of the pill) (Bajos et al. 2014). This crisis was put in the spotlight with the mediatized affair around the serious cardiovascular side effects of third- and fourth-generation pills. Contraceptive pills are categorized in generations according to the kind of progestin they contain. Four generations of progestins have been developed from the 1960s to today, in a quest for effective contraceptive pills with manageable side effects. All progestins bind to progesterone receptors in the body, but they also bind to a lesser degree to other hormonal receptors, producing what are known as side effects. Side effects will also vary according to how individual bodies react to synthetic hormones. Third- and fourth-generation pills caused fewer side effects such as acne, hirsutism (increased hair growth), changes in the metabolism of fats and water retention, but they increased the cardiovascular risks (Davtyan 2012).

In 2012, a young student from Bordeaux, Marion Larat, filed a lawsuit against the pharmaceutical company Bayer, claiming that its third-generation contraceptive pill was the cause of the stroke she had suffered six years earlier with disabling effects. At the time she was twenty-six years old. Over 100 lawsuits from users of third- and fourth-generation pills who had suffered strokes, embolisms and thrombosis with varying severity followed that year. As a result of the *scandale*, the purchase of these pills stopped being reimbursed by public health insurance and doctors were recommended not to prescribe them as a first option.

The crisis of the pill is not only about the last two generations of progestin-only contraceptive pills but also about the contraceptive norm and the place of synthetic hormones more generally. In an article poignantly titled '*C'est pas la pilule qui ouvre la porte du frigo !*' (It's not The Pill that opens the fridge door!, a sentence that invalidates women's experience of pill-related weight gain) Leslie Fonquerne (2021) explains that the unsettling of the contraceptive norm is inscribed in a broader critique and contestation of gynaecological and obstetric violence. Consent, argues Fonquerne, is often violated during contraceptive consultations, where patients are pressured in different ways (by practitioners giving partial information, ignoring complaints related to side effects or having paternalistic attitudes) to accept oral hormonal contraception.

Fonquerne's findings resonate with my own research, where young women (under thirty-five) would often struggle with side effects for years and feel patronized by medical practitioners who would offer to replace one pill with another as the sole solution. Since the French contraceptive norm is articulated around synthetic hormones, the range of non-hormonal methods offered to women in gynaecological consultations and reimbursed by public health insurance is very limited, mostly restricted to copper IUDs and condoms. However, the reluctance of French gynaecologists to prescribe IUDs to women who have never had children (Bajos et al. 2014; Roux et al. 2017) means that choosing a non-hormonal method often proved to be very difficult. Medical practitioners' resistance was such that sometimes moving away from hormonal contraception required women to change practitioners.

There is another factor contributing to the crisis of contraceptive hormones in general and progestins in particular: increasing concerns with the effects of synthetic hormones on bodies and the environment. My interlocutors' journeys towards non-hormonal contraception were deeply informed by a concern about ordinary chemical exposures. Toxicity, suggests Heather Davis (2015: 244), makes the fiction of the independent or impermeable body crumble, as it 'forces us to reveal the ways in which we are multiply composed of plastics, of toxins, of queer morphologies'. Acutely aware of the porosity of the body, the young women I did research with worried that the potentially disruptive effects of synthetic hormones were not contained within humans' bodily boundaries but continued their journey through urine into the sewage system, and then into rivers and the ocean, where they could affect living beings such as fish and marine birds, changing sex ratios and generally turning life upside down.

The popular book *Our Stolen Future* (Colborn, Dumanoski and Myers 1997) reverberated strongly throughout my interlocutors' accounts. Considered by many as the *Silent Spring* of chemically induced hormonal disruption (Johnson 1996), the book assembles a wide array of studies documenting how the hormonal balance of wildlife has been disrupted by chemical by-products of human activity dumped in their habitat. Despite being in their twenties, most of my interlocutors had taken the contraceptive pill for several years, sometimes a decade. Through their interaction with contraceptive hormones, they had acquired a wealth of experience in attuning to hormonal manipulations and perturbations. Because of the obstacles to stepping aside from the contraceptive norm, women who experienced side effects often did so for months or sometimes years. Hormonal tinkering for contraceptive purposes was often experienced as disruptive for bodies and lives, so much so that my interlocutors would refer to the pill as the biggest *perturbateur endocrinien* (EDC, or endocrine-disrupting chemical). In their narratives the two kinds of hormonal interventions – those mediated by progestins and those by EDCs – were often hard to distinguish.

Achillea millefolium: Auto-gynaecology and phytohormones

La crise de la pilule has given way to a contraceptive landscape a little less reliant on progestins (Bajos et al. 2014). Most critically, it has also opened space for a critique of the contraceptive norm and medical practices supporting it. The women's self-help health movement, which originated in the United States and held an important place in the feminist movement during the 1970s and 1980s, had little echo in France at the time (Ruault 2016). These feminist groups aimed to 'seize the means of reproduction' by reclaiming gynaecological techniques from the exclusive hold of the medical realm and reinventing them by 'making photographic diaries of cervical variation, crafting politicized health manuals, examining menstruation with a microscope, building an abortion device with a canning jar and aquarium tubing, forming artificial insemination groups, or turning a living room into a health clinic, among other practices' (Murphy 2012: 1–2). In the past decade, self-gynaecology groups have flourished in France. Aurore Koechlin compares the alliances between medical practitioners and feminists championing the legalization of contraception and abortion services in the 1970s, with current attempts by midwives and intersectional feminists to advocate for women's freedom to make choices about reproductive healthcare (Koechlin 2019).

Between 2019 and 2021 I spent time with the collective Rosae canine, featured in this entry's opening vignette, one of the groups that emerged in this new wave of *auto-gynecologie* (self-gynaecology). The four women composing this feminist collective met when they were following a programme to become herbalists. They live in different regions of the French countryside and get together to create performances and fanzines and to organize guided walks in cities to teach other *meufs*[1] how to identify plants of *usage gynecologique* (gynaecological use). Rosae canine promotes self-gynaecology herbal practices as a way to gain autonomy from institutional gynaecology and pharmaceutical companies that, as they alert in their artistic and communications materials, occupy uteruses and vaginas for power and profit (Rosae canine 2019).

Artemisia vulgaris for period pain, *Verbena officinalis* to support women with postpartum depression and *Filupendula ulmaria rosaceae* to manage heavy flows are some of the plants that can be found in parks, sidewalks or even brownfields in and around big urban centres such as Paris or Marseille. Rosae canine use the plant *Achille millefolium* for its 'progestogenic effects'. They find it useful in managing endometriosis, as sufferers often struggle to find effective relief from biomedicine. Supporting health with herbs is different from treating health conditions with drugs: 'Herbal uterine care doesn't align neatly with event-oriented categories such as abortion, contraception, birth, PMS, etc', points out Andrea Ford when writing about the use of plants in self-gynaecology practices in the United States (2018: 4).

Much like bodily and synthetic hormones, plants can act on the body in various ways, simultaneously. Think for instance of progesterone. This steroid hormone plays a key role in reproduction, particularly menstruation, but it also intervenes in processes affecting other organs such as the brain and the nervous system, the heart, the mammary glands and the skeletal, immune and overall hormonal systems (Carp 2015). *Achille millefolium* has been used in different herbal traditions to treat inflammation, for instance, in conditions such as headaches, malaria and skin injuries (Dalili et al. 2022), in addition to menstrual health. When using plants for sexual and reproductive healthcare, the members of the collective do not focus on specific molecules as active principles but on systemic effects caused by a dynamic combination of molecules, many of which are unknown. The molecular composition of the environment is understood in a similar fashion: diverse, in flux, impossible to fully determine. This understanding is deeply informed by concerns with ambient toxicity and environmental degradation and bears increasing weight in the way women relate to hormones and consequently in their contraceptive choices.

Unlike pharmaceuticals, plants are not designed products carrying a set of previously isolated or manufactured active principles. Plants, like any other organisms, produce myriad molecules of different kinds, which are involved in all vital processes: growth, metabolism, reproduction and so on. Under the lens of biomedicine, some of these compounds have been categorized as phytohormones because despite having different molecular architecture to the hormones produced in mammalian bodies, they act in a similar way, by triggering and regulating physiological processes (Tran and Pal 2014). The molecular contents of plants, like those of any other living being, vary constantly, according to the life stage and in tune with the environment. For instance, metabolic changes take place throughout the seasons.

As permeable beings in permanent communication with their environment, plants' molecular contents include the pollutants present in soil, air and water. *Achille millefolium* for instance has been used as a bioindicator of pollution caused by mining (Nujkić et al. 2020). The herbalist collective's healing practices integrate an awareness of plants' relationships with their environment. Each botanical guided walk ends with a word of caution: since plants are permeable to the compounds accumulated in the soil, air and water they need to grow, vegetal beings used to treat the body should better be collected in less polluted soils. This is something that is not easy to achieve, the members of the group would explain, even in rural landscapes, due to the widespread use of agricultural pesticides and pollutants produced by past and present industrial activity, among other things. In an entry Rosae canine and I wrote together for a collaborative volume creatively exploring human relations with hormones and hormone-like chemicals, Elena writes: 'In the act of harvesting, there are several politics, several rules to apply: do not trample, leave flowers for bees, be careful with animal urine. But one recommendation remains nomadic and potentially inapplicable: do not harvest on polluted land' (Rosae Canine and Rios Sandoval 2022: 64). Healing with plants paradoxically embodies both the promise of healing and bodily autonomy as well as that of sharing in the potentially toxic load of their vegetal allies.

I came across *Achille millefolium* a few other times while doing research on contraceptive practices. Once in a natural gynaecology manual for women written by Rina Nissin (Nissim 2001), a prominent figure in the Mouvement de Libération des Femmes (MLF) of Geneva, particularly active in the struggles for abortion legalization and the self-help movement. I crossed paths with *Achille millefolium* again during an online genital self-exploration workshop I participated in during the first Covid-19 lockdown in 2020. Besides getting to know our anatomies better, we talked about sex, contraception and menstrual periods. One of the international participants mentioned that drinking a yarrow infusion in the last days of her menstrual cycle helped ease period cramps. I was curious about where she had gotten the plant from. She explained she had ordered the seeds online and planted them in a pot by her window.

Concluding thoughts

In the twenty-first century, hormonal conversations have become wildly polyphonic. In addition to the hormones made within individual organisms (humans, in the case featured in this entry) other molecules are engaged in the messaging (sometimes mixed), taking place around the clock to keep vital processes going: synthetic hormones, pharmaceuticals, other manufactured compounds of industrial and household use that have hormonal effects and hormones made in the bodies of non-human organisms such as plants. These complex and diverse molecular interactions challenge the idea of the existence of clear boundaries between different categories of chemicals and between bodies and environments. They also beg for an understanding of chemicals, in this case hormones, as situated objects enmeshed in all sorts of relations, molecular and otherwise.

For the members of the Rosa canine collective, other self-gynaecology groups and all the women making contraceptive choices in my research, compounds as different as contraceptive pharmaceuticals, phytohormones, endocrine disruptors and pollutants travelling in the water or sedimented in the soil belong together because of how they relate and share processes and spaces. Through these understandings, hormones and molecules in general emerge as more fluid objects (Hardon and Sanabria 2017), which are hardly separable into neat categories. Hormones, bodies and health are understood as part of an ecology of diverse and dynamic human and non-human relations that are inseparable from their environment.

Note

1 A slang term meaning women but used in the feminist scene to include genders other than cis women.

References

Bajos, N., A. Bohet, M. Le Guen, and C. Moreau (2012), 'Contraception in France: New Context, New Practices?', *Population and Societies* 492: 1–4.

Bajos, N., M. Rouzaud-Cornabas, H. Panjo, A. Bohet, and C. Moreau (2014), 'The French Pill Scare: Towards a New Contraceptive Model?', *Population and Societies* 511: 1–4.

Bitzer, J. (2015), 'Progestogens in Contraception', in H. J. A. Carp (ed.), *Progestogens in Obstetrics and Gynecology*, 111–27, Tel Aviv: Springer.

Bordenet, C. and S. Gittus (2014), 'Contraception: Ce qui a changé depuis le scandale des pilules', *Le Monde*, 15 October. Available at https://www.lemonde.fr/les-decodeurs /article/2014/10/15/contraception-ce-qui-a-change-depuis-le-scandale-des-pilules _4506401_4355770.html.

Carp, H. J. A. (2015), *Progestogens in Obstetrics and Gynecology*, Tel Aviv: Springer.

Colborn, T., D. Dumanoski, and J. Peterson Myers (1997), *Our Stolen Future: Are We Threatening Our Fertility, Intelligence, and Survival?* New York: Penguin Group.

Dalili, A., S. E. Milani, N. Kamali, S. Mohammadi, M. Pakbaz, S. Jamalnia, and M. Sadeghi (2022), 'Beneficial Effects of Achillea Millefolium on Skin Injuries; A Literature Review', *Journal of Essential Oil Research*, July, 479–89.

Davis, H. (2015), 'Toxic Progeny: The Plastisphere and Other Queer Futures', *PhiloSOPHIA*, 5 (2): 231–50.

Davtyan, C. (2012), 'Four Generations of Progestins in Oral Contraceptives', *Proceedings of UCLA Healthcare*, 16: 1–3.

Fonquerne, Leslie (2021), '"C'est pas la pilule qui ouvre la porte du frigo!". Violences médicales et gynécologiques en consultation de contraception', *Santé Publique* 33 (5): 663–73.

Ford, A. (2018), '(Anti)Institutional Menses: Our Blood, Our Business', *Somatosphere*, May. Available at http://somatosphere.net/2018/antiinstitutional-menses.html/.

Griffith, V. A. S. (2019), *Healers and Patients Talk: Narratives of a Chronic Gynecological Disease*, Lanham: Lexington Books.

Hardon, A. and E. Sanabria (2017), 'Fluid Drugs: Revisiting the Anthropology of Pharmaceuticals', *Annual Review of Anthropology* 46 (1): 117–32.

Hudson, N. (2022), 'The Missed Disease? Endometriosis as an Example of "Undone Science"', *Reproductive Biomedicine & Society Online* 14: 20–7.

Johnson, J. (1996), 'Will Our Stolen Future Be Another Silent Spring?', *Environmental Science & Technology* 30 (4): 168A–170A.

Koechlin, A. (2019), 'L'auto-gynécologie: Écoféminisme et Intersectionnalité', *Travail, genre et sociétés* 42 (2): 109–26.

Löwy, I. (2009), 'L'âge limite de la maternité : Corps, biomédecine, et politique', *Mouvements* 59 (3): 102–12.

Löwy, I. and G. Weisz (2005), 'French Hormones: Progestins and Therapeutic Variation in France', *Social Science & Medicine (1982)* 60 (11): 2609–22.

Nujkić, M., Milić, S., Spalović, B., Dardas, A., Alagić, S., Ljubić, D., and Papludis, A. (2020), 'Saponaria Officinalis L. and Achillea Millefolium L. as Possible Indicators of Trace Elements Pollution Caused by Mining and Metallurgical Activities in Bor, Serbia', *Environmental Science and Pollution Research* 27 (36): 44969–82.

Murphy, M. (2012), *Seizing the Means of Reproduction: Entanglements of Feminism, Health, and Technoscience*, Durham: Duke University Press.

Nissim, R. (2001), *Mamamélis: Manuel de gynécologie naturopathique à l'usage des femmes*, Lausanne: Mamamelis.

Pavard, B. (2012), *Si je veux, quand je veux : Contraception et avortement dans la société française*, Rennes: PU Rennes.

Riche, S. (2013), 'Je Veux Comprendre . . . Le Débat Sur Les Pilules Contraceptives', *MadmoiZelle*, 31 July. Available at https://www.madmoizelle.com/pilules-3eme-4eme-generation-dangers-140924.

Rosae canine (2019), *Jouir*, Fanzine.

Rosae canine, and M. Rios Sandoval (2022), 'Post-Industrial Self-Gynecology Plant Manual', in *Synthetic Becoming*, 68–87, Berlin: K. Verlag.

Roux, A. (2022), *Pilule: Défaire l'évidence*, Paris: Éditions de la Maison des sciences de l'homme.

Roux, A., M. Rouzaud-Cornabas, L. Fonquerne, C. Thomé, and C. Ventola (2017), 'Cinquante ans de contraception légale en France: Diffusion, médicalisation, féminisation', *Population & Sociétés* 549 (10): 1–4.

Ruault, L. (2016), 'La circulation transnationale du self-help féministe: Acte 2 des luttes pour l'avortement libre ?', *Critique internationale* 70 (1): 37–54.

Seear, K. (2009), '"Nobody Really Knows What It Is or How to Treat It": Why Women with Endometriosis Do Not Comply with Healthcare Advice', *Health, Risk & Society* 11 (4): 367–85.

Thomé, C. and M. Rouzaud-Cornabas (2017), 'Comment ne pas faire d'enfants?', *Recherches sociologiques et anthropologiques* 48 (2): 117–37.

Tran, L.-S. P. and S. Pal (2014), *Phytohormones: A Window to Metabolism, Signaling and Biotechnological Applications*, 1 online resource (380 pages): Illustrations vols, New York: Springer.

Ventola, C. (2014), 'Prescrire un contraceptif: Le rôle de l'institution médicale dans la construction de catégories sexuées', *Genre, sexualité & société* 12 (online) (December).

Wright, K. O. (2019), '"You Have Endometriosis": Making Menstruation-Related Pain Legitimate in a Biomedical World', *Health Communication* 34 (8): 912–15.

19 TESTOSTERONE

FABÍOLA ROHDEN

In medical discourses, testosterone is commonly defined as the 'male hormone' and presented as the hormone of desire and aggression. Specifically with regard to sexuality, the focus has been on the association between testosterone and sexual desire. Reviewing the international and Brazilian literature and the dialogue with researchers from several countries, it is possible to conclude that Brazil has become a particular case of intense medicalization and pharmaceuticalization of female sexuality, especially among upper- and middle-class cis women who have access to private medical offices.[1] In Brazil, the treatments of issues related to cis women's sexuality and menopause are largely anchored in the parameters of biomedicine (Sanabria 2010, 2016).[2] As a few recent studies have shown, although the prescription of testosterone is not legally permitted, the hormone has emerged in recent medical events and articles as a special resource that can be indicated for treating problems related to sexuality, especially among older women who are in phases around menopause (Rohden 2013; Faro 2016; Faro and Russo 2017; Manica and Nucci 2017). Thus, we are entering a new entry in the long and complex history of the so-called 'sex' hormones (Oudshoorn 1994; Hoberman 2005; Roberts 2007, 2015; Rohden 2008; Sanabria 2010, 2016; Jordan-Young and Karkazis 2019).

In this entry I discuss the approaches and treatments associated with testosterone used by physicians in a large Brazilian city (Rohden 2018, 2019). The research methodology involved seeking out professionals mainly from the field of gynaecology but also from endocrinology and gerontology, who were indicated for their specialization in treating sexual problems. The twelve specialists interviewed are recognized by their peers as important doctors in their areas of expertise. They have links with universities, hospitals and other educational institutions as well as membership in regional and national medical associations.[3]

In terms of theoretical perspective, I follow the inspiration offered by A. Mol's work. Concerned to emphasize the relevance of both ontologies and normativities, Mol (2012) proposed the term 'ontonorms'. Here I suggest understanding ontonorms as a process of provisional and partial stabilization or framing of a reality. My particular interest in 'ontonorms' means, above all, analysing more closely how normativities are not only embedded in practices but also how they help to produce new materialities. In the specific case that I analyse here, these materialities combine testosterone and sexual desire.

Approaches to and prescriptions for testosterone and desire

The people interviewed were asked what treatments they used for 'female sexual problems'. For most, although they emphasized that sexuality is a multifactorial phenomenon and that female sexuality in particular is highly complex, hormonal treatments were a central reference. This standard is unquestionably associated with differences between men and women that are expressed primarily in terms of biology.

Ivo, a gynaecologist, has a conception that emphasizes a radical difference between genders, based on a binary distinction between sexes, expressed in terms of a natural and evolutionary order. For this doctor, sexuality is related to reproductive factors materialized in the different phases of a woman's life and made concrete in the presence or absence of hormones, especially testosterone. This hormone is seen as the most important factor and, thus, is also presented as the treatment that will resolve nearly all problems. This appears to involve a vision of gender and indeed of the very existence of humans that is based on naturalizing and essentialist perspectives.

At another extreme is a statement by Marcelo, whose trajectory is unique among the doctors interviewed, due to his work with transgender people. According to Marcelo, who is an endocrinologist, gender should not be discussed in binary terms: it is always necessary to pay attention to individual differences and the realities of concrete cases. Nevertheless, when asked about a possible difference in relation to sexuality between men and women, he answered:

I think that, as a rule, men have greater libido. Testosterone has more libido. And this would be a difference related to sexuality, sexual desire; it appears to me that it is much stronger, intense, in men than in women. As a general rule. A man is much more aggressive, and has greater libido.

Even considering the case of transgender people, he continues his line of reflection about the role of hormones in sexuality:

Hormones define libido, we see this clearly because a man has a stronger libido than a woman and the trans man in the same way when he begins to replace testosterone, his libido increases.

What we see with this example is that hormones – specifically testosterone – are identified as absolutely essential agents in the existence and degree of sexual desire. Even if this doctor considers sexuality a phenomenon that cannot be reduced to hormones (he understands that gender is complex and not reducible to biological sex), he does not question the centrality of testosterone to either.

In relation to the treatment of female sexual problems, hormonal prescriptions were the most important reference. In particular, the doctors attest to the recurring presence of testosterone in the field of treatment of sexual problems. They affirm that testosterone treatments are controversial but argue that this is not a reason for them not to be prescribed. Most of them said they prescribed testosterone treatments to older women, despite the fact that this treatment is not legally permitted. Their only consideration was dosage. Even among those most critical of the use of hormones, these substances and their controversial uses and effects occupy a central place in treating older women's sexual problems, such as loss of desire.

Only two of the professionals interviewed were somewhat opposed to prescribing testosterone. Their statements are interesting because they accentuate important aspects of the polemic and different forms of agency attributed to this hormone. Bernardo is a gynaecologist with a long career and is certainly more opposed to suggesting its use. Asked about how he addresses the issue of sexuality, what type of treatments he uses and if they include any hormonal treatment, he responded:

> In my judgment, unless you want to masculinize women, to use hormones, male, in quotes, there is nothing that proves that they will have the intended effect. It is true that with the uses of androgens there is a slight increase in a woman's aggressivity [. . .]. And the increased aggressivity is interpreted as an improvement in the sexual problem, but the effect is transitory.

The interview shows how while the doctor takes a position against the use in women of hormones considered to be male, he also attests that they can have an effect (increasing 'aggressivity') that is mistaken by the doctors who prescribe it as improved 'vitality'. Testosterone, then, is a type of treatment used by professionals who do not have 'serious' knowledge about the issue.

In the same line we also have the statement of Karla, a gynaecologist. She is also quite critical of the use of hormonal treatments and when questioned about the prescription of testosterone by her colleagues, she responded:

> They use it, but they can be sued. It can only be used in cases of removal of ovaries, but they prescribe it nevertheless and in a much larger dosage [. . .].
>
> [Interviewer] And is there [a situation] when the use of testosterone is indicated for women?
>
> No, in women, no indication. So . . . my colleagues want to play God [. . .]. They want to play God. What they do is protect their market, they don't want to send patients to others.

Karla, therefore, in claiming that prescribing testosterone is 'playing God', severely criticizes her medical colleagues. She adds that she is different from other gynaecologists: although she is also trained in this field, she does more specific work with sexual therapy with techniques focused on changing behaviour. But it is revealing that when encouraged to speak about the possible effects of testosterone she affirms that it would improve the libido. Moreover, when she comments on her talk therapy techniques, described later, she believes that they can contribute to improving the levels of endogenous testosterone:

Researchers study what changes with techniques like mine, based on thinking about sex [. . .]. They publish on the effect of thinking of sex to see what changes the hormones. Their research shows what I have already done with my patients, with my technique [. . .]. Things that I have been doing for years with them, they study and prove that they can increase endogenous testosterone.

What is curious here is that although she is critical of the use of treatment based on testosterone, she argues that her therapeutic techniques can increase the levels of this hormone in women's bodies, which would be beneficial, and that this is recognized in the scientific literature. This is not only an assertion that testosterone increases desire but that increased desire (or thinking about sex) is capable of increasing internal testosterone.

Multiple agencies of testosterone: (Un)desired collateral effects

In the group of specialists interviewed, two reported that they also have transgender patients. Their statements are especially important in this entry because they offer an additional perspective about the relationship between the use of hormones, gender and sexuality. When they were asked to discuss the practices they use in clinical treatments, they combined discussions of cis women and trans men.

Janice, in her practice as a gynaecologist, attends to women who come to her for treatment of sexual dysfunctions. She demonstrated affinity with her colleagues, affirming that it is necessary to use different treatments, depending on the case, and that the 'hormonal technique' is used especially for a lack of desire in older women. In this case, testosterone is prescribed in a cream (always prepared to order because she said there is no commercial medication available), or as an injectable, for which there are a few brands available on the market. She said that the official indication that must be used to fill in the forms of controlled prescriptions, according to the International Classification of Diseases (ICD), for the case of testosterone 'replacement' would be 'ovarian insufficiency'. The treatment is justified, according to Janice, 'because it is testosterone that increases sexual desire and libido. It is testosterone, the male hormone'.

Her response to the question about the possible effects of testosterone indicates some ambiguity between the specific role of the hormone and the more general effects of a treatment seeking to improve sexuality:

[The treatment process] increases the libido. They have more desire. Just coming to the office, a sexology clinic, they are already thinking of sex. I always say to the patients 'I am not going to give you a magic pill, and you are not going to get home today and lie down in bed with a heavenly desire'. But just looking for a doctor, speaking of sex, thinking of sex, brings improvement.

Nevertheless, in another sense, she leaves no doubt about her conviction of the concrete effects of the substance. Referring to trans men patients as an exemplary case and contrasting with the patients in 'sexual therapy', she affirms:

My patients that use testosterone, they want the collateral effects. They want the virilisation. Because testosterone is the male hormone. So they want to have a deep voice, they want to have hairs, be more muscular . . . But they want to masculinise. And they use it once a month or once every two weeks [. . .]. These patients in sexual therapy who at times need testosterone, which is to increase the libido, this is the effect that we want . . . so they use a vial, about three a year, quite spaced out. At times it's just to give a trigger and they stop. Just for them to remember how good it is, and then at times they don't need it any more.

Janice added that this could have the effect of masculinization in these women but this does not take place due to the control of the frequency of use and of the different dosages used. It is clear, therefore, that she does not question the effectiveness or the power of testosterone to produce effects considered to be 'naturally' male, such as increased sexual desire and some signs of 'virilization'. It all depends, once again, on the quantities used in each situation to achieve certain ends.

In a similar direction, we have the statement of Marcelo, who was quoted earlier. This endocrinologist is one of the most cautious in highlighting the multiple and unexpected effects of the hormones and the care needed in their use. He juxtaposed and contrasted the hormonal replacement therapy conducted in conformity with the original gender identity to the change in condition of trans people. In the first case, it is about the use of so-called female hormones by cisgender women, which gynaecology and endocrinology have traditionally done for a long time, with the use of hormone replacement therapy. For him, there are not as many doubts or fears about this type of hormonal interference as there are about hormone treatment for transgender people. By referring to the latter case, he describes the patients who come to him:

When does a man come to me for hormonal therapy? When he is not producing testosterone [. . .]. Hormonal replacement therapy for a woman? When? When she is not producing feminine hormones or stopped producing them, menopause. She does not produce them because she does not have an ovary, the ovary does not function, a thousand reasons. Hormonal replacement therapy. We are speaking of hormonal replacement therapy related to gender identity. This has been done for a long time.

Marcelo is therefore saying that the hormonal treatments that medicine has been doing for many decades should also be seen as associated with the production of people's gender. But, in general, this is not thought of. One only thinks about interference in the production of gender in the case of hormone treatment for trans people. What is new, according to Marcelo, are the new hormonal therapies directed at trans people.

When Marcelo was questioned if he was treating cisgender women with testosterone, he first said no. He affirmed that he would only do this in very particular situations of androgenic deficiency: 'when a woman produces no testosterone' there would be a possibility for replacement. He made a point of adding that, with the exception of the latter condition, he did not consider it ethical to conduct this type of treatment, although, he said, there are 'many people doing it'. Upon explaining why this would not be ethical he emphasized:

> It is not ethical because it has some consequences . . . Endocrinology seeks to mimic physiology as much as possible. This is not physiological, to use testosterone for a woman. So it does not promote health [. . .]. We, doctors, follow medical guidelines defined by consensus and there is no consensus about this, to the contrary.

Nevertheless, when speaking about testosterone replacement in menopause to treat low libido, he said this was possible, as long as it involved an 'ethical dose': 'There is a dose that is ethical. It is much lower than the dose that is being used today in gyms, and [being sold] on Facebook.' For Marcelo, the doses used by women in gyms seeking physical performance also have the inconvenience of being ingested orally by means of pills, and 'oral testosterone is harmful'. Moreover, they are associated with increased hair growth, voice deepening, oily skin and even baldness. These effects that would not be felt by patients who take small doses of testosterone, which he recommends in a few cases:

> If you give a cisgender women who wants to improve her libido a bit larger dose and her hair begins to fall out, she goes crazy, she doesn't want this. She wants to improve her libido, but she doesn't want her hair to fall out. And any increase in the dose will have some consequence, so one must be careful. They are very small doses.

Once again we have here the production of a distinction between the suitable or 'ethical' doses that can be prescribed by doctors depending on each situation and the accusation of a certain indiscriminate use of testosterone which is found in cis people at gyms. Ethical doses are characterized by effects that would approach what would be 'natural' or 'physiological' for the body of cisgender women. The central line of differentiation appears to be the volume of the doses and the different intentions of these two groups of users. Some need to replace something they lost or are no longer producing, while others are seeking an 'excess' that is directly manifest in their bodily transformations.

Conclusion

According to these doctors, sexual desire is conceived as being linked or dependent on the existence of a substance, testosterone, the 'male hormone'. It is important to emphasize that although it has been possible to perceive differences between the concepts of the people interviewed, in relation to approval of the use of synthetic testosterone in women, they all attest to the substance's potency. When Bernardo, who was most against its use, affirmed, for example, that testosterone produces virilizing effects and more aggressivity, even in cis women, and that this is confused with desire, he is both problematizing the nature of the substance's effects and continuing to affirm its agency. In the same line, when Karla, who is also against pharmaceutical uses, states that her method of behavioural sexual therapy provokes an increase in the rates of testosterone, she reaffirms the association between increased desire and greater presence of this hormone in women. In different ways, then, testosterone arises as a very powerful material force: in most cases, directly associated to sexual desire.

In terms of the 'collateral effects' there were recurring mentions of the 'exaggerations' of 'too high doses' that go beyond limits considered acceptable by doctors and/or patients. These 'excesses' were often described in terms of risks of virilization as growth of undesired hair, deepening of the voice and increase in the size of the clitoris. Worth noting that in the case of the two professionals who mention treating trans men, these effects even appear as desired or expected effects from the use of testosterone. But in the case of cis women, these corporal indications, interpreted as masculine, are a threat to be avoided. In this sense, the suitable or 'ethical' doses must be monitored so that they do not go beyond established gender borders, as should be correspondingly and binarily evident on the surface of bodies. The other risks, such as the association of hormone treatments with heart problems or cancer, are hardly mentioned.

The main benefit associated with testosterone by most doctors is precisely the 'replacement' or increase of desire not only for older women but also for younger women. Based on the presumption that desire depends on testosterone, they are finding in practice that women who have made use of this hormone have had an increase in desire and improved sex life. It is curious that a few professionals mention that at times merely the fact of being engaged in a treatment to improve sexuality can produce this effect. In this case, it would be difficult to identify what factor (if it would be possible to define or isolate any) is responsible for this 'improvement'. Nevertheless, this result is almost always attributed to testosterone. The fact that is made concrete by these doctors is that women who use testosterone have more desire. And this finding, in turn, helps to reinforce the association between testosterone and sexual desire, characterizing a circular logic between the substance, the multiple entanglements of meaning in play and their concrete effects. However, some questions remain: why and for whom is testosterone 'replacement' being promoted? What are the effects of the reproduction of this discourse that reduces female desire to the presence or absence of the hormone and degree of desire that are conceived as masculine? These issues are certainly associated with many others that form hormonal cascades.

To conclude, we can return to the questions posed by Mol (2012) about ontonorms and versions of reality that are being produced. I propose that the ontonorms that have been presented by the doctors in my study can be translated in these terms: desire is testosterone; testosterone is the male hormone; cis women can use testosterone to increase desire within the limits of non-virilization. In addition, the doctors' efforts can be described as an attempt to account for multiple realities of female sexuality by means of its reduction to an association between desire and testosterone. They therefore seek to generate a certain stability that allows them to intervene concretely through the production of effective results, in relation to the complaints of their patients. At the same time, the at-times contradictory, ambiguous or hesitant character of their statements in relation to the powers of testosterone shows their difficulties in dealing with instabilities in this field of intervention. Moreover, this 'materialization of desire' takes place exactly because it is not precisely defined. It involves a category that generically relates to feelings or sensations and that in practice is very vaguely defined. This is perhaps due to the fact that the more open or vague it remains, the more open it is to highly varied complaints or dissatisfactions that may be targets for new medical treatments.

Notes

1   This entry presents the partial results of the project 'New forms of circulation of knowledge and access to biomedical technologies: contemporary scenarios for corporeal and subjective transformations' supported by the National Council for Scientific and Technological Development (CNPq/Brazil).

2   The term 'cis/cisgender' refers to people who identify with the sex they were assigned at birth. In parallel, the term 'trans/transgender' refers to people who do not recognize themselves in the sex to which they were assigned at birth. The discussion around these terms is relevant here particularly because it calls attention to how all the different forms of expression and materialization of bodies, behaviours and identities are arduously elaborated.

3   Due to ethical considerations the name of the city as well as the real names of the people interviewed remain classified. The project was approved by the Research Commission of the Institute of Philosophy and Human Sciences, Federal University of Rio Grande do Sul.

References

Faro, L. (2016), *Mulher com bigode nem o diabo pode: Um estudo sobre testosterona, sexualidade feminina e biomedicalização*, PhD Thesis. University of State of Rio de Janeiro, Rio de Janeiro.

Faro, L. and J. Russo (2017), 'Testosterona, desejo sexual e conflito de interesse: Periódicos biomédicos como espaços privilegiados de expansão do mercado de medicamentos', *Horizontes Antropológicos* 23 (47): 61–92.

Hoberman, J. (2005), *Testosterone Dreams. Rejuvenation, Aphrodisia, Doping*, Berkeley: University of California Press.

Jordan-Young, R. and K. Karkaziz (2019), *Testosterone: An Unauthorized Biography*, Cambridge, MA: Harvard University Press.

Manica, D and M. Nucci (2017), 'Sob a pele: Implantes subcutâneos, hormônios e gênero', *Horizontes Antropológicos* 23 (47): 93–129.

Mol, A. (2012), 'Mind Your Plate! The Ontonorms of Dutch Dieting', *Social Studies of Science* 43 (3): 379–96.

Oudshoorn, N. (1994), *Beyond the Natural Body: An Archeology of Sex Hormones*, London: Routledge.

Roberts, C. (2007), *Messengers of Sex: Hormones, Biomedicine and Feminism*, New York: Cambridge University Press.

Roberts, C. (2015), *Puberty in Crisis: The Sociology of Early Sexual Development*, New York: Cambridge University Press.

Rohden, F. (2008), 'The Reign of Hormones and the Construction of Gender Differences', *História, Ciências, Saúde-Manguinhos* 15 (June): 133–52.

Rohden, F. (2013), 'Gender Differences and the Medicalization of Sexuality in the Diagnosis of Sexual Dysfunctions', in H. Sivori et al. (eds.), *Sexuality, Culture and Politics: A South American Reader*, 620–38, Rio de Janeiro: CEPESC/CLAM.

Rohden, F. (2018), 'Sexual Desire, Testosterone and Biomedical Interventions: Managing Female Sexuality in "Ethical Doses"', *Vibrant* 4 (3): 1–12.

Rohden, F. (2019), 'Adjusting Hormones and Constructing Desires: New Materialisations of Female Sexuality in Brazil', *Culture, Health & Sexuality* 1: 1–14.

Sanabria, E. (2010), 'From Sub – To Super – Citizenship: Sex Hormones and the Body Politic in Brazil', *Ethnos Journal of Anthropology* 75 (4): 377–401.

Sanabria, E. (2016), *Plastic Bodies: Sex, Hormones and Menstrual Suppression in Brazil*, Durham: Duke University Press.

INDEX